AUTOCOURSE
INDIANAPOLIS
500
& INDY RACING LEAGUE® INDYCAR® SERIES
OFFICIAL YEAR BOOK 2004

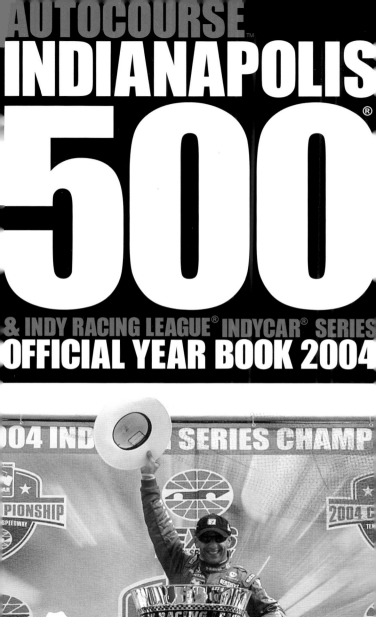

AUTOCOURSE
INDIANAPOLIS 500®
& INDY RACING LEAGUE®
INDYCAR® SERIES
OFFICIAL YEARBOOK 2004
is published by:
Hazleton Publishing Ltd,
5th Floor, Mermaid House,
2 Puddle Dock, London,
EC4V 3DS.

Colour reproduction by Radstock Repro,
Frome, Somerset

Printed in England by Butler and Tanner Ltd,
Frome, Somerset

Hazleton Publishing Ltd is a member of Profile Media
Group plc.

ISBN: 1 903135 46 X

DISTRIBUTORS
UNITED KINGDOM
Vine House
Waldenbury
North Common
Chailey
East Sussex
BN8 4DR
United Kingdom
Tel: (+44) 01825 723398
Fax: (+44) 01825 724188

NORTH AMERICA
Lantech International
Lantec Books,
Box 410,
4567 Bedford Rd.
Sydenham,
Ont. K0H 2T0,
Canada
Tel: 613-376-3100
Toll Free: 1-888-490-1876

REST OF THE WORLD
Menoshire Ltd
Unit 13
21 Wadsworth Road
Perivale
Middlesex UB6 7LQ
Tel: 020 8566 7344
Fax: 020 8991 2439

PUBLISHER
Eddie Taylor

CONSULTING EDITOR
Donald Davidson

MANAGING EDITOR
Stephen Mitchell

ART EDITOR
Richard Lee

DESIGNER
Mandeep Kalsi

PRODUCTION MANAGER
Laura Fell

AUTOCOURSE
WWW.AUTOCOURSE.COM

CONTENTS

Acknowledgements
The Publishers of the Autocourse Indianapolis 500® & Indy Racing League® IndyCar® Series Official Yearbook 2004 wish to thank the following
for their assistance while compiling the 2004 edition: Indianapolis Motor Speedway Historian Donald Davidson; racers Tony Kanaan, Buddy Rice
and Adrian Fernandez; the staff and public relations departments of the Indy Racing League and Indianapolis Motor Speedway; the staff of the
licensing department of the Indy Racing League and Indianapolis Motor Speedway under Nicole Polsky.

Photography
The photographs published in the Autocourse Indianapolis 500® & Indy Racing League® IndyCar® Series Official Yearbook 2004 have been
contributed by the official photographers of the IMS and the IRL.

FOREWORD BY **TONY KANAAN**
2004 INDYCAR® SERIES CHAMPION

KANAAN ON TOP

THERE **WERE MANY, MANY CHALLENGES** that our team had to overcome this season to win our first championship together, but probably nothing was as challenging as trying to put into words what this championship means.

It's really not fair to try to put it on a piece of paper. It's a whole life. It took 22 years to get one thing. It's difficult to describe, especially with the year we had – the laps led, the record of finishing every lap of every race, the string of top-five finishes – all of that.

My whole life I've dreamed of arriving in a top series and being a winner. With all that I went through to get to this point – all the way back to when I was a kid – when I crossed the finish line in Fontana that day, I had all these moments from my life coming back to my mind.

I really don't know how to put into words how big this is and how much this means to me. The best comparison, I would say, is that if you ever dreamed of something that you always thought was almost impossible, almost unreachable – well I got it. That's the way I look at it.

The road was so long and so rough for me that I never expected to make it. I always believed in it, but I didn't know. Then, when I made it and everything looked so bright and so good, came the hard times of not having the results. That's when you go back again and you say, "Well, yeah, maybe I made it, but I will be one more, just like all the other guys that tried. I'm just going to be 'one more'. I'm not going to make history; I'm just going to make it."

Making it is one thing. Making history is a lot different. A lot of years after I started and two years after I signed with the team, we made history. That's pretty cool.

Enjoy the book.
Tony Kanaan

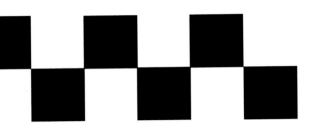

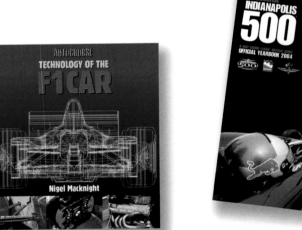
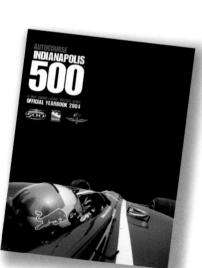

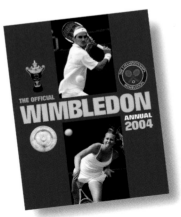

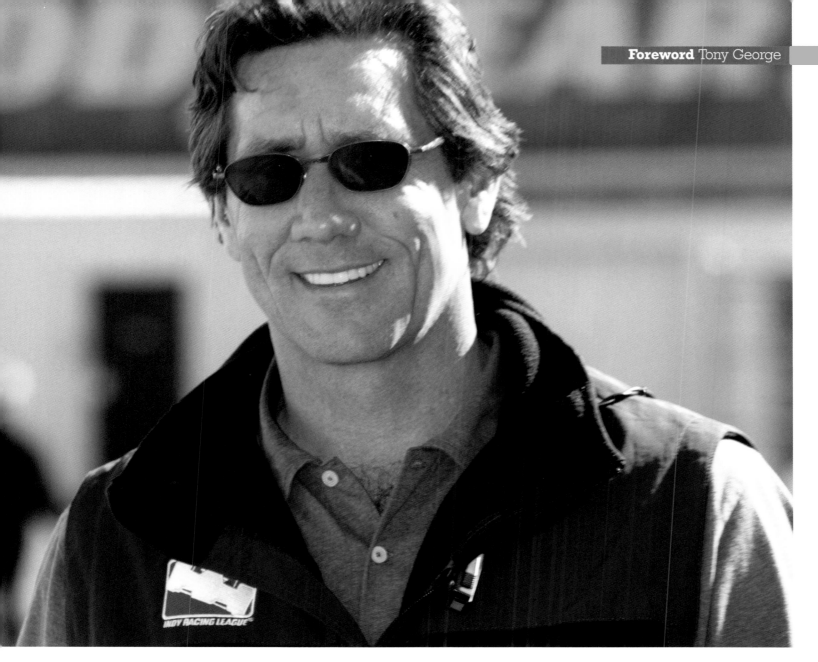

FOREWORD BY

TONY GEORGE

PRESIDENT AND CEO INDIANAPOLIS MOTOR SPEEDWAY CORPORATION

THE 2004 INDYCAR® SERIES PROVIDED WHAT WAS EXPECTED: INTENSE COMPETITION, dramatic moments and more of the close finishes that have become a hallmark of the Series. Most of all, two drivers stood out for their performances and were symbolic of the season: great driving, endurance and a will to win.

In the 88th running of the Indianapolis 500 Mile Race, Buddy Rice drove a masterful race that was interrupted twice by weather and stopped just 50 miles from the end. It was one of the most memorable driving performances in the history of the 500 and brought the Rahal/Letterman team a well-deserved win.

On the road to capturing his first IndyCar® Series win, Tony Kanaan completed every lap – 3,305 in all – of the season, a feat rarely accomplished in the history of racing. He also won three races and had 15 consecutive top-five finishes.

Buddy and Tony were only two of the dramatic stories of the 2004 season. Tenacity, fierceness and gusto for life are shared by Buddy, Tony and all of the drivers of the IndyCar® Series and the Menards Infiniti Pro Series.

I hope you enjoy their stories as you read this annual review.

Tony George

Tony George

Tony Kanaan gathers his thoughts before racing begins.

Kanaan climbs into his machine at Indianapolis; acknowledging his fans; on the winners podium at the Chevy 500 in Texas; receiving his check from IRL President Tony George.

TONY **SUPREMO**

WORDS BY **DAVID PHILLIPS**

THERE **MAY HAVE BEEN OTHER** drivers as respected as Tony Kanaan who had never won a major open-wheel championship in North America. But not many. Sure, he nipped Helio Castroneves for the 1997 Indy Lights crown, but in the years since graduating to Indy-style cars, Kanaan's record was hardly the stuff of legends: two wins; never better than fourth in the Champ Car or IRL IndyCar Series standings.

And yet, there was no shortage of top-rank team owners eager for him to race their cars: Steve Horne, a driving force in TrueSports Racing's rise to prominence in the 1980s and founder of the Tasman Motorsports team that brought Kanaan and Castroneves to America; Morris Nunn, founder of the Ensign Formula 1 team, race engineer par excellence for 1989 Indianapolis 500- and championship-winning Patrick Racing and, later, Target Chip Ganassi Racing's four consecutive titles.

And finally, Michael Andretti, winningest Indy-style driver since 1980 and third winningest of all time. With retirement looming, Andretti joined Kim Green and Kevin Savoree in acquiring Team Green in late 2002. Among their first hires – Tony Kanaan.

Nor were the team owners alone in their regard for Kanaan. Never an organization to let sentiment cloud its fierce will to win, Honda has backed Kanaan in virtually every phase of his career, first with Horne and Tasman and, after the team's start-up season in association with Mercedes-Benz, at Mo Nunn Racing.

Suffice to say Honda, Andretti, Green and Savoree knew what Horne and Nunn knew: despite his unremarkable stats, Kanaan was championship material. Kanaan knew it too. He knew that, ever since he first set foot in an Indy-style car, he had driven for teams long on potential but short on experience. In truth, he also knew he was every bit as good as one particular driver who won 11 races – including two straight Indianapolis 500s – and consistently competed for championships after joining vaunted Marlboro Team Penske.

That would be Castroneves. Kanaan knew he could do just as well as his former Indy Lights teammate/rival/friend, perhaps even better. If only he got the opportunity. Rather than making him jealous, each Castroneves success, each Spiderman routine, underlined Kanaan's belief in himself.

"It helped me," he says. "It made me feel better because I said, 'I'm as good as him. I know if he's doing that well, I just can't become a bad driver from one year to another. Something [else] is going on.'

"So I always knew what I had in my hands. I never, ever doubted what I could do myself. But I knew the situations I was in and I had to wait for the right opportunity. Or that opportunity would never come, or it would come and I would have a chance to prove it again."

That opportunity came with Andretti Green Racing in 2004. And Kanaan proved what he could do. Again. The numbers speak – no shout – for themselves. Three wins, three poles and 15 top-five finishes, ten of them on the podium.

But the statistic that pleases Kanaan most? Completing every single lap in the 2004 IRL IndyCar Series. All 3,035 of them. Only once (an eighth place in the season opener at Homestead-Miami Speedway) did he fail to finish in the top five.

"At the beginning of the season my goal was to complete every lap," he says. "Then that goal started to change to complete every lap in the top ten, then after Homestead I said, 'Maybe complete every lap in the top five.'

"That's a perfect season because you finish every lap of every race and that's what makes you win.

"To look back, it was a championship in which four drivers won three races each, one driver won two races and two drivers won one race. And if I win the championship with three wins that means consistency. So that was my biggest advantage, my consistency. Other people had bad days. I never had one – or when I did have a bad day, I finished fifth!"

Kanaan had some great days, none better than when he led 191 of 200 laps to win at Phoenix or when he led 145 of 200 laps to win at Texas. Then there was that April day when he followed teammate Dan Wheldon home at Twin Ring Motegi, bringing Honda an overdue first victory on home ground.

But it was another second place, the one at California Speedway, which Kanaan recalls as the high point to his season. And not just because he clinched the IRL title with that finish. Bear in mind the fact that Kanaan started an

unrepresentative 21st after suffering mechanical problems in qualifying.

"This year my worst start position was tenth at Richmond, so I never had a lot of work to do in the races, basically," Kanaan recalls. "I was always in the top five. So, especially because I was fighting for the championship [at California], people saw my qualifying and would say, 'Hey, see? Now that the time comes to do it look what happens. Finally. You never had a problem all year, and now we'll see.'

"Five laps into the race and I'm in the top five again."

Recall too that Kanaan needed only a top-four finish to clinch the title. But there he was, battling wheel to wheel with Adrian Fernandez for victory in the closing laps. Yes, he finished second, but it was a racer's second; a thinking racer's second.

"It was the best second place I ever had," he laughs. "But really, I knew the car I had. And to start back there I had to choose to have a lot

of downforce, otherwise I couldn't go through the field. And I knew that could jeopardize my chances of winning the race at the end if I was in the front. But I knew I didn't have to win the race: I had to finish in the top four. So basically, I'm not saying that I didn't race to win because anybody who saw the race knows I raced to win.

"And for the way the race went, we put ourselves in that position. So I wasn't disappointed; the goal wasn't to win the race, it was to win the championship."

There were also frustrating days. May 30 and August 1 in particular, when Kanaan and Andretti Green were second best to Buddy Rice and Rahal Letterman Racing at the Indianapolis 500 and Michigan Indy 400.

"We made mistakes," says Kanaan, "and they were the most important races; obviously Indy is more important than anything. But I knew why I lost at Michigan, and I knew why I lost at Indianapolis. That's how we learned. I know

how I lost it, so let's make sure it doesn't happen again. And if I can prevent that I will. If I can't, I will just maximize what I have."

That task was at once easier and infinitely more complex than it might otherwise have been for an Andretti Green Racing team that fielded four, count 'em, four Dallara/Hondas throughout the season for Kanaan, Wheldon, Dario Franchitti and Bryan Herta. Conventional wisdom has it that two-car teams are ideal, enabling drivers, engineers and mechanics to efficiently share and compare information.

In rare cases a three-car team is successful, with a third data set available to triangulate set-ups and development. But with each additional car, the challenges multiply exponentially. Thus many figured a four-car team was a recipe for disaster.

But Andretti Green proved the naysayers wrong. Not only did Kanaan win the title, team-mates Wheldon, Franchitti and Herta finished second, sixth and ninth, respectively, in the points race.

"We knew it would be a challenge, but we knew what we had to do to make it work," says Kanaan. "So we had the team meeting and we decided, 'We're going to make it work. We're going to make it happen.'

"And I think we did make it succeed a lot, with the help of a lot of people within the team. It's easier when you have three team owners, I think, because one does one thing, one does another and so forth. And we had plenty of engineers and four good drivers that get along pretty well.

"But I tell you, it's definitely not easy. We have our moments, we had a few *discussions* but that's normal.

"But I never believed that it was not gonna work, because I worked with Bryan and Dan all last year and Dario was a good friend of mine. So I said, 'It couldn't be better than that. They're all good drivers, they're all good people and they all understand what the team is all about.' "

The final factor in the success of Kanaan and company in 2004 is, of course, Honda. Competitive – only just – in its rookie season of IndyCar competition, Honda reloaded for 2004 and promptly got trounced by Toyota in the season opener. And when Kanaan won at Phoenix and Honda dominated at Twin Ring Motegi in the swan-song of the 3.5-liter engine, the critics scoffed, saying Honda had concentrated so much of its energy on winning before the home crowd that there would be hell to pay when the 3.0-liter engine regulations kicked in at Indianapolis.

As was the case with the four-car Andretti Green operation, Honda got the last laugh, winning 12 of the first 13 races in the 3.0-liter era, running away with the IRL manufacturers championship and taking all but two of the top nine positions in the drivers' points race.

Honda's one-two punch may have surprised some observers. But Kanaan, who has driven Honda-powered cars in all but one season since 1998, was not among them.

"I've been with Honda for a long time and I know how capable they are and how much they can do," he says. "So I never disbelieved what they could achieve. At the end of last year we knew we were behind, but you have to look back and say, 'Hey, they just joined the program in November of 2002; Toyota was running that engine already for a year.'

"I knew over the winter they were gonna work so hard. They proved so many times, everywhere, in F1 and CART, so I knew it was gonna come. Obviously people expected more problems. They said, 'Yeah they're concentrating on the 3.5, you'll see when the new rules come in,' but that wasn't the reality."

The reality is that Honda was up to the challenge. Like Kanaan himself. And if he was the happiest man in racing when he clinched the title that day in Fontana, California, he had plenty of company. In the ensuing days he fielded phone calls from as far away as New Zealand, Monaco and Thailand; from old mentors and friends like Horne and Rubens Barrichello, with whom Kanaan lived for a spell when they were young go-karters in Brazil.

Facing page: Another lightning pit stop. Clockwise from top left: Kanaan holds aloft the Phoenix trophy; celebrating the 2004 Championship, Texas style; in the pace car during pre-race preparation at the Texas Speedway.

The calls were filled with congratulations and not a little good-natured ribbing. "Steve Horne called me twice, [Alex] Zanardi called me the day that I won; Rubens called, he was in Thailand on vacation. Jimmy [Vasser], Oriol [Servia]... all the people I really care about called.

"Some were in Fontana. My sister who lives here. My mother came, my in-laws as well, my wife. Cristiano da Matta called as well. A lot of people called congratulating me, giving me a hard time: 'If it wasn't for Honda giving you the big engines you'd never win...' But I don't care what they say: it's mine!!!"

All it took was the right opportunity.

RICE TO THE OCCASION

WORDS BY **JOHN OREOVICZ**

DURING **THE SECOND HALF OF THE**
Month of May, when it became apparent
that he had become one of the favorites
to win the 2004 Indianapolis 500, Buddy Rice
began to joke about staying under the radar. But
that was nothing new for the 28-year-old Phoenix
native, who had more than his fill of laying low
after winning the CART-sanctioned Toyota
Atlantic Championship in 2000.

Of course, Rice went on to score a solid
victory in what many observers considered
the most highly competitive Indianapolis race
in recent memory – certainly in the past decade.
In the space of a few hours, Rice was vaulted
from relative obscurity to the spotlit ubiquity
that is part and parcel of becoming an
Indianapolis 500 champion. And to his credit,
he successfully used that Indianapolis triumph
as a springboard to challenge for the IRL IndyCar
Series championship and firmly establish himself
as one of the League's most competitive and
combative drivers.

Rice has come a long way since he won that
Atlantic title, learning in the process that while
American open-wheel racing may have a ladder
system, the top rung isn't necessarily definable
or reachable. In Buddy's case, that meant

abandoning his plan of racing Champ Cars
in favor of the oval-track world of the IRL.
He certainly adapted quickly, coming very close
to winning his very first IndyCar Series race
in August 2002 for Team Cheever.

But after a fairy-tale debut, reality set in for
Rice when he was replaced by Alex Barron.
After sitting idle through 2001 and the first half
of 2002, Rice took a seat on the sidelines once
again in the middle of 2003, and plotted his
next move.

His destination turned out to be Rahal
Letterman Racing, rekindling a spark that dated
to late 2001 when Bobby Rahal tried to put the
pieces together to run Rice in CART. That seat
eventually went to Michel Jourdain Jr..

In early 2004, even before he made the
decision to devote all of his team's attention
and resources to the IRL, Rahal needed a driver
to substitute for the injured Kenny Bräck in his
IndyCar Series entry. Remembering how highly
he rated Rice in 2001, Rahal made the call that
changed Buddy's life.

"I always thought highly of Buddy and he was
certainly on the A-list," Rahal reflects. "I guess
I felt pretty good, but when we went to
Homestead and he put it on the pole, I thought,

'Wow!' It was clear he was going to run up
front, it was clear that he and the engineer,
Todd Bowland, were communicating well and
obviously Honda was providing us with very
good engines. You saw that the ingredients
were there."

The Homestead pole didn't translate into
a win, but Rice's solid performance in the year's
first two races, coupled with complications
to Bräck's recovery, meant that Rahal confirmed
to Rice prior to the race at Motegi, Japan, that
the Pioneer/Argent car was his for the rest
of the season. Beyond that would depend
on the unknown.

"Getting the year off to a good start was
important, but at the same time I knew what
was expected of me before I showed up at
Homestead," Rice relates. "When we had our
first test with the [Panoz] G Force, I was trying
to get up to speed with the G Force/Honda
package and my engineer, and so was the team.
We knew what we expected. We were hoping
we were going to be competitive and quick
but I think we even shocked ourselves a little
bit with our qualifying run there."

Rice was thrilled simply to have his first
opportunity to race for a truly top-line team.

The professional approach at RLR seemed to relax Rice, even if it meant cutting his hair and abandoning his traditional practice of wearing his sponsor hat backward.

"I drove for two awesome Atlantic teams and thought I knew what it took, but to be able to hook up with a top-tier team like this to see how it's done and how it all works was shocking," he says. "[At Cheever] I was in a position where things happened a certain way and they said one thing, then decided I couldn't get the job done. Then I showed up here with even more of a difficult task than what was handed to me before. But the group had a plan and knew what we were trying to accomplish. We excelled at that and moved forward. It's just nice to be able to go to a team that you know will be competitive and run up front like they are supposed to do. You're not constantly guessing where you stand or what's happening."

A setback came in late April, when Rice crashed hard in Turn Four in pre-race testing at the Indianapolis Motor Speedway. Rahal believes the crash helped Rice focus his approach for the Month of May, which eventually paid huge dividends.

"I take full responsibility for that deal," Rice comments. "We knew there was a strong chance it was going to be cool all month long. I got after it and it got away when we were definitely pushing for speed, and were in qualifying trim. But stuff happens. It was probably a little bit of a detriment but it helps you focus a little bit more and makes you work on certain things. It made me stay on top of my game."

That ability came to the fore in Indianapolis qualifying, where Rice was the only driver who topped 222 mph on a day marked by tricky conditions to secure the pole position.

"We always thought Buddy had talent and that he could win races," noted RLR's chief operating officer, Scott Roembke. "But watch his qualifying run at Indy – I don't think anybody has hung it out like that for a long time. But he did it when he needed to do it. He's not the guy who's going to win the free steak for having the fastest lap each day, but he sat on five poles this year. He knows when he has to push the button."

On Race Day, Rice didn't panic when he stalled during a mid-race pit stop and dropped to 16th place. He calmly and methodically picked off the cars in front of him, moving from fifth to first by

passing his fastest competitors during the key stint from laps 137 to 151.

"One thing I like about Buddy is that he doesn't get excited in the cockpit – just listen on the radio," remarked Rahal. "I don't want to say he's laid-back, I think he's just outwardly very unemotional and that allows you to step up the pace when you need to and understand where you are. It allows you to control a race rather than have it control you. At Indy and some other races, when it's time to go... boom. It's almost as if he races with something in hand."

During June and July, Rice established himself as Tony Kanaan's chief championship threat. The Rahal team's Panoz G Force/Honda package excelled in particular on the 1.5-mile superspeedways, and Rice added excellent victories at Kansas Speedway and Michigan International Speedway. The Kansas win came in a photo finish with Rahal Letterman teammate Vitor Meira.

As a backdrop to that sustained run of success, Rice embarked on a punishing media and publicity tour that comes with being a modern-day Indianapolis 500 champion. Aside from making the rounds of the New York talk shows,

Rice threw out ceremonial first pitches at Yankee Stadium and Cincinnati's Great American Ball Park; attended the ESPN X-Games, where he reconnected with several motocross and BMX riders he competed against as a youth; and drove a Bradley land pursuit vehicle with the U.S. Army's 7th Infantry Division.

All of that paled in comparison with the very rare honor bestowed upon Rice and his team that not every Indianapolis 500 champion receives: an invitation to the White House to meet President George W. Bush.

"That was the pinnacle," Rice acknowledges. "It's really hard for me to put into words the fact that I was able to shake hands with the most powerful man in the world and that he took time out of his busy schedule with all that is happening in the world to meet with us. I was nervous at first but he's a great guy and easy to get along with. He's easier to talk to than some of the bosses I've had."

Bush admitted that he paid attention to Rice's win because Buddy was the first American driver since Cheever in 1998 to win at Indianapolis. Rice hopes it may lead to a resurgnce of American drivers in the race. "It depends on how the kids perceive it," Rice says. "I hope it gives somebody the drive to go do that. Probably one of the biggest things I've heard since I won the 500 was that an American had won it. If Indy is something they want to strive to go do, they know the Americans can do it. I think there has been a big resurgence in the American driver. We fell behind a little bit, and maybe our training ground or proving ground wasn't as complete as we thought, but right now, the kids who are very good are getting a shot or an opportunity and they're moving forward."

Rice's championship challenge took a hit in mid-August when he crashed on the first lap at Pikes Peak International Raceway. Four months later, the Turn Two incident still has Buddy scratching his head.

"It was a freak deal, to be honest," he notes. "Tomas Scheckter came from the back and had a monster run on everybody around the outside. They looked at the data and the car lost almost 25 percent of its downforce when he went by me because of the blast of air that comes off the cars. The air across the wing actually put the car in yaw, because it came across the wing diagonally. The whole car lifted up and spun on its own. It was crazy because it happened so quick that I didn't know what happened."

The aerodynamic sensitivity of the current generation of IndyCars was on graphic display at Chicagoland Speedway where, late in the 400-mile race, Rice's car locked wheels with Darren Manning's Panoz G Force and was propelled into

Facing page: winning at Michigan International Speedway. This page, clockwise from left: ringing the closing bell at the New York Stock Exchange; always a team effort; meeting President George W. Bush; victorious at the Kansas Speedway.

the air. Rice's machine, though, was able to return to earth without hitting the catch-fence, and therefore avoiding serious injury to the driver. Although Buddy was unhurt, his championship hopes took a fatal hit and he eventually lost second place in the standings to Dan Wheldon.

But all in all, 2004 was a breakout season for Rice in every sense of the word. Now he faces the challenge of living up to the expectations that come with entering into a new season as championship and fan favorite.

"I think for everything to happen the way it did for myself and the team made for a huge year," he notes. "Between what happened in the team and with myself in 2003, to come together in 2004 and to have the success we did with all the reshaping just shows how strong the Rahal team is. I was finally in a proper situation where

I could go out and do the job I know I've been able to do. I didn't change my approach from the start of this season to the end and that's not going to change. We're starting to build and I think we learned from each other and that helped our consistency."

For now, Rice plans to spend his off-season just being Buddy – cruising around Phoenix with his girlfriend or his dad in a car from his hot rod collection, maybe shagging a few ground balls on the baseball diamond. In that respect, Buddy Rice is a throwback to the glory days of American championship racing, when rough-hewn drivers like A.J. Foyt and the Unser brothers ruled the roost.

"I haven't changed and I'm not gonna change," Rice laughs. "I'm not going to go out and sell my pickup truck just because I won the Indy 500. I leave that stuff about image up to the fans and the media because I know it comes with the territory. It's part of the deal. But I don't look at myself as someone who's looking to have the camera in my face 24/7 like some people do. I'm there to do my thing. Racing is what I want to do and that's where I want to be."

Above: Al Unser, Jr., the day after winning at Indianapolis in 1992, with his son, Al III, who could conceivably be a 500 driver before long.

THE UNSER DYNASTY

WORDS BY **DONALD DAVIDSON**

ON WEDNESDAY, JUNE 30, 2004, Al Unser Jr. sat in the interview room at the Indianapolis Motor Speedway and announced to the world that his race driving days were over.

It had been approximately ten years, one month and two weeks since the day his famous father had done exactly the same thing.

Of all the surnames associated with the Indianapolis Motor Speedway over the years, surely only a handful have been held in as much reverence as that of Unser. Since 1958, drivers by that name have appeared in the starting lineup no fewer than 71 times, and there has only been one race since 1963 in which the famous racing household did not appear.

But unless a promising 22-year-old fourth-generation racer from the Menards Infiniti Pro Series – yet another Al Unser (who some observers dearly wish would avoid confusion by agreeing to be known as Al Unser III) – makes an attempt to run in the 500 a year earlier than had generally been anticipated, then there will not be an Unser in competition on Race Day 2005.

This is, of course, assuming that his father does not rethink his recent decision, as others have been known to do in the past.

Six members of the Unser clan have competed in the 500 thus far, and three have emerged victorious. In fact, between 1968 and 1994, this trio was able to land racing's most coveted prize a total of nine times, thus averaging one win every third year for almost 30 years. And in the 28 races held between 1967 and 1994, only on nine occasions did an Unser fail to finish either first, second or third.

So just exactly who are these people? Well, in a nutshell, the close-knit family hailing from Albuquerque, New Mexico, has been represented by three brothers – Jerry, Bobby and Al – each of whom have had one son follow in their tire-tracks, Johnny, Robby and Al Jr., respectively.

The three winners have been Bobby (1968, 1975 and 1981), his younger brother Al (1970, 1971, 1978 and 1987) and Al's son, Al Jr. (1992 and 1994).

The first Unser to face the green flag in a 500 was Jerry – or to be more specific, Jerry Jr. – back in 1958. But he wasn't the first Unser to be *entered* at Indianapolis. That honor fell to his Uncle Louis, an eventual seven-time winner of the Pikes Peak Hill Climb, who took a portion of his "rookie" test, before time ran out, in 1940. Uncle Louis returned over several subsequent years, but always as a crew member rather than as a driver, and he remains the only Unser to have been entered at Indianapolis and not earn a starting position.

But even Uncle Louis wasn't the first with *intentions* of running at Indianapolis. A decade earlier, the Coleman Motors Corp of Littleton, Colorado, a truck-building concern that was attempting to get into the passenger car business, built three massive front-drive cars to be driven at Pikes Peak in 1929 by Louis and two other brothers, Jerry Sr. and Joe. A rare photo shows the three of them seated in these cars, and family lore has it they were planning on going to Indianapolis in 1930 until Joe lost his life while practicing with one of them on an open road in Colorado. In deference to the legend, the cars in the photo appeared a little unwieldy for anything that would have been entered for the 500, even under the considerably relaxed regulations of 1930.

But a photo is known to exist of Jerry Sr., plain as day, posed outside a building in one of the two sleek front-drive cars Coleman also built for Lou Moore and Phil Shafer to drive at Indianapolis that year. Whether or not Jerry and his brothers were lined up to accompany them as potential relief drivers on these cars and whether or not the death of Joe may have put an end to this through pressures from the family remains a mystery. But the typically stern-appearing Jerry

looks perfectly at home in a white uniform, the straps of his cloth helmet hanging lazily about his shoulders, and a menacing glare on his face indicating that he means business.

While Jerry never did make it to Indianapolis as a driver, he had three sons who did. After the successful qualification run by Jerry Jr. in 1958, along came Bobby in 1963, followed two years later by Al.

Also in the mix in those days, to complicate matters still further, was a fourth brother, Louis J. Unser, who was Jerry Jr.'s twin. Yet another Pikes Peak specialist, Louis J. served as Jerry's race day crew chief in 1958 and was named co-chief on Al's car in 1965 by George Bignotti in order that Bignotti could concentrate on lead driver A.J. Foyt. This Louis, who dearly wanted to drive alongside his brothers, was already in the early stages of battling multiple sclerosis, but even while wheelchair-bound went on to become one of American racing's most respected engine builders. He passed away on March 2, 2004 at the age of 71.

In 1983, the Unser family made history when 21-year-old Al Unser Jr. became the very first driver ever to race against his own father in the same 500. (This was not the first father/son combination to be entered, however, that "first" having occurred six years earlier when young James McElreath was just a fraction too slow to join his father, Jim, in the 1977 field). Johnny Unser, son of Jerry Jr., made it for his first of five consecutive starts in 1996, and Unser number six, Bobby's son Robby, joined Johnny in 1998 and 1999.

Jerry Jr., a Pikes Peak Hill Climb specialist, as were all of the Unsers, had been the 1957 USAC Stock Car Champion. He only had a brief career at Indianapolis but he left behind a lasting legacy. In 1958, he was lucky to escape with only a dislocated shoulder when the chain reaction in a huge multi-car accident on the very first lap

sent him sailing completely over the third turn wall; but no sooner had practice begun for the 1959 race than his luck ran out.

Fire-retardant uniforms were not yet mandatory and Jerry was dressed only in slacks and a short-sleeved shirt when he hit the wall on May 2. While suffering burns on his arms, he did not appear to be injured that seriously at first; but his condition worsened, blood poisoning set in, and to the utter shock of those who had been up to visit him, he passed away on May 17.

From that day on, the choice of driving apparel was no longer up to the drivers. The use of fire retardant uniforms, recommended for years but never enforced, was now mandated permanently.

The debut of "Little Al" in 1983 was truly memorable. After starting fifth, but running into delays during the event, the supremely talented youngster lined up for a late-race restart, several laps down but placed directly behind the drivers who were running first and second. They just happened to be his father, already a three-time winner, and Tom Sneva, a three-time runner-up who had not yet won.

Just as the green flag was about to be displayed, "Little Al" took it upon himself to jump the restart and pass the two ahead of him. He then allowed his father to re-pass but made it less than easy for Sneva to do the same. The hampered challenger was eventually able to pass regardless, and soon after made fairly short work of "Big Al" on his way to the win.

"Little Al" ran out of fuel at the very end, and while he didn't win the Rookie of the Year award – that honor went to Teo Fabi – the grinning youngster had clearly made his mark.

Rather ironically, "Little Al" is not alone in having been an Unser who lost out to another driver for the coveted Rookie of the Year award. As unlikely as it may seem, no member of the Unser family has ever won it; not even Robby, who finished fifth after running third for many laps in 1998.

It is also somewhat noteworthy that none of the Unser wins came as part of a long-standing driver/car owner "magic" combination relationship such as there had been, for instance, with Jim Clark and Colin Chapman, or Rick Mears and Roger Penske. Bobby's three wins each came for a different owner; namely Leader Cards, Inc., in 1968, Dan Gurney's All American Racers in 1975 and Penske in 1981. After Al scored back-to-back wins for the Vel Miletich and Parnelli Jones team in 1970 and 1971, he then won for Jim Hall in 1978 and Penske in 1987. The wins for Al Jr. came with Rick Galles in 1992 and Penske in 1994.

Another irony is that in spite of the abundance of Unser family members at Indianapolis over the last 40 years, there have never been any more than two in any one race. Bobby and Al

An all-star cast greets Al after he qualifies for his first 500 in 1965. At left is his father Jerry Unser Sr. and brother Bobby. Third brother, Louis J. is crouched behind the windshield next to Foyt and Bignotti, with co-owner Bill Ansted behind them. Standing next to the right front wheel is Lujie Lesovsky, the famed builder and fabricator.

Al becomes a four-time winner in 1987. Facing page, clockwise from top: Johnny, Robby and Al Unser Jr.; Seven bas-relief sculptures of Bobby and Al appear on the Borg-Warner trophy; May 11, 1998 and Bobby prepares to take a lap of honor in his restored 1968-winning mount as son Robby cherishes the moment.

faced each other a total of 16 times between 1965 and 1981 – Al did not start in 1969 because of injuries received in a motorcycle accident – but the debut of Al Jr. in 1983 did not come until just after Bobby had retired. By the time Johnny arrived in 1996, "Big Al" had also retired and "Little Al" was on a 500 hiatus, due to the decision of his car owner, Roger Penske, not to enter the 500 for a few years. Robby came along to join Johnny in the lineup in 1998 and 1999, but, as luck would have it, was unable to qualify in 2000, the year in which Al Jr. made his return. A disappointing qualifying run by Robby prevented the trio of extremely close first cousins from competing against each other and finally having three Unsers start in the same 500.

The stats this family leaves behind at the Indianapolis Motor Speedway are truly amazing. For instance, Al Unser's total of 644 leading laps is more than any other driver in history, while his total of 27 starts ranks third only to A.J. Foyt (35) and Mario Andretti (29). Bobby led 440 laps and Al Jr. 110 for a total of 1,194 between the three of them.

In addition to winning four times, Al was also runner-up three times and third-place finisher four times. There aren't many drivers who can boast 11 Indy 500 starts during their career. Al finished that many among the top three!

With five top-three finishes by Bobby and another three by Al Jr., the total number of podium appearances by Unsers has been a staggering 19. The total number of finishes among the top ten is 37, Al having 15, Bobby and Al Jr. ten each, and Robby two.

The dynamic Bobby, whose inspired all-out qualifying runs were always a joy to behold, failed to rank among the fastest 12 qualifiers only once in 19 starts, and on no less than nine occasions he qualified for the front row, twice on the pole.

In the nine 500s between 1986 and 1994, Al Jr., who inherited his father's uncanny knack of being able to "bring them home," completed 1,770 out of a possible 1,800 laps. The 179 laps he completed in 2004 (rain halted the leaders at 180 instead of the full 200) pushed his total to 2,867 and moved him above Johnny Rutherford for sixth in the all-time standings. In fact, should he reconsider his retirement, it would be possible for him to pass both Arie Luyendyk and Mario Andretti in 2005, while an average of only 146 laps per race over the next two would move him past Gordon Johncock and into third place. Only his father (4,356) and A.J. Foyt (4,909) would have a greater number of laps completed.

And, oh, the memories. There was the sterling victory by Bobby in 1968 when the turbine of

Joe Leonard failed with only nine laps to go... and Bobby was severely hampered by having lost all but top gear.

There was Bobby's extraordinary qualifying run in 1972, when, during the first year in which bolt-on rear wings were permitted, he raised the single lap record from 179.354 mph to 196.678 mph, an increase of a phenomenal 17 miles per hour – close to ten percent – in one year.

There was the amazing upset run by Al in 1987, when he was invited back onto the Penske team after having been released the previous winter, substituted for the injured Danny Ongais, and scored his record-tying fourth Indy 500 win by nursing home a year-old car which had started out the month on display in the lobby of a Pennsylvania hotel!

There was the epic wheel-to-wheel battle in 1989 between Al Jr. and Emerson Fittipaldi in which their tires touched with just over one lap to go, sending Unser into the wall. His reward would come three years later when he held off challenger Scott Goodyear to win by about half a car length – a margin of 0.043 of a second – which to this day remains the closest finish in 500 history.

And who could ever forget the parents of Jerry Jr., Louis J., Bobby and Al, who were so much a part of the scene in the mid-1960s? "Pop" and his devoted wife, the beloved Mary "Mom" Unser, were faced with the predicament of deciding with which tire company they should place their allegiance, considering that Bobby was contracted to Goodyear and Al to Firestone. Someone solved the dilemma by taking one of each jacket, cutting them up the middle and sewing the opposite halves together. From the back, the blue and red one read "Goodstone," the red and blue one, "Fireyear."

Mom, who had such a magical presence in front of an audience, was best known for her chili, a lethal concoction not recommended for those with sensitive stomachs. Rumor had it that the recipe, on certain occasions, included tequila. Whether true or not, her chili bashes were truly legendary and they raised thousands of dollars for charity.

It's been a terrific ride.

And yet, keep an eye on young Al Unser III (or "Just Al," or "Mini Al" as he was known as a kid). The amazing run of the Unser racing family dynasty may not be quite at an end.

FROM **ROOKIE** TO **POWERHOUSE**

WORDS BY **MATT CLEARY**

AFTER **MAKING A BELATED DECISION** to join the Indy Racing League, longtime Champ Car competitor Adrian Fernandez and his team had a lot to overcome in 2004. But despite a difficult start, the veteran Mexican driver found success on the track, enjoyment in the paddock, and established his Fernandez Racing team as a bona fide championship contender in the IRL ranks.

The Fernandez Racing squad was not entirely new to IndyCar racing. It had contested the 2003 season with Roger Yasukawa in a partnership with ex-Formula 1 racer Aguri Suzuki under the Super Aguri Fernandez Racing banner, which operated out of the Fernandez Racing shop in Indianapolis. For 2004, however, after Super Aguri Fernandez Racing had tabbed the highly talented young Japanese driver Kosuke Matsuura, it wasn't until the very last minute that Fernandez made up his mind to join the IRL himself.

Fernandez decided to join the IRL so late, in fact, that he missed the opening race of the season at Homestead as well as two open series tests. He faced a true baptism by fire as he lined up on the grid for the second race of the season at Phoenix International Raceway, just 11 days after making the announcement that he would be racing in the IndyCar Series.

The team worked some late nights to prepare a car for the Copper World Indy 200, but despite its best efforts, the debut weekend at Phoenix was a disaster. Fernandez qualified a credible 13th but failed even to complete a lap. He was so unfamiliar with his Panoz G Force/Honda that he broke the transmission coming up to speed for the start of the race.

The team traveled next to Twin Ring Motegi, Japan, where Fernandez had twice emerged victorious in CART competition. Honda,

meanwhile, was still seeking an elusive first win on home soil and was determined to pull out all the stops. Hopes, therefore, were high, but the team was still working to overcome its many challenges, and the frustration continued. Fernandez lined up 18th on the grid and finished in the same position after encountering a motor problem.

"That was definitely the low point of the season," Fernandez reflects. "We had no preparation, no knowledge of the car for myself, and I wasn't even adjusted to the car physically – it was completely uncomfortable to even be in – so the first two races were incredibly difficult for us as a team."

Meanwhile, the Super Aguri side of the team was displaying some promising signs. Matsuura, who had impressed in testing, was the highest-finishing rookie in each of the first three races. He also took an impressive fourth on the grid at Motegi in just his third IRL race. Fernandez was anything but downhearted.

"Yes, it took some time to catch up to the environment, but for me, it was only a question of when it was going to all come together," he says. "We have an unbelievable team and you have to keep in mind that it's just the fourth year for us, so we are continuing to improve as a group, and this IRL move was just another challenge for us to take on as a team."

After the long trip back from Japan, the team had some time to regroup and prepare for one of the biggest challenges in racing – the Month of May at Indianapolis. Remarkably, Fernandez Racing was able to convert the challenge into a turning point, as the team posted times in the top five nearly all month, was a threat to win the pole, and scored a solid race finish.

"We're still a young team, still learning," noted Fernandez, competing at Indianapolis for the first time since 1995, "but hopefully this will be a team that a lot of people will talk about in the future."

The team indeed got people talking. On just the third day of practice, Matsuura turned the fastest lap of the day and Fernandez was right behind him in second place. And as the first week

22

This picture: Running well at Indianapolis. Right: Fernandez and crew are pleased with practice results. Below right: In the pits during practice at Indianapolis.

of practice progressed, both men proved that had been no fluke.

Pole Day qualifying didn't go as Fernandez had hoped. He settled for a spot on the outside of row two with a four-lap average of 220.999 mph, despite having run several laps in the 222 mph range earlier in the month. The team had clearly established itself as a contender, however, and with Matsuura netting the best qualifying position of any rookie, ninth, that status was shared by both facets of the team.

Despite their pace in the days leading up to the race, difficult race day conditions caught the team out, keeping Fernandez from translating any of his speed from the month into success on race day.

"It just happened that the race day was much colder than anything we'd experienced all month, and we just couldn't get the car to turn well," recalls Fernandez. "So the result of seventh was, of course, very frustrating. But still, to be so competitive all month long, and so fast, it was

tremendously satisfying to feel as though we were truly capable of winning the race."

After seeing his team step up to the challenge through an arduous start to the season and begin to show improvement on the race track, Fernandez was now looking forward to the rest of the campaign. It turned out to be perhaps the most competitive year in the League's history, with 11 races being decided by less than one second.

The extreme closeness of the competition demanded the most from every member of the team – including Fernandez.

"Everything is different in the Indy Racing League," he says. "You have to learn to race side by side for a lot of laps, and the spotter makes a huge difference in those kind of conditions, so it was just a matter of getting used to it. Also, the difference between cars is a lot smaller than

"IT WAS TREMENDOUSLY SATISFYING TO FEEL AS THOUGH WE WERE TRULY CAPABLE OF WINNING"

it'd been in the past, and we had to adapt as a team to that."

Following the Indianapolis 500, a fifth-place finish at Texas Motor Speedway kicked off a run of five straight top-ten finishes for Fernandez as his team learned the nuances of a fiercely competitive category, and established itself as a threat to win on a regular basis.

"Results are a combination of having all 50 people pulling in the same direction every day of the week," team co-owner and managing director Tom Anderson says. "This is probably the most competitive league that Adrian and I have ever participated in, and a little bit means an awful lot."

Despite the string of top-ten finishes, Fernandez was frustrated not to be winning, and pushed his team to find more speed.

"I have to give all the credit to the team, because they just put their heads down, went testing, and were able to find the speed we needed to be competitive," says Fernandez. "After that Kentucky test, things just came together so much better. That test put us in the position we were in for the rest of the season – we went on to win that race, and from there, we never finished out of the top six for the rest of the season."

It can't be forgotten that 2004 was all about Honda, which netted an impressive 14 wins in the 16-race season.

"We simply wouldn't have had the success we did this season without Honda power," Fernandez declares. "I am tremendously proud to be part of this great year of success with Honda, and of what my team was able to contribute to the effort."

The hard work helped Fernandez savor success on the track, but he was enjoying himself outside of the car as well. Reunited with many of his former CART rivals, Fernandez found himself thriving in the paddock environment and felt as though that experience helped him produce something he has never had – an incident-free year.

"It was my most relaxed season ever, no question," he says. "I knew most of the guys I was racing against, and that was important because the racing is so incredibly close that you have to be able to trust the guys around you."

Fernandez's switch seems to have given him a new lease of life, and the competitive Mexican claims he has no thoughts of hanging up his helmet just yet.

"Everything is about enjoyment," he says. "Even if you enjoy driving and can be

"We had the same [Panoz G Force/Honda] package as Rahal [Letterman Racing], and yet we weren't getting the results that they were at that point," notes Fernandez. "I was really frustrated, and let my guys know."

After the Mexican had finished a disappointing 12th at Michigan, the team went right back to work after the race, heading south for a test at Kentucky Speedway in early August. Finally, the team found what it was looking for in terms of speed.

A little more than one week later, Fernandez headed back to Kentucky and led more than 50 laps in the Belterra Casino Indy 300 on his way to taking a breakthrough win by just 0.0581 of a second over Rahal Letterman Racing's Indianapolis 500 Champion, Buddy Rice. The margin of victory was the slimmest ever at the track, and the ninth closest in IndyCar Series history. Matsuura underscored the team's vault to prominence by finishing fourth – his best result of the season.

competitive, if you cannot give your whole concentration and focus, you know, maybe it's time to stop. I'm 41 years old now, and with no doubt I am living the best moment in my career as a professional race car driver."

The 2004 season produced some memorable moments for Fernandez – both as a driver and a team owner – but his personal highlight came at California Speedway, where he won over 2004 IRL Champion Tony Kanaan by a scant 0.0183 of a second – the seventh closest finish in series history.

"It was just fantastic, an absolutely unbelievable feeling to take that win," he enthuses. "It's a big satisfaction for everyone who is part of the organization, because after three years of hard work we are now at a level where we can fight against the best.

"To be able to have this success as not only a driver but with your own team just makes it all the more special, and to be competing – and winning – against established championship-winning teams like Ganassi and Penske is so completely satisfying."

Fernandez can be justifiably proud. The team gelled impressively, despite its hesitant start, earning three race wins as well as Rookie of the Year honors with Matsuura. The second half of the season firmly established Fernandez Racing as one to be reckoned with in the Indy Racing League, and Fernandez is relishing the chance to build on that momentum.

"I am thrilled with our first season in the IRL and I am already looking forward to 2005," he says, a glint in his eye. "I believe we will be challenging for the championship next year."

MATSUURA MAKES THE GRADE

WHEN THE 2004 INDY RACING LEAGUE season began, not many race fans in North America were familiar with the name Kosuke Matsuura. By year's end, however, not only did they know who he was, but many had even learned how to correctly pronounce it (Ko-skay Mat-sur-ah).

Before making his IRL debut with Super Aguri Fernandez Racing, Matsuura had been impressively quick both in Japan and Europe on his way up the road-racing ladder, showing enough speed to take wins, if not the consistency it takes to claim championships.

Intense in the cockpit, but quick to smile out of it, Matsuura was faced with a laundry list of

new things to learn heading into the 2004 season – the team, the language, and the fact that every turn was going to be left.

Matsuura had taken an unusual path toward his new career in oval racing. He began in the karting ranks in his native Japan, before moving up to win the Formula Dream Series championship in 2000. After attracting the attention of noted talent-spotter Suzuki, and intent on seeking the toughest competition he could find, Matsuura moved to Europe and scored second in the German F3 championship in 2002. He stepped up to the Formula Renault V6 Eurocup ranks in 2003, powering to third in the championship on the strength of eight podiums and three wins. Then came the opportunity to test for Super Aguri Fernandez Racing.

Team principals Aguri Suzuki, Adrian Fernandez and Tom Anderson liked what they saw at Phoenix International Raceway and took him under their wing to replace Roger Yasukawa. Matsuura soon confirmed the promise he'd shown in testing, beginning his rookie IRL campaign with two consecutive 11th-place finishes and proving that he knew not only how to drive the ovals, but also how to race on them. In just the third race of the season, at Twin Ring Motegi in Japan, Matsuura raised eyebrows once again as he qualified an impressive fourth, and went on to take his first top-ten, with eighth at the finish.

Matsuura continued to show that he was a quick learner in Indianapolis, where he was fast all month. He was the only rookie to finish, in 11th, and afterward declared it his best race ever. It was the fourth race in a row that he'd finished as the top rookie, and earned him the coveted Bank One Rookie of the Year Award.

After Indianapolis, a run of tough finishes (16th, 14th and 18th) frustrated Matsuura, but he rebounded to claim ninth at the one-mile Nashville Speedway. Two races later, he converted a tenth-place qualifying effort into his season-best finish of fourth at Kentucky

Speedway, behind race-winning teammate Adrian Fernandez.

"Today is the day I believe Kosuke Matsuura grew up," Super Aguri Fernandez Racing managing director Tom Anderson said after the Kentucky race. "He had an opportunity to throw it all away a couple of times and he didn't. He waited. He was patient."

Matsuura's learning curve was also helped by having a veteran teammate in Fernandez, who had thousands of miles of lessons to pass on to Matsuura despite the fact that it was also his first IRL season.

"Kosuke is a great guy to work with," says Fernandez. "He caught up very quickly and started to understand why you need to use your head and why you need to be patient."

Matsuura went on to win the Indy Racing League Bombardier Rookie of the Year Award. His feat was even more impressive given the fact that his primary competitors all had extensive experience on ovals, with both Ed Carpenter and Mark Taylor having emerged from the Menards Infiniti Pro Series.

It wasn't just the fans and his team that he impressed. Matsuura's competitors also noted his quick adaptation to the IRL.

"I was in Kosuke's position last year," notes Andretti Green Racing's Dan Wheldon, the 2003 Bombardier Rookie of the Year. "When you come into this series, it might look a little bit easier than it really is. So you have to give this guy a lot of credit because he's been exceptional, and I'm sure he'll be a factor next season."

Matsuura faced an almost vertical learning curve in 2004, but despite a tough midseason, he showed he was up to the task. He has been retained by the team for 2005 and has his sights aimed high.

"It was a very exciting but tough rookie year for me," says Matsuura. "I wanted to finish the season stronger, but I am looking forward to next season already and I hope I will be able to lead the team to our first win."

REACHING OUT...
TO THE **RIGHT**

WORDS BY **MATT CLEARY**

AFTER **TEN YEARS OF RACING** exclusively on ovals, the IndyCar Series will expand its schedule to include three road and street races in 2005, highlighting a series-high 17 events for the season. With races taking place on a temporary street circuit in St. Petersburg, Florida, the long course at Infineon Raceway in California, and at historic Watkins Glen in New York, the road racing-tuned IRL machines will see action on three very different types of tracks across the United States.

Most of the drivers in the IRL have extensive backgrounds in road racing, and are enthusiastic about the addition of the new races to the schedule. While the trademark razor-thin winning margins that the series has become famous for in its oval races are unlikely to be replicated on

the road courses, the drivers are looking forward to the new challenge.

"I'm thrilled and I'm sure that a lot of our fans, teams and drivers share this sentiment," said Helio Castroneves, who won seven times on road courses in Champ Car competition before becoming king of the Indianapolis 500 in the IRL. "I can't wait to turn right again!"

Teams began preparing for the new challenge even before the 2004 season had been concluded as the IRL hosted tests to begin work on making the changes needed to the cars and to the tracks for next season. 2004 Indianapolis 500 winner Buddy Rice recorded the first official road-course lap in an IndyCar Series car during a private test on September 22 at Homestead-Miami Speedway, and the test left him looking forward to the new races.

"It's a big learning curve to take these cars that have been made to predominantly just go left and try and sort everything out, but I think it's going quite well," Rice said. "The biggest change is the braking – trying to get the thing to brake and get that to work as good as you can."

Rice, who blazed a trail through the Toyota Atlantic ranks on his way to the Indy Racing League, shares his fellow drivers' enthusiasm for the new events.

"Everyone was looking forward to running on road courses," he said. "Everyone wanted to get back to it, and I'm excited about it. It's fun to go back and be turning right."

The IRL was equally pleased after the initial tests, as the cars responded well to the changes, despite unfavorable weather conditions.

"Not only did our cars turn right for the first time, we got an opportunity to run in the rain," said IRL President Brian Barnhart. "The guys got to test the Firestone Firehawk [tires] in the rain, and they performed well. Overall, it was a very good day."

It was anticipated that the stresses of road racing would cause some problems for the oval-oriented cars, but they proved to be up to the task in the initial tests.

"I'm like a kid in a candy store," said Castroneves. "I'm extremely happy to be turning right and left again. They did a hell of a job with the braking and the downshifting. Normally, they call me 'the termite' because I destroy

Buddy Rice tests at Homestead. Below: Tony George.
Facing page: The twists and turns of Infineon Raceway.

gearboxes, but so far, I'm doing very good, so that means it's a great package."

Series founder Tony George was proud to see the IRL grow its product beyond its oval traditions, and he believes that the new venues will provide added interest in the series.

"I think that road racing is something that we've always had on our agenda from the time we started with the Orlando race in 1996," George said. "Between 1994 and 1996, we were sort of developing a vision for the Indy Racing League as it came to be known. All along we had contemplated running road courses and street circuits possibly at some point in time, with a real focus on preserving and protecting the open-wheel oval-racing aspect of major league open-wheel racing."

The Dallara and Panoz G Force chassis used by the teams were originally designed to compete exclusively on ovals, so changes will be needed to prepare the cars for road racing. Most of the attention will be focused on the powertrain, cooling, suspension and braking systems. The lower speeds and reduced airflow that the cars will carry on the road courses in comparison to the ovals means that keeping the engine cool will be a new challenge.

However, IRL officials emphasize that radical changes to the IndyCar Series formula won't be needed to go road racing, and that keeping the costs associated with the adaptation down would be a priority.

"We're doing everything we can to maintain our principle of cost containment while allowing for these specifications and the changes necessary to make the cars," said Barnhart.

In addition to mandating that teams use the same wing package as they already have for short ovals, another important element of the cost-containment measures will be limiting testing to only the open tests hosted by the IRL.

The IRL's first-ever right-hand turn in competition will be at the Honda Grand Prix in St. Petersburg, Florida. The city has shown an appetite for road racing, hosting SCCA Trans-

Am events from 1985-1990 as well as in 1995 and 1996, and most recently staging the season-opening Champ Car event in 2003.

The 12-turn, 1.806-mile long track will use an airport runway for the main straightaway, and will wind its way by the South Yacht Basin, Bayfront Center and Progress Energy Park. After visiting the track for the first time, Andretti Green Racing's Dario Franchitti thinks it will make for some close racing.

"I think the combination of street and airport is going to make for a fabulous course," said Franchitti. "There are a number of places for

Clockwise from main picture: Buddy Rice and Sam Hornish Jr. testing at Homestead; IRL President Brian Barnhart; Watkins Glen; the Florida sunshine of St. Petersburg. Facing page: The streets of St. Petersburg.

passing, which all the drivers will like. I think it's a terrific setting, it's exciting and I'm looking forward to it."

While Franchitti didn't get any laps in at St. Petersburg, he did get the chance to test at Infineon Raceway. The track, once known as Sears Point, has benefitted from major investments that have been made to upgrade the facility in recent years. The facility, constructed on 720 acres north of San Francisco, staged its first official event in late 1968, with the last major open-wheel race taking place there in 1970, when Dan Gurney took the checkered flag in the USAC IndyCar 150.

The track has a variety of configurations to accommodate the different kinds of racing it hosts – from AMA motorcycle races to the American Le Mans Series and the track's annual NASCAR Nextel Cup visit. After Franchitti did some initial testing on the track, IRL officials decided to use a 12-turn, 2.2-mile layout.

The track will see some modifications to ensure that the high-speed IRL cars have enough run-off room in some critical corners, and the IRL confirmed that it will use Turns Four to Six of the traditional road course, including the sweeping, 200-degree Carousel as well as

modified versions of Turns Nine and 11. Grading will be completed at Turns Two and Three to provide more run-off, while additional k-wall and tire packs will be placed around the course.

Infineon's tight turns and drastic elevation changes will increase demand on the cars' brakes and transmissions – and drivers too. Indeed, Franchitti was surprised by the physical demands it imposed.

"This course is really challenging and I was quite taken aback at first," said Franchitti, who in mid-November was the first IndyCar Series driver to test on the facility. "The corners are very quick, which makes it difficult. These cars accelerate very quickly, so you're coming into the corners very fast and you have to be prepared."

The IRL's second road course visit will be to Watkins Glen in upstate New York – and will represent the historic venue's first major open-wheel race in nearly a generation.

The towns has a tremendous history in the sport, hosting the first post-World War II road race in the United States in 1948 on the streets of charming Watkins Glen. NASCAR first ran a Grand National Stock Car event there in 1957, and the circuit still welcomes the NASCAR Nextel Cup to its corners each season.

The Glen, as it is affectionately known, also staged the United States Grand Prix Formula 1 World Championship race from 1961 through 1980, and the IRL's September 25 race date is a nod to the gone-but-not-forgotten fall open-wheel classic. The track will also require some modification to host the IRL cars, which will have significantly higher cornering speeds than the NASCAR stockers.

True road race fans will relish seeing the open-wheelers in "the boot," which is part of the traditional Grand Prix circuit, and track officials are excited to add the IRL to their schedule.

"Given our open-wheel heritage and unique track history as the home of American road racing, our staff, fans and surrounding communities have been anxiously awaiting the opportunity to return Watkins Glen International to its roots," said Watkins Glen International President Craig Rust.

"I think with Watkins Glen's history and tradition, the fact that it's a natural terrain road circuit, in a geographic area of the country that we really weren't in, all made sense," added Tony George.

With a growing schedule, and the new challenge of road courses, the teams and drivers of the IRL are looking forward – and left and right – to the 2005 season.

ANDRETTI GREEN PROMOTIONS

The St. Petersburg event will be overseen and developed by Andretti Green Promotions, a collaboration between Team Green Investments, IndyCar Series team Andretti Green Racing and sports marketing giant CSS-Stellar. Former Champ Car team owner Barry Green will direct the venture, and it's not the first time he has played this role, having been involved for several years in the promotion of the CART event in Toronto.

"When I came down to St. Petersburg and met with Mayor Baker and his team, I just saw how enthusiastic these folks were, and how much they wanted an IndyCar [Series] race in this city," said Australian-born Green.

Green also has a long history with Honda, which has signed on as the title sponsor for the event.

"We won a lot of races with Honda, so I am excited to be working with them again in St. Petersburg," said Green.

Left: Rodger Ward in Victory Lane for his
second 500 win in 1962.

RODGER WARD

WORDS BY **DONALD DAVIDSON**

RODGER **WARD, WHO PASSED AWAY** on July 5, 2004 at the age of 83, was quite simply one of the most outstanding drivers ever to appear at the Indianapolis Motor Speedway, not to mention having been one of motor racing's finest ambassadors and spokesmen.

Twice winner of the Indianapolis 500 (1959 and 1962), he enjoyed an extraordinary six-year run between 1959 and 1964 in which he never finished worse than fourth, placing first, second, third, first, fourth and second respectively.

His rankings in the USAC National Championship standings were perhaps even more impressive. He jumped from fifth in 1958 to the title in 1959, and almost won it again in 1960, dropping out of the final race and being narrowly out-pointed by 25-year-old A.J. Foyt. In 1961, while Foyt successfully defended, Ward slipped to third, barely being nudged out of second in the standings by runner-up Eddie Sachs. Ward came back to outpoint Foyt in 1962 (in spite of starting only nine of 13 races) and then was runner-up to the Texan in both 1963 and 1964.

In 89 starts between 1957 and 1964, he racked up 23 wins, ten seconds and eight thirds, therefore having placed among the first three in practically every other race for seven years.

And but for coming up shy of edging Sachs for second in 1961, he would have placed either first or second in six consecutive seasons.

"You know what?" Rodger once chuckled after having been introduced at a function with these statistics, "If it hadn't been for that Foyt, I would have had a hell of a record."

The record is even more remarkable considering that in most years Ward did not run the entire schedule. It was never quite clear as to whether he did not care for the promoter at the extremely treacherous one-mile dirt track at Langhorne, Pennsylvania, or whether he simply did not care for the track itself, or a combination of both, but one way or another, even with a championship hanging in the balance, Rodger did not return after 1958.

In 1962, there were two races at Langhorne and he was absent from both.

He was, to be sure, a pretty complex human being. His very emergence as racing's elder statesman, eloquent spokesman and cagey, steadily-driving master strategist came as a surprise to many, because during the early days of his career and his first half-a-dozen years on the National Championship trail, he had been anything but.

Right: Obvious affection and respect between two great champions as Ward congratulates Brabham upon qualifying in 1961. Below: Posing on the bricks the day after winning in 1959. Facing page: First 500 victory in 1959.

Right: Obvious affection and respect between two great champions as Ward congratulates Brabham upon qualifying in 1961. Below: Posing on the bricks the day after winning in 1959. Facing page: First 500 victory in 1959.

He had copped an attitude and not everybody was a Rodger Ward fan.

He swaggered, was cocky, sarcastic, and he had a reputation for being a carouser. He ran hard and won a pair of National Championship races in 1953 – Detroit and Springfield – but he also found himself in the unenviable position of being a marked man. He was right in the middle of two major racing tragedies, and while others might have been exonerated, Rodger realized he had few supporters to whom he could turn.

In the closing stages of the 1954 dirt track 100-miler at DuQuoin, Illinois, he tangled with the J.C. Agajanian-owned car of Chuck Stevenson and spun into the pit side guardrail. Stevenson's own mechanic, the legendary Clay Smith, lost his life in the ensuing accident.

Just months later, in the 1955 Indianapolis 500, it was his car – ironically the ex-Agajanian, Clay Smith-wrenched 1952-winning car of Troy Ruttman – which caught the wall and began the chain-reaction accident which resulted in the demise of the great two-time defending 500 winner, Bill Vukovich.

According to Rodger, he climbed into the grandstands later that night and sat alone in the dark, vowing right there and then to make changes in his life.

"I had a reputation for being a heavy drinker, for one thing," he once confided, "but while it is true I did hit the sauce, my problem was that I had a low tolerance for alcohol. The crowd I ran with drank a lot. But it didn't take much to get me going. So I stopped."

"IF IT HADN'T BEEN FOR THAT FOYT, I WOULD HAVE HAD A HELL OF A RECORD"

After five years of not finishing the 500, and with a fresh outlook on life, he managed to convince car owner Ed Walsh and mechanic Harry Stephens that he was up to the task. They gave him a chance and he finished the full 500 miles in 1956 in eighth place.

For 1957, he joined the team of sportsman Roger Wolcott, and drove Herb Porter-prepared cars to five National Championship wins during the next two years. Of the five, it was perhaps the win in the August 1958 Milwaukee 200 which got the most attention. Even so, not everybody was prepared for what happened next.

A.J. Watson, chief mechanic for 500 winner Bob Sweikert in 1955 and for Pat Flaherty the following year, had suddenly become racing's most successful car builder. He had recently left car owner John Zink after a disagreement and was hired by Milwaukee enthusiast Bob Wilke for the purpose of forming a brand-new team and building cars. With Jim Rathmann and George Amick, their first choices, already being committed to others, attention turned to Ward, and no one was more surprised than Rodger himself when Wilke sought him out to offer a deal.

The combination of Watson, Ward and Wilke soon became known as "The Flying Ws" and

they made plenty of history during the next half a dozen seasons.

Unlike many of his colleagues at the time, Ward had diversified interests in racing and not nearly enough credit has been given to him as a road racer. He competed in numerous sports car events and even drove a BRM in the U.S. Grand Prix at Watkins Glen in 1963. When he famously won a 150-mile Formula Libre race at Lime Rock, Connecticut, driving Kenny Brenn's Offenhauser-powered midget in 1959, it was actually in retaliation to the fact that he was supposed to have driven a Cooper Monaco. When the Cooper was re-assigned at the last minute to road racer John Fitch, who was promoting the event, Ward became so incensed that he was obsessed with going up there in anything in order to beat Fitch.

And while his spirited attempt at driving Bob Wilke's Offy-powered midget in the inaugural U.S. Grand Prix at Sebring, Florida, in December 1959 was much maligned and less than successful, he struck up a friendship which would have far reaching effects on American oval track racing.

The concept of a rear-engined car at Indianapolis was not new. There had been various attempts between 1937 and 1951, but only four such cars had ever qualified and none of them had made it past 47 laps. But Ward was so impressed by the agility of the tiny World Championship-bound rear-engined Cooper-Climax cars of Jack Brabham and Bruce McLaren at Sebring that he struck up a friendship with

THE INDIANAPOLIS NEWS

WARD WINS THE '500'

4th EXTRA

John Cooper and his drivers and suggested they try a car at Indianapolis.

On October 5 and 6, 1960, Brabham and Cooper showed up for the exploratory laps, which would result in the landmark 500 entry the following May. In addition to helping make the arrangements, Rodger took the Cooper out himself, and it is understood that Brabham's overnight stay in the city was at Ward's house!

It was at around that very time that he was having quite a profound effect, with little or no notoriety, on another race track in the vicinity. Not only did Ward design the 2.5-mile road course at Indianapolis Raceway Park – he was one of the original partners in the IRP project – he also designed the 5/8-mile oval. "He drew it out on a napkin," recalls former broadcaster Charlie Brockman. "The idea was to try and achieve three distinct grooves, so instead of a parabolic curve, he worked it so that the angle of the bank would keep increasing in stages. Not only did he design it, but he even rode the grader while the construction people were laying it down. Remember how great the midget and sprint races were on the ESPN Thunder shows? They have Rodger Ward to thank for that."

Rodger was always an excellent speaker and he became known as a great ambassador for the sport. Speedway owner Tony Hulman began calling upon him with some frequency and he always made himself available. Around 1957, Rodger had even gone to the extra effort of taking a course in public speaking – something he really didn't need to do – and he was extremely critical of colleagues who showed up at functions shabbily dressed and ill-prepared for making an appropriate presentation.

Over the years he became an outstanding raconteur, the real surprise coming when he would discuss drivers and incidents from periods earlier than those with which one would generally associate him. Even with the knowledge that, yes indeed, he was already at Indianapolis by 1951, one could be rather taken aback at hearing him tell stories about Chet Miller, Joe James, Cecil Green, Johnny McDowell and numerous others who were already deceased by 1953. He was simply a marvelous resource for those historically inclined.

And he was very balanced in his opinions, giving plenty of credit to others when he felt credit was due. "Parnelli [Jones] was the moral winner of that one," he said of the 500 in 1962. "He had it in the bag until his brakes failed. I was down on power and was just out there running. I simply backed into it."

In retrospect, Rodger could well have been a *five*-time winner, and *not* necessarily by his own admission. In the cockpit of his A.J. Watson-built rear-engined car in 1964, a lean-rich switch, which had been sticking into his leg during practice, was reversed for race day; but the two tags indicating "direction" were not. Additionally upset over the terrible second-lap

accident, which took two of his friends – Eddie Sachs and Dave MacDonald – he inadvertently ran most of the race on a full-rich fuel mixture, causing him to make five pits stops to winner Foyt's two. He was lucky to salvage second.

Perhaps he could have won in 1966. Driving a rear-engined Lola for John Mecom, and with George Bignotti as crew chief, Rodger was less than happy because teammates Graham Hill and Jackie Stewart had been given V-8 Ford engines whereas his allotment was a supercharged Offy. There were a variety of other factors but the end result is that Rodger came in and parked after 74 laps, claiming handling problems.

The following evening, the entire audience at the Victory Dinner was aghast when he concluded his remarks by completely choking up and saying, "A long time ago I told myself that if ever this stopped being fun I'd quit. Well, yesterday, it just wasn't fun anymore. So, see you all."

There were those who felt there was nothing wrong with the car at all and, considering the rate of attrition that day, he probably could have won.

And then there was 1960. He was one of the two principals in what was undoubtedly the greatest two-man battle the Indianapolis Motor Speedway has ever seen. There may have been closer finishes but there was never a contest to compare with this one. There was a record total of 29 lead changes (still unbeaten), 14 of which took place during the second half of the race between Ward and Jim Rathmann, who had been runner-up to him the year before. Lap after lap, these two were never any more than a few feet apart, first one leading and then the other.

The very running of the 500 was entirely different in those days in that there were no spotters, no two-way radios, no pace car to pack up the field during caution periods; and in fact,

Rodger Ward
Indianapolis Motor Speedway
= 1953 =

darn few caution periods to begin with, only a fairly major occurrence calling for such a measure.

It was simply Rathmann and Ward out there on this memorable day, two masters sizing each other up and trying to out-guess and out-fox the other.

There is much to be told about the 1960 race, but suffice to say that tire wear was Ward's undoing. A tell-tale strip of white began to appear in the center of his right front tire with about four laps to go, indicating that the cord was beginning to show through. He had stalled on his first pit stop and had placed additional stress on his tires during the effort to catch up. While others may have stopped for a change, several years of experience as Firestone's test driver told Ward he could slow down and still save second, which he did.

In spite of the loss, he always considered this to have been his greatest race.

Clockwise from top right: The M.A. Walker Offy with which Rodger won Detroit and Springfield in 1953; A pit stop on the way to second in 1960; The "Flying Ws" – Ward, Bob Wilke (standing left) and A.J. Watson in 1961.

As intense and smoldering as he may have been as a young man, he made this marvelous transition into a sedate and respected icon, so that racing enthusiasts of more recent years could hardly believe their good fortune when he would sit with them and reminisce.

By then a delightful master of the understatement, his grinning response to a radio interviewer's request in May 1992 that he discuss some of the details of a dinner at which he was to be a special guest a couple of nights hence was, "Well, the 500 Oldtimers Club has decided, this year, to honor all of the living drivers from the 1962 500, and I, er, just happened to have been in that one."

As indeed he was. He won it, as a matter of fact.

A YEAR TO REMEMBER

WORDS BY **JOHN OREOVICZ**

THE **FRUITS OF THE INDY RACING** League's steady, measured growth were on display for all to see in 2004. The year in which the IRL IndyCar series ran its 100th event will be remembered mainly for Honda's dominance; Honda engines won 14 of the season's 16 races, capped by a faultless run to the title by Tony Kanaan and Andretti Green Racing. But in truth, the IRL came of age in 2004, demonstrating a new level of professionalism at the team and manufacturer level that garnered unprecedented respect and worldwide attention for Tony George's series.

Fittingly, the season was highlighted by what many observers called the best Indianapolis 500 in recent memory. Despite persistent rain showers that shortened the race to 450 miles, the 500 served up some classic racing and ended with the man who was demonstrably fastest on the track seeking shelter in a makeshift Victory Lane. The storyline wasn't hurt by the fact that Buddy Rice was the first American driver to win at Indianapolis in six years and only the third in the last decade.

Rice also found himself at the center of two of the most breathtaking moments of the IndyCar season. At Kansas Speedway in July, he edged Rahal Letterman Racing teammate Vitor Meira in the second-closest finish in IndyCar Series history – 0.0051 secs, or about six inches. Then at Chicagoland Speedway two months later, Rice's Panoz G Force/Honda was launched into the air after wheel-to-wheel contact with Darren

Manning's Toyota-powered Panoz G Force. Fortunately, Rice's machine came to rest intact, and the 28-year-old escaped without harm.

In fact, the most significant aspect of the 2004 IndyCar season was how safe it was. Thanks to continual development and refinement of the cars and the widespread adoption by oval tracks of the SAFER Barrier pioneered by the Indianapolis Motor Speedway, IndyCar Series drivers sustained no major injuries this year and only a handful of starts were lost to minor ailments. With the exception of Rice's incident at Chicago, aerodynamic changes implemented by the IRL for 2004 proved effective, creating a more stable race car in turbulence without sacrificing the League's trademark side-by-side racing.

Intended to slow the cars down, the relatively minor aero changes were driven by a pair of devastating accidents at the end of 2003. For the first three races of 2004, the IndyCars were also forced to race with a slot cut in the air intake of their 3.5-liter engines in an effort to restrict power, prior to the introduction of downsized 3.0-liter powerplants at the Indianapolis 500. The League's goal was to drop speeds by 5-8 mph, especially in superspeedway trim.

"We cut the downforce and drag numbers back to coincide with the horsepower output to make it more of a challenge to drive around a place like Texas," said IRL President Brian Barnhart. "Our goal was to reduce the excess downforce to a point where we do create a little separation between the cars. In the past, we actually

Facing page: Buddy Rice climbs into his ride. Top: Sam Hornish Jr. began the season on winning form. Above: Team owner Michael Andretti had a hugely successful 2004.

Scotsman Dario Franchitti
hits the pits.

artificially created 'pack racing' where they couldn't get away from each other. You would literally get stuck side by side and as exciting as that may be, it's really not in the best interest of anybody to get cars stuck side-by-side. If one guy is quicker than another, he needs to be able to pull out and pass."

The new rules did what they were supposed to at the season-opener at Homestead-Miami Speedway – and for the rest of the year, for that matter. Rice, occupying the injured Kenny Bräck's seat at Rahal Letterman Racing, gave an indication of things to come by surprisingly claiming the Homestead pole. In the race, Marlboro Team Penske teammates Helio Castroneves and Sam Hornish staged an epic

"THE SEASON WAS HIGHLIGHTED BY WHAT MANY CALLED THE BEST INDIANAPOLIS 500 IN RECENT MEMORY"

duel, with two-time series champion Hornish emerging the victor after an inside pass into Turn Three on the final lap. It was a dream start for the vaunted new Hornish/Penske combination; could they keep it up?

The answer was no, mainly because Penske had tougher competition in the IRL in 2004 than ever before. Just prior to the start of the season, 1986 Indianapolis 500 winner Bobby Rahal decided to focus all of his team's attention on the

IndyCar Series. And in mid-March, Adrian Fernandez followed suit, dropping his plans to run in the Champ Car World Series. Supported in their move by Honda, the arrival of these top-level teams accelerated the rising level of professionalism in the IRL paddock, to the consternation of some of the smaller teams like Kelley Racing, Dreyer & Reinbold Racing and even Panther Racing which found themselves shuffled to the back of the grid.

Kanaan repeated his 2003 victory at Phoenix International Raceway, leading 191 of the 200 laps. Hornish was his strongest challenger until the hard-driving Ohioan spun and tapped the wall before half-distance. Dan Wheldon then took what was arguably Honda's most important victory, leading Kanaan in an Andretti Green one-two on Japanese soil at the magnificent Twin Ring Motegi complex.

At that point, rival competitors Toyota and Chevrolet put Honda's advantage down to the Japanese manufacturer's desperate desire to win at Motegi; a track it constructed in 1997 but never mastered with a victory. Honda's total focus has been on the 3.5-liter engine, they said. Wait until the 3.0-liter engines come on board at Indy.

By the time Rice led Honda's sweep of the top seven slots on the Indianapolis grid, it was obvious that Toyota and Chevrolet were the ones lagging. Honda's advantage with the 3.0-liter engine was estimated at up to 40 horsepower, earning the prestigious Schwitzer Award for the development teams at Honda Performance Development and Ilmor Engineering. Rice stormed on to a popular Indianapolis victory, with Honda powering the top eight finishers. The $1.7 million that Rice took home established a new Indianapolis 500 record.

A clean and virtually incident-free Month of May prompted the IRL to adopt the Indianapolis aero specification for the remainder of the season's high-speed ovals. It was also announced that the qualifying procedure at Indy will be changed for 2005, with a fourth qualifying day making a surprise return in an effort to encourage participation and further spice up the show. Drivers will be allowed to make multiple attempts at earning one of the eleven spots up for grabs on each of the first three days, capped by a traditional "Bump Day."

Toyota and, to a greater extent, Honda successfully ratcheted up their attack to another level in 2004, leaving the Chevrolet-powered runners firmly in their wake.

Honda's considerable advantage over the competition remained a constant factor throughout the summer as a succession of drivers won races with the California-built V-8s. Kanaan added victories at Texas Motor Speedway and Nashville Superspeedway, while Wheldon won at Richmond International Raceway and Nazareth

Speedway, the latter in the IRL's 100th event. AGR colleague Dario Franchitti also broke into the win column at Pikes Peak International Raceway and the Milwaukee Mile in what amounted to the Scotsman's first full season of IRL competition. Rice notched up a third win at Michigan International Speedway.

Perhaps most impressive of all was the late-season rise of Fernandez. Thrown in at the deep end at Phoenix in a new series without any pre-race testing, Fernandez muffed a gearshift and didn't even complete a lap at speed. At Indianapolis, the 41-year-old Mexican was often fast in practice but wasn't a factor on race day. A midseason test gave the owner-driver more confidence in the Panoz G Force/Honda package

Clockwise from top: Tomas Enge was a late arrival to the 2004 season; Dario Franchitti returned to the IRL after major back surgery; Adrian Fernandez made a dramatic impact on the latter half of the year; Tony Kanaan with Tony George at the Chevy 500.

and he responded with solid victories at Kentucky Speedway, Chicagoland Speedway and California Speedway to finish fifth in the overall series standings – all while tutoring Kosuke Matsuura to "Rookie of the Year" honors.

Meanwhile, Kanaan kept finishing races. The 29-year-old from Sao Paulo completed all 3,305 laps of competition in 2004 and after his eighth-place run in the opener at Homestead, he never again finished out of the top five. It was

a remarkable season in terms of its consistency, exceeded only by Michael Schumacher's 2002 F1 season, when the German ace finished on the podium in every grand prix.

While Wheldon ended up second in the standings, Kanaan's closest and toughest rival in the quest for the IRL championship and its corresponding $1 million payday was Rice. The pair disputed victory in several midseason events, and Kanaan was particularly gutted when he lost the Michigan Indy 400 to his American rival after dominating most of the contest. Toward the end of the season, some bitter words were exchanged between the duo as they argued about etiquette on the track, and it will be interesting to watch this 200 mph rivalry intensify in the future.

The youth movement sparked by Kanaan, Rice and a whole host of 20-something drivers prompted a pair of the IRL's elder statesmen to hang up their helmets. Robbie Buhl ceded his

seat at Dreyer & Reinbold Racing to Felipe Giaffone prior to the Indianapolis 500, while an uncompetitive series of races in IRL newcomer Patrick Racing's Chevrolet-powered car caused two-time Indianapolis winner Al Unser Jr. to throw in the towel after the Richmond race in June.

Andretti Green's success in running four cars convinced several other team owners that the economies of scale are worth pursuing. Bobby Rahal will field three full-time entries in 2005, with female Toyota Atlantic Championship standout Danica Patrick joining Rice and Meira, while 2003 series champion Target Chip Ganassi Racing is set to run a third car for the Toyota-backed Australian Ryan Briscoe. Interestingly, Penske Racing has decided to buck the "superteam" trend and will stick with two cars for Hornish and Castroneves.

With all the success Honda and its teams enjoyed in 2004, there were inevitably failures. The Penske team was usually best of the rest;

Clockwise from top left: Darren Manning in his #10 Panoz G Force/Toyota; Tony Kanaan in triumphant mood; Dan Wheldon gets the full treatment from his Andretti Green Racing crew.

indeed, aside from Hornish's victory in the opener at Homestead, Castroneves earned the only other non-Honda win by claiming the season finale at Texas Motor Speedway. Most notable was the Ganassi team's surprisingly weak title defense. After finishing second at Phoenix to Kanaan, Dixon was never a factor and in the second half of the season, the New Zealander was often outclassed by his "rookie" teammate Darren Manning. However, the Englishman was criticized on numerous occasions by rivals for what they perceived as his over-exuberance on the track and a dangerous propensity for blocking.

Toyota is expected to bounce back in 2005, but such a scenario is unlikely for Chevrolet in what amounts to a lame duck season.

In October, General Motors announced that it intends to pull out of the IRL at the end of 2005, citing rising costs and diminishing returns for struggling teams. Morale within the Chevrolet ranks hadn't been helped by a dismal 2004 season that produced only one podium finish (for Red Bull Cheever Racing's Alex Barron at Phoenix) and an almost unbelievable series of setbacks and retirements for the marque's lead driver, Tomas Scheckter.

A few days after the Chevrolet pullout was announced, Toyota Racing Development General Manager Lee White also made some critical remarks concerning the rising cost of engine development in the IRL, a topic that George addressed when he served on a business panel at the SAE Motorsport Conference in December.

"Our goals have always been to keep racing affordable for sponsors, teams and fans, while providing the opportunity for all teams to enter the sport at a reasonable level," George said. "We began the Indy Racing League as a production-based platform; after three years, we evolved into a race-purpose engine. That was part of our evolution and part out of necessity. However we have continued to control our engine costs, despite what some may say.

"RACING IN THE IRL IS A MUCH MORE SERIOUS BUSINESS THAN IT WAS FOUR OR FIVE YEARS AGO"

"The costs today to compete – and that's important, to *compete* – in the Indy Racing League are about the same as they were in 1997, adjusted for inflation. There are a number of additional costs that enter into it, some that the manufacturers have been bearing, but they are part of making the overall experience of what I guess it needs to be. That includes driver salaries and development programs. But we have worked very hard at controlling the amount of things to be engineered to produce what we feel are negligible changes. We can't always legislate how people who have money spend it."

George added that one of the IRL's main challenges in moving forward is to gain relevance in an increasingly crowded sports and entertainment marketplace. To that end, the IRL is adding road racing in 2005, starting with a street race in St. Petersburg, Florida, promoted by 1995 Indianapolis 500 winning team owner Barry Green and a new company known as Andretti Green Promotions. Additional road races are planned on traditional natural-terrain road courses at Watkins Glen, New York, and Sonoma, California, much to the pleasure of the IndyCar series' drivers, most of whom hail from a road racing background. However, the schedule will be capped at 17 races because the IndyCar Series will make only one visit to Texas Motor Speedway, and Nazareth Speedway has been dropped from the rotation.

Car count is expected to remain about the same in 2005, but there will be a consolidation of teams. Many of the smaller teams that created the core of the IRL in its early days have found it impossible to compete with the manufacturer-backed multicar superteams. While the higher level of professionalism that pervades the IRL paddock these days can only be considered positive, part of the rationale for the League's creation was the notion of opening up competition to the "little guy," as exemplified by rookie Marty Roth's shoestring effort at Indianapolis. In every respect, racing in the IRL is a much more serious business that it was even four or five years ago.

That said, the racing world in general takes the IRL itself a lot more seriously than it did in the League's early days. In terms of sponsor and manufacturer expenditures, the IndyCar Series has developed over the last couple of years into America's premier form of open-wheel racing. At Nazareth Speedway, on the eve of the IRL's 100th event, George reflected on the past and

Facing page: Series champ Tony Kanaan keeps focussed. Top and above: "Rookie of the Year" Kosuke Matsuura on the track and at the wheel.

the future of the League, which he formed back in 1994.

"Right now, it's easy to say I would have envisioned the League being where it is today four or five years ago, but hindsight is 20/20," he said. "We're pleased with where we're at and we just stay focused on where we are today and where we want to be tomorrow, not worry about what could have been.

"I think the addition of road courses to our schedule next year sort of ushers in a new era for the League," George added. "We'll try to continue to provide close, exciting racing on-track and see what opportunities a new discipline and new markets will present us with. I think we have to do a better job of telling our story and getting connected with the public. That's our biggest challenge."

Adrian Fernandez picked up three wins in the final six races.

2004 IRL INDYCAR® SERIES
FACTS AND FIGURES

P	Driver	Nat.	Entrant	C/E/T	Homestead	Phoenix	Motegi	Indianapolis	Texas I	Richmond	Kansas	Nashville	Milwaukee	Michigan	Kentucky	Pikes Peak	Nazareth	Chicago	California	Texas II	Points
1	Tony Kanaan	BR	Andretti Green Racing	D/H/F	8	1†	2	2	1†	5	3	1	4	2P†	5†	5P	2	3	2	2	618
2	Dan Wheldon	GB	Andretti Green Racing	D/H/F	3	3P	1P†	3	13	1	9	13	18	3	3	3	1	4	3	3	533
3	Buddy Rice	USA	Rahal Letterman Racing	G/H/F	7P	9	6	1P†	15	6	1P†	6P	2P	1	2P	22	4	14	5	20	485
4	Helio Castroneves	BR	Marlboro Team Penske	D/T/F	2†	6	3	9	12	3P	7	3	12	10	12	6	5P†	10P	7P†	1P†	446
5	Adrian Fernandez	MEX	Fernandez Racing	G/H/F	–	20	18	7	5	7	6	10	8	12	1	2	7	1†	1	5	445
6	Dario Franchitti	GB	Andretti Green Racing	D/H/F	17	17	7	14	2P	12†	4	20	1†	22	6	1†	3	20	6	15	409
7	Sam Hornish Jr.	USA	Marlboro Team Penske	D/T/F	1	15	19	26	4	13	8	2	3	4	14	18	11	6	4	17	387
8	Vitor Meira	BR	Rahal Letterman Racing	G/H/F	–	–	17	6	6	2	2	12†	5P	5	7	7	10	5	21	4	376
9	Bryan Herta	USA	Andretti Green Racing	D/H/F	13	7	14	4	19	4	5	18	9	6	9	9	8	2	17	16	362
10	Scott Dixon	NZ	Target Chip Ganassi Racing	G/T/F	18	2	5	8	14	8	12	8	DNS	7	13	20	9	7	8	6	355
11	Darren Manning	GB	Target Chip Ganassi Racing	G/T/F	6	5	4	25	8	20	11	4	19	13	10	4	6	15	DNS	–	323
12	Alex Barron	USA	Red Bull Cheever Racing	D/C/F	16	4	12	12	3	22	10	17	7	11	11	10	12	12	18	14	310
13	Scott Sharp	USA	Kelley Racing	D/T/F	9	13	9	13	18	9	20	14	15	9	17	4	13	21	21	13	282
14	Kosuke Matsuura (R)	J	Super Aguri Fernandez Racing	G/H/F	11	11	8	11	16	14	18	9	20	20	20	19	17	13	14	12	280
15	Tora Takagi	J	Pioneer Mo Nunn Racing	D/T/F	4	8	10	19	10	19	21	11	22	11	14	8	11	20	11	12	263
16	Ed Carpenter (R)	USA	Red Bull Cheever Racing	D/C/F	12	19	22	31	21	16	14	22	11	14	8	11	20	11	12	21	245
17	Mark Taylor (R)	GB	Panther Racing	D/C/F	19	12	16	30	17	18	–	–	–	–	–	–	–	–	–	–	232
			Access Motorsports	G/H/F	–	–	–	–	–	–	–	7	14	21	19	14	22	17	10	7	
18	A.J. Foyt IV	USA	A.J. Foyt Enterprises	D/T/F	15	14	15	33	22	11	13	16	16	15	18	21	15	16	19	10	232
19	Tomas Scheckter	SA	Panther Racing	D/C/F	5	16	13	18	20	17	15	19	21	19	22	17	13	19	15	18	230
20	Felipe Giaffone	BR	Dreyer & Reinbold Racing	D/C/F	15	9	10	15	9	10	16	15	13	16	16	16	16	8	20	11	214
21	Townsend Bell	USA	Panther Racing	D/C/F	–	–	–	–	–	–	17	5	6	8	21	12	18	22	9	9	193
22	Jaques Lazier	USA	Patrick Racing	D/C/F	–	–	–	–	–	–	–	21	17	18	15	8	14	18	–	–	104
23	Greg Ray	USA	Access Motorsports	G/H/F	14	10	20	27	7	15	–	–	–	–	–	–	–	–	–	–	99
24	Robbie Buhl	USA	Dreyer & Reinbold Racing	D/C/F	10	18	21	–	–	–	–	–	–	–	–	–	–	–	–	–	44
25	Al Unser Jr.	USA	Patrick Racing	D/C/F	–	–	–	17	11	21	–	–	–	–	–	–	–	–	–	–	44
26	Roger Yasukawa	USA	Rahal Letterman Racing	G/H/F	–	–	11	10	–	–	–	–	–	–	–	–	–	–	16	13	39
27	Tomas Enge (R)	CZ	Patrick Racing	D/C/F	–	–	–	5	–	–	–	–	–	–	–	–	–	–	–	–	31
28	Bruno Junqueira	BR	Newman Haas Racing	G/H/F	–	–	–	16	–	–	–	–	–	–	–	–	–	–	–	–	30
29	Jeff Simmons (R)	USA	Pioneer Mo Nunn Racing	D/T/F	–	–	–	16	–	–	–	–	–	–	–	–	–	–	–	–	26
			Patrick Racing	D/C/F	–	–	–	–	–	–	19	–	–	–	–	–	–	–	–	–	
30	Richie Hearn	USA	Sam Schmidt Motorsports	G/T/F	–	–	–	20	–	–	–	–	–	–	–	–	–	–	–	–	12
31	Sarah Fisher	USA	Kelley Racing	D/T/F	–	–	–	21	–	–	–	–	–	–	–	–	–	–	–	–	12
32	Robby McGehee	USA	PDM Racing	D/C/F	–	–	–	22	–	–	–	–	–	–	–	–	–	–	–	–	12
33	Buddy Lazier	USA	Dreyer & Reinbold/Hemelgarn Racing	D/C/F	–	–	–	23	–	–	–	–	–	–	–	–	–	–	–	–	12
34	Marty Roth (R)	CAN	Roth Racing	D/T/F	–	–	–	24	–	–	–	–	–	–	–	–	–	–	–	–	12
35	P.J. Jones (R)	USA	CURB/Agajanian/Beck Motorsports	D/C/F	–	–	–	28	–	–	–	–	–	–	–	–	–	–	–	–	10
36	Robby Gordon	USA	Robby Gordon Motorsports	D/C/F	–	–	–	29*	–	–	–	–	–	–	–	–	–	–	–	–	10
37	Larry Foyt (R)	USA	A.J. Foyt Enterprises	G/T/F	–	–	–	32	–	–	–	–	–	–	–	–	–	–	–	–	10

*Relieved by Jaques Lazier after red flag restart.

Black type indicates car still running at finish.

Legend: P – pole position; † – led most laps; DNS – did not start; R – IndyCar Series Rookie.

Chassis legend: D – Dallara (15); G – Panoz G Force (7). Engine legend: C – Chevrolet (6); H – Honda (9); T – Toyota (7). Tire legend: F – Firestone (22).

Buddy Lazier slots in at Dreyer & Reinbold Racing. Right: Fourth placed Helio Castroneves. Below right: Top rookie Kosuke Matsuura.

POLE POSITIONS

1=	Helio Castroneves	5
	Buddy Rice	5
3=	Tony Kanaan	2
	Dan Wheldon	2
5=	Dario Franchitti	1
	Vitor Meira	1

DRIVER **STATISTICS**

Driver	Starts	Best Start	Best Finish	Laps Comp. (3305 poss.)	Top 5 Finishes	Top 10 Finishes	Laps Led	Season Earnings ($)
Alex Barron	16	2	3	2930	2	5	3	931,990
Townsend Bell	10	7	5	1885	1	5	0	398,600
Robbie Buhl	3	11	10	415	0	1	0	128,000
Ed Carpenter (R)	16	7	8	2359	0	1	0	779,085
Helio Castroneves	16	1	1	3299	6	13	505	1,314,790
Scott Dixon	15	2	2	2813	2	10	3	975,890
Tomas Enge (R)	2	15	13	388	0	0	0	74,500
Adrian Fernandez	15	4	1	2856	6	12	173	1,159,540
Sarah Fisher	1	19	21	177	0	0	0	208,740
A.J. Foyt IV	16	6	10	2677	0	1	0	776,435
Larry Foyt (R)	1	22	32	54	0	0	0	192,485
Dario Franchitti	16	1	1	2883	5	8	349	1,100,890
Felipe Giaffone	13	12	8	2648	0	3	5	711,140
Robby Gordon	1	18	29	88	0	0	0	192,420
Richie Hearn	1	30	20	178	0	0	0	207,740
Bryan Herta	16	3	2	3120	4	10	67	1,057,740
Sam Hornish Jr.	16	2	1	3000	6	8	301	1,042,140
P.J. Jones (R)	1	31	28	92	0	0	0	195,490
Bruno Junqueira	1	4	5	180	1	1	16	296,240
Tony Kanaan	16	1	1	3305	15	16	889	1,911,990
Buddy Lazier	1	28	23	164	0	0	0	212,240
Jaques Lazier	7	9	8	1244	0	1	0	250,400
Darren Manning	14	5	4	2611	4	8	12	872,990
Kosuke Matsuura (R)	16	2	4	2864	1	4	11	901,540
Robby McGehee	1	33	22	177	0	0	0	202,740
Vitor Meira	14	1	2	2841	6	11	152	1,019,340
Greg Ray	6	2	7	995	0	2	3	452,585
Buddy Rice	16	1	1	2886	7	12	342	2,689,040
Marty Roth (R)	1	32	24	128	0	0	0	203,990
Tomas Scheckter	16	3	5	2495	1	1	32	790,040
Scott Sharp	16	12	8	2964	0	6	5	870,940
Jeff Simmons (R)	2	19	16	351	0	0	0	258,090
Tora Takagi	16	9	4	2752	1	4	0	838,790
Mark Taylor (R)	15	3	7	2456	0	3	4	746,890
Al Unser Jr.	3	17	11	496	0	0	0	292,740
Dan Wheldon	16	1	1	3215	12	13	433	1,640,790
Roger Yasukawa	2	12	10	378	0	1	0	322,840

RACES LED

1	Tony Kanaan	13
2=	Sam Hornish Jr.	11
	Dan Wheldon	11
4	Helio Castroneves	9
5	Buddy Rice	8

RACE WINS

1=	Adrian Fernandez	3
	Tony Kanaan	3
	Buddy Rice	3
	Dan Wheldon	3
5	Dario Franchitti	2
6=	Helio Castroneves	1
	Sam Hornish Jr.	1

BOMBARDIER ROOKIE OF THE YEAR

1	Kosuke Matsuura	280
2	Ed Carpenter	245
3	Mark Taylor	232
4	Tomas Enge	31
5	Jeff Simmons	26
6	Marty Roth	12
7	Larry Foyt	10

TEAMS & DRIVERS OF THE 2004 IRL INDYCAR® SERIES

WORDS BY **JOHN OREOVICZ**

ANDRETTI
GREEN
RACING

BASE: Indianapolis, Ind.

DRIVERS: Tony Kanaan, Dan Wheldon, Dario Franchitti, Bryan Herta

SPONSORS: 7-Eleven, Klein Tools, Jim Beam, ArcaEx, XM Satellite Radio

EQUIPMENT: Dallara/Honda/Firestone

BEST FINISH: 8 wins (Kanaan 3, Wheldon 3, Franchitti 2)

BEST QUALIFYING: 5 poles (Kanaan 2, Wheldon 2, Franchitti 1)

TOTAL POINTS: 1,922 (Kanaan, 618 – 1st; Wheldon, 533 – 2nd; Franchitti, 409 – 6th; Herta, 362 – 9th)

THIS **WAS A SEASON THAT SIMPLY** belonged to Andretti Green Racing. Tony Kanaan's near-perfect year on his way to capturing the IRL IndyCar Series drivers' title was as much a reflection of the team's brilliance as that of the Brazilian himself. And thanks to its home-grown protégé, Dan Wheldon, AGR completed a one-two finish in the championship standings, while Dario Franchitti and Bryan Herta also ended the season well inside the top ten in points.

With three wins and three poles in the first five races, the organization quickly established its Dallara/Hondas as the performance benchmark for the series, and between them AGR's four drivers ended up taking eight wins – exactly half the races contested.

The 2003 season had been one of learning the IRL ropes for the AGR team, following the buyout of Barry Green's Champ Car squad by race veteran Michael Andretti, longtime team manager Kim Green and businessman Kevin Savoree at the end of 2002. But having established the team's operating procedures in that learning year, AGR arrived at the start of the 2004 season as a well-oiled machine with all the necessary pieces in position for immediate success.

The key word was continuity. Kanaan and Wheldon remained with their #11 and #26 teams respectively, while even the biggest off-season change was a case of AGR keeping what it had. The decision was taken to add an extra team, making Andretti Green the first full-time, four-car operation in modern major open-wheel racing. With Franchitti returning from injury to reclaim his seat in the #27 Dallara/Honda, the new #7 team was formed to run Herta, the Scot's 2003 fill-in, in his own car.

With all of AGR's senior managerial and technical staff staying on for the new campaign,

the group was confident they had the structure of communication and ability to cope with the logistics of running four cars. Under Kim Green (who also oversaw Kanaan's #11 car in races), Tino Belli remained as technical director. General manager Kyle Moyer also oversaw the #27 in races, while team manager Tony Cotman made the calls for Wheldon's #26. George Klotz was then given overall responsibility for Herta's new #7 car and the special development role it would play.

The data-gathering benefits of having four cars piloted by top-line drivers proved to be enormous, and rivals' skepticism soon turned to envy at what

AGR had at its disposal. All this information – be it on set-up, fuel loads, track conditions or race strategies – was then pooled, processed and used to maximize each drivers' chances come race day. It worked perfectly.

The system's success was in large part due to the trust and cooperation that existed between the drivers. The personal chemistry required to make this happen was uppermost in the mind of Michael Andretti when he brought each on board during 2003, but it was as an established quartet this year that the team bonded, both at the track and away from it, better than even Andretti could have hoped for.

BRYAN HERTA

7

Born: May 23, 1970
Hometown: Warren, Mich.
Resides: Valencia, Calif.
Ht./Wt.: 5-10/155
Previous INDY 500 starts: 2 (1994-95)

TONY KANAAN

11

Born: December 31, 1974
Hometown: Salvador, Bahia, Brazil
Resides: Miami, Fla.
Ht./Wt.: 5-5/145
Previous INDY 500 starts: 2 (2002-03)

Honda's ascendancy in the engine war was clearly also a huge factor in Andretti Green's championship-winning season. The team has a deeply integrated relationship with the manufacturer's US motorsport arm, California-based Honda Performance Development, to the point that one of the key roles of Herta's fourth AGR car was to be a test mule for new HPD engine developments. Honda's advantages, not just in sheer power, but also in driveability, fuel economy and reliability, all ensured that the AGR drivers were constant contenders. Still, the team was not alone in enjoying HPD's hardware, yet it – and Kanaan – came out on top.

The Brazilian's blend of consistency and speed was astonishing – he completed every single one of the season's 3,305 racing laps and strung together 15 consecutive top-five finishes.

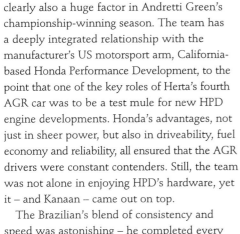

A formidable achievement that required *every* element involved in the #11 AGR operation to be working perfectly. It was.

Kanaan has always been strong on ovals; his aggressive style and bravery are well-suited to the challenges of the 200 mph side-by-side IndyCar racing. And he had learned from his maiden IRL season in 2003 that consistency alone is not enough to win the title, and altered his approach for this season – always push for race wins, but if you have a fifth-place car on a given day, accept it. It's a fine line to tread, but as a man in his prime, it was Kanaan's time. He displayed unrelenting focus to achieve his title goal with a perfect balance of experience and hunger, confidence and caution.

After a quiet eighth at the season-opener in Miami (his worst result of the year!), he bounced back with a win at Phoenix, then took second places at Motegi and Indianapolis. The Brickyard classic established that Honda's new 3.0-liter motor was markedly better than the opposition, and Kanaan capitalized on AGR's superiority next time out at Texas to take a dominant win, and with it a points lead he would never lose.

It was never easy, though. Wheldon and Buddy Rice were close in the points all summer and both then won races after Texas, but a major turning point occurred at the halfway mark in Nashville. Kanaan – by his standards having a relatively uncompetitive day – inherited victory late on after his rivals Wheldon and Rice clashed. The breathing space this afforded him in the point standings allowed him to play the

percentages from then on; but he still always got the best from what he had.

There were, of course, days when Kanaan and his long-time engineer, Eric Cowdin, did not get their car perfect. At Milwaukee his car setup was poor, but Kanaan pulled out what he called his drive of the season to drag out a fourth place. The team also made its lone error next time out at Michigan. Kanaan had been utterly dominant, but in the dying laps the team mistakenly told Kanaan to let Rice pass, believing the American would run low on fuel. But the fact that second place was a bad day says it all. A string of four podiums over the final quartet of races meant he sealed the title with a race still to run.

Rivals pointed to Kanaan being blessed with good luck – and that's true to a point. But by consistently qualifying at the front (average position: fourth), racing at the head of the pack (he led for over a quarter of the season), and having a team that gave him a race car with 100 percent reliability and smooth pit stops, Kanaan and AGR never gave bad luck a look in.

Second place in the championship represented a stellar season for Dan Wheldon. Last season's Rookie of the Year did not quite achieve Kanaan-levels of perfection, but in many seasons his three wins and eight third places would have reaped a title. From the start it became clear the Englishman had made the step up from being a headstrong and occasionally wild sophomore to a fully-fledged championship contender. Third places at both Miami and Phoenix were followed by a brilliantly dominant victory at Motegi – giving Honda its first victory at its home track. An equally impressive third at Indy emphasized his growing maturity, and he ended the first quarter of the season at the top of the point standings.

Wheldon freely admitted that he profits most from the spirit of cooperation in the AGR camp. What he gained from listening to three top-line, experienced drivers proved invaluable, and as his friendship with them blossomed – especially Kanaan – so did his confidence.

AGR team manager Cotman's brilliance with mid-race tactical calls for the #27 car was a major factor in Wheldon's other two wins at Richmond and Nazareth, but short tracks were also an area where Dan improved massively. Still, there's

room for improvement. There were a few days, such as at Kansas, when he was not a factor, and his qualifying form was inconsistent. But he never misted his mind with "title talk," and he can look at a gearbox failure at Texas in June and an electrical problem at Milwaukee as reasons that separated him from being much closer to Kanaan's tally.

Unlike his title-contending teammates, Dario Franchitti went through a sweet and sour season, two wins punctuated by a series of mechanical failures and mishaps. Having run just three races in 2003 because of a back injury, his first full IndyCar Series season started badly with a brace of retirements. After a disappointing 14th at Indy, he then took pole and a second place at Texas. But far from kick-starting his season, he was then taken out of a race at Richmond he might have won, and suffered gearbox failure at Nashville. Four DNFs in eight races meant any title aspirations were ruined.

The second half of the season was much the same – quick everywhere, he took two dominant short track wins at Milwaukee and Pikes Peak, but three more mechanical failures meant he did well to finish sixth in points.

Still, his experience and technical input is key to the team, and he enjoyed being an essential part of a winning organization. Most important of all was that he knew he'd made the right decision to undergo major back surgery to return to the cockpit.

Bryan Herta might stand out as the one AGR driver who didn't win a race in 2004, but the significance of his selfless dedication to the team's cause cannot be underestimated. Like Franchitti, he provides superb, detailed technical feedback and his development work on the Honda engines was crucial in a series with so little testing. He's still quick, though, and came very close to winning at Chicago – it's a matter of when, not if, that he returns to Victory Lane.

The success of AGR's multi-car line-up can be gauged by the fact that many of their rivals plan to expand their operations for 2005. As for AGR, it is keeping all elements intact for its title defense, and Kim Green insists there's room for improvement. A sobering thought for the opposition.

26 DAN WHELDON

Born: **June 22, 1978**
Hometown: **Emberton, England**
Resides: **Indianapolis, Ind.**
Ht./Wt.: **5-9/157**
Previous INDY 500 starts: **1 (2003)**

27 DARIO FRANCHITTI

Born: **May 19, 1973**
Hometown: **Edinburgh, Scotland**
Resides: **Nashville, Tenn.**
Ht./Wt.: **5-9/153**
Previous INDY 500 starts: **1 (2002)**

RAHAL LETTERMAN
RACING

BASE: Hilliard, Ohio

DRIVERS: Buddy Rice, Vitor Meira, Roger Yasukawa

SPONSORS: Pioneer, Argent Mortgage, Centrix Financial, Sammy

EQUIPMENT: Panoz G Force/Honda/Firestone

BEST FINISH: 3 wins (Rice)

BEST QUALIFYING: 6 poles (Rice 5, Meira 1)

TOTAL POINTS: 900 (Rice, 485 – 3rd; Meira, 376 – 8th; Yasukawa, 39 – 26th)

WHEN **THE RAIN CLOUDS FINALLY EMPTIED THEIR** contents onto the Indianapolis Motor Speedway last May, it signaled the emergence of Buddy Rice as one of America's brightest new motorsports stars. The Rahal Letterman Racing driver then went on to push Tony Kanaan harder than anyone else for the title through the rest of the IndyCar Series season, and cemented his position as a major force in U.S. open-wheel racing.

The Indianapolis 500 victory made it a big year for Bobby Rahal's team, too. But for Rice, it was huge, as he completed a great American sporting tale of triumph over adversity. Discarded by Cheever Racing before the end of the 2003 season, Rice was facing the prospect of being unemployed for

2004. But Rahal's team needed a replacement for its star driver Kenny Bräck, who was seriously injured in the 2003 season finale at Texas. Rice got the drive and capitalized on the opportunity.

Even putting Bräck's accident aside, Rahal's team had endured a difficult 2003. The former CART champion and his team principal Scott Roembke regrouped over the winter, switching from a Dallara to Panoz G Force chassis. Then, at the second IndyCar Series race at Phoenix, the team announced it would concentrate all its efforts on the IRL, turning a parallel one-car Champ Car operation into a second IndyCar Series entry. With a two-car team now under the Rahal Letterman Racing banner and the support of Honda, it emerged as a major player.

In retrospect, the signs of Rice's stellar season were there from the first race at Homestead-Miami when he took pole position – the first of five through the year. He was seventh in the race, before a quiet day at Phoenix netted ninth and a competitive run at Motegi – the day Vitor Meira joined him in the second car – resulted in sixth. A solid start, but his meteoric form at Indy was still a surprise to many. All through practice Rice was quick, then he stormed to pole position. Still he was not the race favorite, but Rahal was learning he had a star on his hands.

Rice's temperament is one of controlled but open aggression at all times, and he races with a matter-of-fact calmness that makes him both consistent and unflappable. This meant he wasn't fazed by his new-found status of being aboard a potential winning car. His performance at Indy was nothing short of superb, his speed and passing ability unmatched as he charged to a victory that all rivals agreed he deserved. Thrust into the media spotlight, Rice began a dizzying run of public appearances that perhaps took their toll by the season's end. But aside from being an Indy 500 winner, he was also now confirmed by Rahal for the rest of the year and propelled into the thick of a title fight.

A competitive run at Texas proved that his Indy form was to continue, but a damaged suspension knocked him out of contention. He was sixth at Richmond, and then embarked on a run of two wins (Kansas and Michigan) and two runner-up spots (Milwaukee and Kentucky) in five races that made

him Kanaan's closest title challenger. This spell began with the Kansas win over his teammate Meira, and the next time out at Nashville the duo were again the pick of the field.

Rahal's team was by now setting the pace for the summer. What Buddy was left to rue, however, was only finishing sixth at Nashville – a late race yellow had negated his lead and at the restart he clashed with Dan Wheldon, damaging his front wing. At a time when Rahal held the upper hand, Rice had been foiled from taking maximum advantage, and Kanaan inherited the Nashville win. But it was at Pikes Peak at the end of August that things truly unraveled, as Rice spun out on the opening lap. It was a rare mistake, but was followed at Chicago by a 200 mph flip. As Rice's inverted machine came to a halt half a mile down the track, so did his title challenge. But it won't be his last.

Meira, like Rice, was a man who grabbed opportunity with both hands in 2004. Roembke had a list of potential drivers for the additional second seat, but Meira – without a drive since the demise of Team Menard at the end of 2003 – chased it harder than anyone else and won his chance. He didn't disappoint. The quiet Brazilian was impressive all month at Indy, and while Rice stole the headlines, he took a solid sixth. Second places at Richmond and Kansas followed, enough to persuade Rahal to keep him on for the year as it became apparent that Bräck was not ready for a comeback. With the security of a proper contract, he left the entire field behind at Nashville, leading the first 113 laps in imperious fashion before airjack and then gearbox problems ruined his day. After that, however, he never again properly led a race, and failed to register any more top-three finishes. A good eighth in the final points, he'd done enough to land a multi-year contract with Rahal by the end of the year, and the continuity will benefit him. But he needs to step up a notch to establish himself as a regular race winner in 2005.

The team added a third Panoz G Force/Honda at Motegi and Indy for Japanese-American Roger Yasukawa. A solid 11th was backed up by tenth at the Brickyard. The squad expands to three cars full-time in 2005, with Toyota Atlantic star Danica Patrick joining Rice and Meira. Headlines are guaranteed.

ROGER YASUKAWA

16

Born: October 10, 1977
Hometown: Los Angeles, Calif.
Resides: West Hollywood, Calif.
Ht./Wt.: 5-7/150
Previous INDY 500 starts: 1 (2003)

BUDDY RICE

15

Born: January 31, 1976
Hometown: Phoenix, Ariz.
Resides: Phoenix, Ariz.
Ht./Wt.: 5-8/150
Previous INDY 500 starts: 1 (2003)

VITOR MEIRA

17

Born: March 27, 1977
Hometown: Brasilia, Brazil
Resides: Brasilia, Brazil
Ht./Wt.: 5-7/141
Previous INDY 500 starts: 1 (2003)

MARLBORO TEAM PENSKE

BASE: Reading, Pa.
DRIVERS: Helio Castroneves, Sam Hornish Jr.
SPONSOR: Marlboro
EQUIPMENT: Dallara/Toyota/Firestone
BEST FINISH: 2 wins (Hornish 1, Castroneves 1)
BEST QUALIFYING: 5 poles (Castroneves)
TOTAL POINTS: 833 (Castroneves, 446 – 4th; Hornish, 387 – 7th)

FOR **AN ORGANIZATION WITH** a towering record of success such as Marlboro Team Penske, the 2004 season will not go down as one of its best. Amid a year that was bookended by a brace of lone victories for its pair of Toyota-powered Dallaras, there was plenty of frustration. But given that, for once, Roger Penske's team suffered from an unfair *disadvantage* in not having Honda engines, it displayed many qualities as it spearheaded the opposition all season.

One of Penske's great strengths over the years has been continuity of personnel, and all major areas of operation, from president Tim Cindric downward, remained unchanged for 2004 – bar one glaring exception. The team had pulled off the biggest coup of the winter by signing double IRL IndyCar Series champion Sam Hornish Jr. to replace the retired Gil de Ferran. Much fanfare followed the arrival of the IRL's "poster boy" at U.S. motorsport's greatest team, and his progress up against the established Penske ace, two-time Indianapolis 500 winner Helio Castroneves, was one of the most eagerly anticipated aspects of the year ahead. The 2004 season was just two hours old before Hornish gave the most emphatic of answers.

Hornish and Castroneves qualified an unspectacular seventh and tenth respectively for the first event at Homestead-Miami, but once the race was underway it became apparent that the Penske juggernaut had hit the ground running. The duo rapidly carved its way to the front of the field, with Castroneves doing the lion's share of leading. It came down to a straight fight between them, and on the penultimate lap Hornish pulled off a stunning passing maneuver inside his new teammate to become the first driver to win on his debut in a Penske open-wheel car.

Given their dominance at the Florida race, no one could have predicted that it would not be until the Texas finale, a whole eight months later, that a Penske car would again enter Victory Lane. Even though Honda's giant team, Andretti Green Racing, laid the foundations for the Japanese manufacturer's 14-race winning streak with victories at the following two events, the Penske duo were far from outclassed in terms of performance. Hornish was hot on Tony

Kanaan's tail at the Phoenix short oval before spinning into the wall, while Castroneves only lost second place to Kanaan at Motegi at the final restart.

The team had every expectation that Toyota – the dominant engine manufacturer in 2003 – would again come out on top when the new 3.0-liter units were introduced at Indianapolis, as Penske strove for a record fourth consecutive 500 victory. But once the Hondas began sweeping the time sheets at the Brickyard, their hearts sank. In typical Penske fashion, they put up a brave fight against the odds, with Hornish leading early on (he was the only driver to pass eventual winner Rice for the lead), before he was taken out in an accident. Castroneves salvaged ninth.

The race set the tone for the rest of their season, as Penske regularly proved its mettle by being the only Toyota-powered team – Ganassi included – to consistently challenge Honda's major players. The team usually maximized everything it had to negate its rivals' advantage in power, torque and fuel economy. Penske found the sweet spot on the Dallara chassis on the short ovals, where the strong Phoenix form continued. Its pit stops were consistently as good as any team's, and its two talented drivers always gave their all behind the wheel, despite little reward. Only at Kansas and Kentucky did its cars appear to be off the ultimate pace. The paradox is that the team strove against the odds to put itself in a winning position so well that, by its own standards, its conversion rate of potential race wins into actual victories was certainly lacking.

The stats also suggest that Penske, despite its underdog status, should have taken more than two wins. Castroneves led the second most laps of any driver all year, while Hornish led at some point or other in no less than 11 races! They also qualified well, both driver's average position bettered only by Kanaan and Rice.

Races they could have won included Pikes Peak, where Hornish led much of the way but, as at Phoenix, ended the day crashing as he chased the leader. Both Penske drivers also led for long spells at Milwaukee and Nazareth, where Hornish's chances were ruined by a pit lane miscue that caused a fire. And by rights, Castroneves *should* have won at the other short oval, Richmond, where he took pole and was the quickest out there in the race until he was foiled only by AGR's inventive fuel strategy. Hornish was rudely blocked when he had a run on race winner Kanaan at Nashville, but the most cruel miss came at the penultimate race at California. Castroneves led three-quarters of the race only for late yellows to give his rivals a chance. A sluggish restart cost him the win but, of course,

he redeemed himself two weeks later with an emphatic victory at the Texas finale.

The ground that Toyota gained on Honda toward the end of the season certainly helped Penske leap into contention, and Castroneves – with his wings trimmed right down and taking some deep breaths – ended the year with four straight poles.

His qualifying ability is one of the reasons the Brazilian came out marginally on top in a straight comparison to Hornish. He also made fewer mistakes, being the only driver other than Kanaan to finish every race of the year, and his fourth place in the final points, plus the Texas triumph, was some reward for an impressive year.

Perhaps Hornish losing out in the consistency stakes was to be expected as he adapted to his new environment, but at least the Phoenix and Pikes Peak errors proved he was pushing right to the limits. And his brave, incisive passing remains second to none; the road courses will now be the next fascinating test.

For next year, Penske is resisting expanding beyond its traditional two-car operation, and with Hornish and Castroneves back on board, it has proved itself the best-placed team to take full advantage of the expected Toyota revival.

SAM HORNISH JR.

6

Born: **July 2, 1979**
Hometown: **Defiance, Ohio**
Resides: **Defiance, Ohio**
Ht./Wt.: **5-11/165**
Previous INDY 500 starts: **4 (2000-03)**

HELIO CASTRONEVES

3

Born: **May 10, 1975**
Hometown: **Sao Paulo, Brazil**
Resides: **Miami, Fla.**
Ht./Wt.: **5-8/147**
Previous INDY 500 starts: **3 (2001-03)**

FERNANDEZ
RACING

BASE: Indianapolis, Ind.
DRIVERS: Adrian Fernandez, Kosuke Matsuura (R)
SPONSORS: Quaker State, Telmex, Tecate, ARTA, Panasonic
EQUIPMENT: Panoz G Force/Honda/Firestone
BEST FINISH: 3 wins (Fernandez)
BEST QUALIFYING: 2nd (Matsuura)
TOTAL POINTS: 725 (Fernandez, 445 – 5th; Matsuura, 280 – 14th)

FERNANDEZ **RACING WAS ONE OF THE** great success stories of the 2004 IRL IndyCar Series, navigating a year that began in turmoil and ended in triumph. The team's owner/driver Adrian Fernandez arrived late to the series chased by controversy, but by the end of the season had racked up three wins and established himself as one of the IndyCar Series' leading players.

The plans for Super Aguri Fernandez Racing were set long before the season began. Fresh from a move into new premises in Indianapolis, that team, overseen by Fernandez co-owner Tom Anderson, would return to the IRL for a second season. Only this time it would have Japanese rookie Kosuke Matsuura as its driver in place of Roger Yasukawa, and trade the Dallara chassis for a Panoz G Force to go with its Honda engines. That much was straightforward.

The complication came after the IndyCar season had already started. Adrian Fernandez himself was to continue with a sister team in Champ Car but, left without assurances of the series' future, he decided to switch his effort, Mexican sponsors and all, to the IRL. That move, which sent shockwaves through the US open-wheel and Mexican racing fraternities, came on March 11. Just ten days later, Fernandez was sitting on the grid at Phoenix.

Adrian himself looked drawn and harried at the Arizona short oval. The decision to switch codes had been a hard one and he was dismayed by the negative reaction within his Mexican fan-base. But, with the strong support from Honda on offer,

the opportunity to meld his and the Super Aguri operations into one unit, and the security of the IRL's future, he was adamant – and still is – that it was the right business decision at the time.

On the track, however, it was an inauspicious start. His day at Phoenix ended right away at the green flag when the gearbox broke, and then he retired early at Motegi with an engine problem.

In reality, therefore, Fernandez's season started at Indianapolis, where he had a month of practice to get himself and the team's engineers – led by experienced campaigners John Ward and John Dick – truly familiar with the needs of the Panoz G Force.

The 41-year-old's experience began to take effect, and he and the increasingly-impressive Matsuura were among the very fastest at the Brickyard all month – helped, of course, by the advantage Honda had over the opposition with its new 3.0-liter engine. In the race, Fernandez was quick but unlucky to fall from fourth to seventh in the shuffle of the final stops. Still, a corner had been turned.

A fifth place next time out at Texas started a run of five straight top-ten finishes that elevated Fernandez to 12th in the points at the season's halfway mark. But he was never a major threat for victory and, seeing the Rahal Letterman team turn its Panoz G Force/Honda combination into the hottest cars around, frustration grew. Then, a strong run at Michigan was ruined by Fernandez himself making an uncharacteristic error by spinning in the pit lane. As a result, Fernandez urged himself and his team to make a leap forward.

At the ensuing Kentucky test, that's exactly what they did, discovering some major gains in their car's performance. From then, the blue touch paper was lit and the Mexican ace hit supreme form. At Kentucky he was a factor at the front all day, and in the closing stages he pulled off a great passing maneuver to take three cars and a lead he would hold to the flag. With Matsuura in fourth place, it was a day for the whole team to cherish.

Second place at Pikes Peak was followed by a seventh at Nazareth – a slow final stop costing three places. By now, however, rivals reckoned Fernandez's car was *the* strongest out there, and he reeled off two more wins at Chicago and California. A fifth place at the Texas finale meant Adrian ended the year fifth in the points. Given his slow start, it was a fantastic effort.

It was a year that showed Fernandez is still at the top of his game, his fitness, bravery and zeal defying his age, and he heads into 2005 on a high.

The team's good year was completed by Matsuura, an oval novice, securing rookie-of-the-year honors at the Texas finale.

He showed a genuine speed and fearlessness from the start and, alongside F1 star Takuma Sato, is the most exciting new talent in Japanese motorsports. By the third race at Motegi, he was able to qualify fourth and race to eighth, and he applied himself extremely well at Indy.

However, from that great platform he might look back with a tinge of disappointment on the rest of the season. Beyond the Kentucky result there were only two more top-ten finishes, and although he suffered two mechanical failures, there were weekends when he was simply unable to unravel the secrets of oval racing. Still, he is a buoyant and popular character and, after being re-signed by Fernandez for 2005, has the potential to make a major impact on the US racing scene.

5 ADRIAN FERNANDEZ
Born: **April 20, 1963**
Hometown: **Mexico City, Mexico**
Resides: **Paradise Valley, Ariz.**
Ht./Wt.: **5-8/145**
Previous INDY 500 starts: **2 (1994-95)**

55 KOSUKE MATSUURA
Born: **Sept 4, 1979**
Hometown: **Aichi, Japan**
Resides: **Indianapolis, Ind.**
Ht./Wt.: **5-6/150**
Previous INDY 500 starts: **0**

TARGET CHIP GANASSI RACING

BASE: Indianapolis, Ind.
DRIVERS: Scott Dixon, Darren Manning
SPONSORS: Target
EQUIPMENT: Panoz G Force/Toyota/Firestone
BEST FINISH: 2nd (Dixon)
BEST QUALIFYING: 2nd (Dixon)
TOTAL POINTS: 678 (Dixon, 355 – tenth; Manning, 323 – 11th)

THERE'S **NO GETTING AWAY FROM IT: BOTH EMOTIONALLY** and statistically this was Target Chip Ganassi Racing's worst season for 12 years. Scott Dixon, having won the 2003 IRL IndyCar Series crown, could only manage tenth in the points, with his teammate Darren Manning positioned one place behind. And between the two of them there was not a single victory.

Indeed, bar Dixon's early-season form, the pair of Toyota-powered Panoz G Forces never even looked like winning a race. The team remains a model open-wheel operation, but the year did not live up to Ganassi's own high standards. There was plenty of head-scratching and analytical self-examination, but few concrete conclusions.

Clearly, as the season settled in, it became apparent that anyone without a Honda engine was at a considerable disadvantage. But that doesn't quite cover an explanation, for Ganassi's yardstick could still be seen as Toyota's

other primary squad, Team Penske. And more often than not, its cars were genuine factors at the front. The same cannot be said for Ganassi's boys.

Of course, the team entered the season still privately coming to terms with the loss of its new signing Tony Renna, killed in a testing accident at the end of 2003. The young American was never forgotten, but the whole squad got on with its job with a dignity and professionalism that was exemplary.

That one tragic factor aside, one of the causes for consternation over the lack of victories was that so little had been changed from the formula that took Dixon to the '03 title. The team was using the same Panoz G Force/Toyota package. Its long-term management remained unchanged, with the vastly experienced Mike Hull running the show day-to-day under Chip Ganassi's ever-present eye. Dixon stayed with his chief engineer Julian Robertson, and the only new factor was Renna's replacement, Darren Manning, who was placed under the charge of long-time race engineer Bill Pappas. So why weren't they winning?

In fact, while the 3.5-liter engines where still in service during the first three races, the signs didn't look too bad. At the Homestead-Miami opener, Dixon's was the only car able to live with two Penske cars at the front, and was running third when he suffered a nasty accident, losing control and hitting the tires at the end of the pit wall as he entered the pits. Manning finished sixth.

Then at Phoenix, Dixon chased winner Tony Kanaan home, with Manning in fifth. A heavy crash in practice at the Twin Ring Motegi left Dixon with a fractured ankle, but he raced through the pain to fifth – one place behind the ever-improving Manning.

But then, come the arrival of the new 3.0-liter engines at the Indianapolis 500 in May, the Honda teams left the rest trailing. Dixon, on the back of signing a new multi-year deal with Ganassi just before the race, was the best of the rest in eighth. From then on, Dixon and Manning gradually slid from fifth and sixth in the points to the foot of the top ten.

As the established star, Dixon was expected to lead the way, but after Homestead he would not lead another lap all season. A major problem for the team was a lack of qualifying speed. This meant that week after week both drivers had their race setups and strategies compromised, and were exposed to the risks of life in the midfield as they tried to work their way to the front.

To try to make up for the power deficit, Ganassi trimmed off more and more downforce from the Panoz G Force chassis, but this came at a price – it became nervous and difficult to drive. Dixon was twice caught out at Milwaukee. Two big crashes left him with a sprained ankle and broken thumb, and he missed the race. The Kiwi took this low-point as a warning, and admits that he then stopped trying to push the car beyond its limits, because he alone was never going to make up the deficit. He was right – in oval racing, a touch of pragmatism will always prevail over sheer heroism in the long run.

There was some encouragement at the end the year, with four straight top-tens. But while Toyota had a late-season revival that allowed Penske to win the Texas series finale, Dixon had to make do with sixth. The Kiwi's own analysis was that they were maybe victims of their own 2003 success – trying to replicate year-old methods on a car that had substantially changed. Still, it was a season to forget, but with a talent as big as his, he's bound to bounce back in 2005.

Being up against Dixon was not an easy task for Manning, but the Englishman came out smelling of roses. The weight of overall expectation was always going to be lower on him, and with only three Champ Car oval races under his belt there was a steep learning curve at first. Confident and quick, rivals were at first wary, and Manning did initially cling to a road racing mentality of diving down the inside to "claim a corner."

But with time his driving became more sympathetic and consistent, and he got quicker and quicker. His talent for passing cars produced some excellent drives through the field, especially on short ovals where his natural car control also came to the fore. In the second half of the season, his fourth places at Nashville and Pikes Peak were highlights, and he often put Dixon in the shade in both qualifying and race situations.

A sizeable accident during qualifying at the penultimate round in California meant he missed the final two rounds, but by then the team had already exercised its option to retain Manning for 2005. He deserves it, and progress could be spectacular.

Chip Ganassi – and Toyota – does not take kindly to failure. All the stops, including a likely third car, will be pulled out for '05, and Dixon and Manning will convert the progress into results.

SCOTT DIXON

1

Born: **July 22, 1980**

Hometown: **Auckland, New Zealand**

Resides: **Indianapolis, Ind.**

Ht./Wt.: **5-10/150**

Previous INDY 500 starts: **1 (2003)**

DARREN MANNING

10

Born: **April 30, 1975**

Hometown: **North Yorkshire, England**

Resides: **Indianapolis, Ind.**

Ht./Wt.: **5-9/135**

Previous INDY 500 starts: **0**

RED BULL CHEEVER RACING

BASE: Indianapolis, Ind.
DRIVERS: Alex Barron, Ed Carpenter (R)
SPONSORS: Red Bull
EQUIPMENT: Dallara/Chevrolet/Firestone
BEST FINISH: 3rd (Barron)
BEST QUALIFYING: 2nd (Barron)
TOTAL POINTS: 555 (Barron, 310 – 12th; Carpenter, 245 – 16th)

THE RED BULL CHEEVER RACING squad endured a season that on paper promised much, but ultimately delivered very little tangible reward. Lead driver Alex Barron did score the sole podium finish for a Chevrolet-powered car – a third place at the Texas race in June – and ended as GM's highest points scorer in 12th overall. But still, an ambitious team boss like Eddie Cheever exited the season contemplating far more lows than highs, along with a sizeable accident damage repair bill.

After a trying 2003, the ebullient Cheever made a raft of changes over the winter that appeared to set his operation up for a far stronger year in 2004. With the stable financial platform provided by energy drinks company Red Bull's third successive year of primary sponsorship, the squad was expanded from one to two full-time cars.

Two-time IRL race winner Barron, who had been brought in to replace Buddy Rice for the final three races of 2003, was retained to spearhead the driving roster aboard the Chevy-powered Dallaras. An all-American line-up with a mix of youth and experience was completed by rookie Ed Carpenter, the stepson of Indy Racing League founder Tony George, who made the move up from the Menards Infiniti Pro Series.

Former Indy 500 winner Cheever elected to not drive at all himself during the year to devote all his energies to running the team, and former Roush Racing leading light Max Jones continued as managing director. The team's 2003 R&D liaison with the disbanded Team Menard had dissolved, but in February Cheever announced a major new technical partnership with the Montreal-based automotive giant Mecachrome, previously a Formula 1 engine builder. With all this in place, and status as one of Chevrolet's two primary teams, the elements looked set for a strong season.

Things started badly at Homestead when Barron was taken out by newcomer Darren Manning, but he immediately bounced back with an encouragingly competitive fourth place at Phoenix.

The Month of May proved quite a struggle for the whole team as Chevy's new Cosworth-built 3.0-liter engine was, like the Toyota, left trailing in the wake of the new all-conquering Honda unit. Still, Barron buckled down to the task in hand on race day to take 12th, highest GM runner once more.

In the slipstreaming mix of Texas, which masked certain power and torque issues, Barron guided the car to third place, but from then on there was little to shout about. Barron's best form came at the short ovals, with a seventh at Milwaukee the highlight of his remaining three top-ten finishes. In between there were four more crashes, all but one caused by the Californian being collected by another's crash – the type of bad luck that running in the midfield can attract. But when he did manage to finish, it was always in the top 12.

The alarming thing from Barron and Cheever's point of view was that the team rarely matched the pace of fellow Chevy users Panther, and although Tomas Scheckter received the latest engine developments first, it showed there are improvements to be made. Barron is still a quality driver, though, and it was good that he found a permanent home with Cheever after a transient 2003. That he remained in the top ten of points for much of the year was a testament to his consistency at bringing the car home.

For his part, Ed Carpenter only had one top-ten finish to show for his efforts, along with quite a few wrecked cars. But, with Barron as his barometer, there's no doubt that Carpenter showed flashes of genuine pace; in qualifying terms over the course of the season there was little to separate him from his team leader. And he proved to be a good racer with the ability to overtake, with a few events where he outshone his teammate in the early stages during moves through the field and into the top ten.

He was also at a disadvantage in that his schooling was in short-track midgets. This may have taught him the art of car control, but both the finesse required to drive a high-downforce open-wheel car and the technical knowledge and feel needed to set it up were not areas heavily covered on his apprenticeship path. It turned out he had a very steep learning curve, and some of the accidents were a case of losing a battle against an ill-handling car.

Combine this with the severest testing restrictions ever in the series, 16 tracks to learn and an ever-increasing standard of entry, and this rookie was truly up against it. Any mistakes were both heavily punished and very public, but he improved and scored six finishes in the second half of the year.

Cheever has not renewed Carpenter's deal for 2005, but ignore skeptics who put his presence in the series purely down to family ties. He deserves another shot at this level.

After the lack of success, Cheever has shown he's not afraid to rip it all up and start again. Some may question his frenetic leadership style, but he seems to have landed the goods for 2005. Toyota will be his third engine supplier in four years, he's boosted the technical staff with the arrival of ex-F1 technical director Henri Durand, and Mecachrome's increasing involvement has brought in French-Canadian Champ Car ace Patrick Carpentier. In 2004, the team had some excuses. No more.

51 ALEX BARRON

Born: **June 11, 1970**
Hometown: **San Diego, Calif.**
Resides: **Menifee, Calif.**
Ht./Wt.: **5-10/150**
Previous INDY 500 starts: **2 (2002-2003)**

52 ED CARPENTER

Born: **March 3, 1981**
Hometown: **Indianapolis, Ind.**
Resides: **Speedway, Ind.**
Ht./Wt.: **5-9/165**
Previous INDY 500 starts: **0**

PANTHER RACING

BASE: Indianapolis, Ind.
DRIVERS: Tomas Scheckter, Mark Taylor (R), Townsend Bell
SPONSORS: Pennzoil, Menards, Johns Manville
EQUIPMENT: Dallara/Chevrolet/Firestone
BEST FINISH: 5th (Scheckter, Bell)
BEST QUALIFYING: 3rd (Scheckter, Taylor)
TOTAL POINTS: 502 (Scheckter, 230 – 19th; Bell, 193 – 21st; Taylor, 79 of 232 – 17th)

THERE **MUST HAVE BEEN TIMES DURING 2004 WHEN THE** five-strong ownership team at Panther Racing wondered what they did wrong in a previous life, because fate certainly dealt them the worst possible hand all year.

For the first time in six years they went through a season without a win; but that was just the tip of the iceberg for the two-time IndyCar Series champion team. Indeed, the string of bad luck which dogged lead driver Tomas Scheckter defied belief. Time and again the South African's Dallara/Chevrolet was one of the fastest cars on the track, yet he finished a dismal 19th in the points table, with just one top-ten finish and no fewer than ten retirements. Humbling stuff.

The team had started the year in optimistic mood with Panther CEO John Barnes promising that, with Panther's guidance, Scheckter would add consistency to his prolific speed and mount a serious championship challenge. The team also took the increasingly important step of becoming a multi-car team with the addition of the #2 Menards entry for rookie Mark Taylor. With the stability of its engineering staff, led by technical director Andy Brown, and the strong late-season form in 2003 of the Cosworth-built Gen IV Chevrolet engine, Scheckter's title aspirations appeared justified.

The year started well with a strong performance at Homestead-Miami, where Scheckter led early on and only fell from third to fifth at the final round of pit stops. A certain third place was lost at Phoenix when he was hit from behind in the late stages by Dario Franchitti. A fuel miscalculation cost a strong result at Motegi, before a late-race pit mix-up at the Indy 500 dropped Scheckter from tenth to 18th. If those first four races had gone to form, he would have sat fifth in the points. As it was, things went from bad to worse.

Over the next 12 races, Scheckter saw the checkered flag on just three occasions, and even in those he suffered some mishap that kept him out of the top ten. There was never one single weak link that went wrong; one week it would be a gearbox, the next a halfshaft; or there were the three occasions he was innocently caught up in other's accidents, two more when he was hit by other cars.

Amid the craziness, a pattern emerged. On seven occasions, Scheckter suffered a misfortune early on that sparked a stirring comeback drive through the field – no one can have passed more cars all year. His struggles became a rolling sideshow – mishap, stunning recovery, terminal problem. Sport can be the cruelest form of theater.

At both Michigan and California he made up a whole lap to get into the top five, while at Kentucky he went a lap down and fought back to the lead. Each time, however, fate would whip the carpet from under Scheckter's feet and everyone's efforts came to naught.

It is to Panther's eternal credit that the team stuck it out. They exonerated Scheckter even when he had got it wrong. But this loyalty was a reflection on Scheckter himself, whose mistakes were rare and who became a true leader, a positive and talented talisman in which the team never lost faith. He never stopped trying, never stopped passing – and the maturity that Barnes sought out emerged. When good luck beckons, the rest had better watch out.

The pressure that Scheckter's troubles brought made life difficult for Mark Taylor in the sister car. The reigning Infiniti Pro Series champion showed some speed, but suffered from the restrictive testing rules and made his mistakes in public. When his fifth shunt in six races at Richmond also took out Scheckter, the guillotine dropped and the Englishman was gone.

In stepped Townsend Bell. Calm, confident and with oval experience, he immediately started chalking up top-ten finishes – three in his first four races – including a fifth at Nashville. As a foil to Scheckter's perennial misfortune, it was exactly what the team needed.

The Californian's intelligence and feedback contributed a lot to the engineering side, and although he didn't always match Scheckter's raw speed, he sometimes wasn't benefiting from GM's latest developments. Bell also suffered mishaps over the final six events - not helped by bizarrely being taken out by Scott Sharp in consecutive races - but fully deserves a full season in the series, which could establish him among the IRL elite.

4 TOMAS SCHECKTER

Born: September 21, 1980
Hometown: Cape Town, South Africa
Resides: Cape Town, South Africa/Indianapolis, Ind.
Ht./Wt.: 5-11/160
Previous INDY 500 starts: 2 (2002-03)

2 MARK TAYLOR

Born: December 16, 1977
Hometown: London, England
Resides: Indianapolis, Ind.
Ht./Wt.: 6-0/170
Previous INDY 500 starts: 0

2 TOWNSEND BELL

Born: April 19, 1975
Hometown: San Luis Obispo, Calif.
Resides: San Luis Obispo, Calif.
Ht./Wt.: 5-11/165
Previous INDY 500 starts: 0

KELLEY RACING

BASE: Indianapolis, Ind.
DRIVERS: Scott Sharp, Sarah Fisher
SPONSORS: Delphi, Bryant Heating & Cooling, Cure Autism Now
EQUIPMENT: Dallara/Toyota/Firestone
BEST FINISH: 8th (Sharp)
BEST QUALIFYING: 12th (Sharp)
TOTAL POINTS: 294 (Sharp, 282 – 13th; Fisher, 12 – 31st)

ONE **OF THE FEW REMAINING "ORIGINAL" IRL INDYCAR** Series teams at the start of the season, Kelley Racing found its status slip from major player to backmarker during 2004. The Indianapolis-based squad of car dealership mogul Tom Kelley had won races in each of its six previous seasons, including two in 2003, but found itself unable to muster the resources to match the step-up in performance of the growing IndyCar giants. After losing its Corteco backing of Al Unser Jr.'s entry following the 2003 season, Kelley's effort was reduced to one car, with long-time driver Scott Sharp retained for a seventh season to pilot the Delphi-backed Dallara/Toyota overseen by experienced team manager Paul "Ziggy" Harcus. The year started in reasonable fashion with a ninth place at the season-opener at Homestead, which Sharp repeated two races later at Twin Ring Motegi.

With Sarah Fisher as a teammate in a one-off second entry for the Indianapolis 500, Sharp took a solid enough 13th-place finish at the Brickyard. But it was also the day when it became apparent that, with the switch to the new 3.0-liter engines, anyone without a Honda was at a distinct disadvantage. Given that handicap, Sharp was never even a contender at the front for the rest of the year.

There's no doubt that Kelley, having been one of the original Toyota teams in 2003, was never given the same status as the Japanese manufacturer's topline squads Penske and Ganassi, but it never came close to matching their efforts to take on the Honda brigade. Sharp struggled particularly in qualifying – 12th in Japan remained his best effort – and there were regularly days when he was no more than an also-ran, finishing several laps down. Still, the likeable American maintained his smiley demeanor throughout, and used his experience to produce a good finishing record – only three DNFs all year – that resulted in a slightly flattering 13th overall in the points.

Given a chance to use his drafting knowledge on fast tracks, he pulled out a couple more top-tens: eighth at Michigan and ninth at Chicagoland represented good efforts by all involved. But Sharp was also still prone to unfathomable mistakes, such as crashing just as the green flag fell at Kansas and nudging Townsend Bell into the wall at Chicago.

Long before the end of the season it became clear that Tom Kelley had had enough. His team couldn't match the manufacturer-backed big guns, and he was unwilling to pour in the extra resources needed to do so. A "For Sale" sign was on the squad's equipment before the final race. Still, the team signed off in good fashion at the Texas finale. With Toyota's late-season improvements finally reaching its single-car teams, Sharp pulled out a good eighth-place finish. Sponsor Delphi remains stoutly loyal to its driver, and insists on giving him another chance with a different team in 2005.

8 SCOTT SHARP
Born: Feb 14, 1968
Hometown: Norwalk, Conn.
Resides: Jupiter, Fla.
Ht./Wt.: 5-8/155
Previous INDY 500 starts: 9 (1994-96, 1998-2003)

39 SARAH FISHER
Born: Oct 4, 1980
Hometown: Commercial Point, Ohio
Resides: Indianapolis, Ind.
Ht./Wt.: 5-3/120
Previous INDY 500 starts: 4 (2000-03)

MO NUNN
RACING

BASE: Indianapolis, Ind.
DRIVERS: Tora Takagi, Jeff Simmons (R)
SPONSORS: Pioneer
EQUIPMENT: Dallara/Toyota/Firestone
BEST FINISH: 4th (Takagi)
BEST QUALIFYING: 9th (Takagi)
TOTAL POINTS: 277 (Takagi, 263 – 15th; Simmons, 14 of 26 – 29th)

MO NUNN RACING BEGAN THE 2004 SEASON WITH HIGH hopes that Japanese driver Tora Takagi would achieve great things but, by the end, all parties were simply wishing to see the back of the year.

Veteran engineer Mo Nunn's squad had won a race in each of its two previous IRL campaigns and had enjoyed some promising moments with Takagi in 2003. In his maiden IRL season the ex-Formula 1 driver had scored nine top-tens, including a third at Texas, and placed tenth in points. Many predicted that his speed would translate into a visit to Victory Lane at some point during 2004.

Having flip-flopped between chassis in 2003, Takagi had opted to make his preferred Dallara a permanent choice. And even the fact that over the winter Nunn lost the Brazilian Hollywood backing that had funded his other car – which left Takagi's Toyota-powered example as its sole entry – did not dent the quiet optimism.

The year started well, too, with Takagi taking full advantage of clever late-race pit strategy to finish a close fourth at Homestead. That was a rare day that favored Toyota-powered runners, but he backed it up with an eighth at Phoenix and then a gutsy tenth place at Motegi after a heavy practice crash. But then at Indianapolis Takagi really struggled. Toyota's new 3.0-liter engine was no match for the Honda. Even so, Takagi never looked comfortable. When Nunn put Jeff Simmons in a second car as an Indy one-off, the American newcomer immediately matched Takagi's speed, and then outshone him in the race.

Perhaps it was a combination of the Motegi crash and having his speed called into question by a rookie, but from then on Takagi's performances became ever more lackluster. He began routinely qualifying and running at or near the back, and while whatever gains Toyota made certainly did not head in the Nunn team's direction first, it was a disappointing performance.

Takagi's poor command of English – despite having raced in the US for four years – made it very difficult for his engineers to interpret his feedback, a problem exacerbated in 2004 by the lack of a second car for comparison.

Engineers Iain Watt and then Jeff Britton both eventually left, leaving their colleague Yoshi Iwashita to download Takagi's instructions in Japanese.

Confidence crumbled on both sides of the pit wall, so that by the time of the Chicago race in September, Takagi was running around out of the draft – a sure sign of a man who simply didn't want to be there.

He returns to Japan next year, where he'll hopefully rediscover a spark to go with his talent. Meanwhile, the Nunn team is regrouping and will hope to benefit from Toyota's major push to improve in 2005.

12 TORA TAKAGI

Born: Feb 12, 1974
Hometown: Shizuoka, Japan
Resides: Los Angeles, Calif.
Ht./Wt.: 5-9/135
Previous INDY 500 starts: 1 (2003)

21 JEFF SIMMONS

Born: Aug 5, 1976
Hometown: Hartford, Conn.
Resides: East Granby, Conn.
Ht./Wt.: 5'10/160
Previous INDY 500 starts: 0

DREYER & REINBOLD RACING

BASE: Carmel, Ind.
DRIVERS: Robbie Buhl, Felipe Giaffone, Buddy Lazier
SPONSORS: Purex
EQUIPMENT: Dallara/Chevrolet/Firestone
BEST FINISH: 8th (Giaffone)
BEST QUALIFYING: 11th (Buhl)
TOTAL POINTS: 270 (Giaffone, 214 – 20th; Buhl, 44 – 24th; Lazier, 12 – 33rd)

THE HARDY DREYER & REINBOLD TEAM NAVIGATED ITS WAY through a tough year as the stakes rose again in the IRL IndyCar Series. A long-standing IndyCar participant, it could never match the resources and performance of some of the newer, giant operations, but always made the best of what it had to produce a handful of worthy results.

Loyal sponsor Purex remained the primary backer of its lead car, to be piloted by co-owner/driver Robbie Buhl. But the cash was never forthcoming for the team to run the second Chevrolet-powered Dallara that had been campaigned by Sarah Fisher through 2003. But with Buhl's experience, and a management backbone led by John O'Gara and veteran engineer Owen Snyder, the drop to a lone entry was not a major drawback.

When GM had introduced its new Cosworth-built, Gen IV engine at the end of 2003, Buhl had looked strong, and carried optimism into 2004. The veteran American driver started much as he left off, taking a solid tenth place in the season-opener at Homestead-Miami. An accident ended his day at Phoenix, and then he retired again at Motegi. It would be his last race. Buhl abruptly announced on his return from Japan that, after 20 years in the cockpit, it was time to hang up his helmet.

The 40-year-old, who had two IRL wins from 78 starts to his name, elected to concentrate all his energies on his team's survival, and hired a proven race winner in Felipe Giaffone to take over driving duties from Indy onward. The Brazilian, without a ride after losing his Hollywood backing at Mo Nunn Racing at the end of 2003, took a solid 15th first time out at Indy, and then followed this up with top-tens at both Texas and Richmond.

D&R couldn't have asked for a more solid start. With a Chevy engine and limited resources, it was always going to be a tall order to improve greatly on those performances. But the amiable Giaffone gelled well with the team and, although often towards the back, ended up with an enviable finishing record; only a gearbox failure at California broke his run of race completions. And there was a high point at Chicago, where he led five laps when out of sync in the drafting mix and finished an excellent eighth. The jury is still out on whether he has quite regained the form he'd shown before breaking his pelvis at Kansas last year, but he fully deserves a place on the IndyCar grid.

Former Indy 500 winner Buddy Lazier joined the team to drive its second car at Indy, but retired late with a fuel problem. A move back to two cars full-time for 2005 would be a welcome step forward for D&R, but the priority for this spirited operation is still survival.

24 ROBBIE BUHL

Born: September 2, 1963
Hometown: Detroit, Mich.
Resides: Cleveland, Ohio
Ht./Wt.: 5-9/150
Previous INDY 500 starts: 8 (1996-2003)

24 FELIPE GIAFFONE

Born: January 22, 1975
Hometown: Sao Paulo, Brazil
Resides: Orlando, Fla.
Ht./Wt.: 5-8/145
Previous INDY 500 starts: 3 (2001-03)

91 BUDDY LAZIER

Born: October 31, 1967
Hometown: Vail, Colo.
Resides: Vail, Colo.
Ht./Wt.: 6-0/175
Previous INDY 500 starts: 11 (1991-92, 1995-2003)

ACCESS MOTORSPORTS

BASE: Indianapolis, Ind.
DRIVERS: Greg Ray, Mark Taylor (R)
SPONSORS: University Loft
EQUIPMENT: Panoz G Force/Honda/Firestone
BEST FINISH: 7th (Ray and Taylor)
BEST QUALIFYING: 2nd (Ray)
TOTAL POINTS: 252 (Taylor 153 of 232 – 17th; Ray, 99 – 23rd)

FORMER **INDYCAR SERIES CHAMPION** Greg Ray's robust team again navigated a year of highs and lows, lurching from one financial crisis to another but always displaying a terrific survival instinct to carry on and produce a handful of giant-felling performances.

A year on from its foundation in 2003, Access Motorsports remained the minnow of the IRL teams. Driver/owner Ray was still at the helm, supported by Ted Bitting (team manager) and Jamie Nanny (chief mechanic), and his hardcore band of seven full-time staff was resilient as ever. The team maintained the Panoz G Force/Honda package it pioneered in 2003, but the main concern for the single-car effort was money. Ray had to sit out over half of the allocated pre-season testing as sponsorship was sought, but was duly on the grid at Homestead come March. A tenth-place finish at Phoenix was a fillip, and then Ray pulled out one of the qualifying performances of the year to take the outside front row spot in front of the Honda top brass at Motegi.

In keeping with his rollercoaster fortunes, a touch from another car early on ruined his chances, but a major point had been made.

Things took a dive at Indy, where again the lack of a major sponsor forced Ray to sit out the majority of practice – he didn't need to spend money on practice when he knew he could comfortably make the show come Bump Day. In the race he got caught in an accident, but then bounced back next time out with typical style to take seventh place at his home event in Texas, the team's best-ever result. But by the time of the

Kansas race in July, the financial problems overflowed. A wrangle with Honda over engine payments resulted in Access being barred from competing, and the team's trucks rolled out of the track before a racing wheel had been turned. It was a bitter pill, but Ray is not an easy man to keep down. Within two weeks he had the whole thing back on its feet again, having made a big sacrifice himself by vacating the driver's seat.

Panther Racing had discarded rookie Mark Taylor after six races, so the Englishman combined his resources with Ray's new sponsor, University Loft, to return Access to the action. And what a return it was, with the duo thumbing

their noses at the establishment as Taylor took seventh place first time out at Nashville. Some hard luck stories followed through the second half of the season, although Taylor routinely out-paced better funded operations. Given one-to-one nurturing by Ray, Taylor's form and confidence improved; and despite a nasty fiery accident at Chicago, he ended the year with a tenth at California and another excellent seventh at Texas.

Ray remains committed to returning to the driver's seat next year, and hopes to accommodate Taylor again in a second car. If anyone can make it happen, Access can.

13 MARK TAYLOR
Born: December 16, 1977
Hometown: London, England
Resides: Indianapolis, Ind.
Ht./Wt.: 6-0/170
Previous INDY 500 starts: 0

13 GREG RAY
Born: August 3, 1966
Hometown: Plano, Tex.
Resides: Plano, Tex.
Ht./Wt.: 6-0/160
Previous INDY 500 starts: 7 (1997-2003)

A.J. FOYT
RACING

BASE: Waller, Tex.
DRIVERS: A.J. Foyt IV, Larry Foyt (R)
SPONSORS: Conseco
EQUIPMENT: Dallara/Toyota/Firestone (A.J.) & Panoz G
Force/Toyota/Firestone (Larry)
BEST FINISH: 10th (A.J.)
BEST QUALIFYING: 6th (A.J.)
TOTAL POINTS: 242 (A.J. Foyt IV, 232 – 18th; Larry Foyt, 10 – 37th)

AT FIRST GLANCE, ONE TOP-TEN FINISH AND AN
unspectacular 18th in the points was not a stellar performance
by A.J. Foyt IV, but by the end of the 2004 season the green shoots
of a genuine talent were beginning to emerge. Just 19 years old when the
season started, the grandson of the legendary A.J. Foyt Jr. was easily the
youngest and least experienced driver in the IRL IndyCar Series. Driving
for his grandfather's team, the weight of expectation on the younger Foyt's
shoulders came as much from within his own family as the outside world.
And given the brusque demeanor of his indomitable boss, that wasn't
always the easiest position to be in.

Adding to A.J. IV's difficulties was that, for the first time, the Foyt team
was down to entering a single car in 2004, giving him no teammate for
comparison. He was helped, however, by the Toyota-powered team opting
to use the Dallara chassis full-time this year, having alternated with a Panoz
G Force through his rookie campaign in 2003. In a series with severely
restricted testing, however, Foyt was forced to once again do his learning
in public. Still, he began the year with three finishes. But then youthful
impatience got the better of him, and he crashed after just 12 laps at Indy
and after 38 laps in Texas.

The team lacked the solid engineering backbone and technical resources
of rivals. Foyt was often left to bravely wrestle with an ill-handling car, and
demonstrated some true car control. Still, there were some promising
efforts: at Richmond he was 11th, and at Kansas netted a 13th. His growth
in confidence as a driver and a personality was plain to see as the year
progressed – his average qualifying was better than that of Scott Sharp and
Tora Takagi in the other single-car Toyota teams. Then veteran engineer
Tim Wardrop came on board for the final three races. The results were
immediate: at Chicago Foyt qualified sixth, the second fastest Toyota-
powered car, and he ran well in the race before a mechanical failure caused
a crash. Sure, the improvement of the Toyota engine was a factor, but the

effect of the additional technical input was undeniable. Foyt then qualified
seventh at California and was headed for a top-ten before unfortunately
crashing 22 laps from home. But finally he got his reward at the Texas
season-closer with a tenth-place finish.

Likely to stay with the family team in 2005, there's still a feeling his true
potential cannot be determined until he gets a ride with a larger squad.

Stock car regular Larry Foyt, big A.J.'s youngest son, joined the team
to make his major open-wheel debut in its Panoz G Force chassis at the Indy
500. Amiable and articulate, he learned steadily throughout the month of
practice and successfully qualified 22nd. Sadly, he completed a bad day
for the team by being the next driver to retire after A.J. IV when he too
hit the wall after 54 laps.

14 — A.J. FOYT IV
Born: May 25, 1984
Hometown: Hockley, Tex.
Resides: Hockley, Tex.
Ht./Wt.: 6-0/155
Previous INDY 500 starts: 1 (2003)

41 — LARRY FOYT
Born: February 22, 1977
Hometown: Houston, Tex.
Resides: Huntersville, N.C.
Ht./Wt.: 5-9/170
Previous INDY 500 starts: 0

PATRICK RACING

BASE: Indianapolis, Ind.
DRIVERS: Al Unser Jr., Jeff Simmons (R), Jaques Lazier, Tomas Enge (R)
SPONSORS: Stacker 2
EQUIPMENT: Dallara/Chevrolet/Firestone
BEST FINISH: 8th (Lazier)
BEST QUALIFYING: 9th (Lazier)
TOTAL POINTS: 191 (Lazier, 104 – 22nd; Unser, 44 – 25th; Enge, 31 – 27th; Simmons, 12 of 26 – 29th)

THE MAIN STORY INVOLVING PATRICK Racing during 2004 was the retirement of its driver, two-time Indianapolis 500 winner Al Unser Jr. That caught all the headlines, but also served to thrust the single-car effort into a messy season during which it worked through three more drivers.

After 24 years in Champ Car, veteran team owner Pat Patrick – one of that series' founders – elected to move his team to the IRL IndyCar Series for 2004. One of the key motivations behind such a shift was the opportunity to link up for the first time with 42-year-old driving legend Unser Jr., who had lost his 2003 drive with Kelley Racing. The deal was not struck until after the season had begun, however, so the duo inaugurated their union with a lone Chevrolet-powered Dallara at the Indianapolis 500 in May,

with the intention to then complete the following 12 races.

Much of Patrick's existing infrastructure had been disbanded at the end of 2003, so the IRL effort was housed at Walker Racing's Champ Car base in Indianapolis, with many of the latter's mechanics moonlighting on the IRL effort overseen by Steve Krisiloff and Steve Newey. The team clearly did not have the commercial platforms of other operations – it only landed a primary sponsor for the Indy 500 itself – and Patrick had to bankroll the effort. The small operation was a sound one, but with these compromised beginnings it stood little chance of matching the big guns in the increasingly competitive IRL environment – especially when Chevrolet's new 3.0-liter engine proved no match for the Honda.

Unser Jr. put in a solid Month of May, qualifying 17th and finishing 17th, but it was hardly a performance worthy of one of America's greatest open-wheel racers. Next time out at Texas Unser trailed to an 11th-place finish as the last car running. Two weeks later at Richmond he was again at the back, and enough was enough. "Little Al" parked it and the next day announced his retirement.

Patrick's initial replacement was young American Jeff Simmons, who'd made a great impression on his IRL debut at Indy. He ran solidly at Kansas before getting caught in a three-way sandwich at Turn One and crashing into the wall. Seeking experience, Patrick then turned to former IRL race winner Jaques Lazier, who ran the next seven races. He did a competent job and was often ahead of other single-car entries. The highlight was an eighth place at Pikes Peak.

Looking to next year, the team put Czech driver Tomas Enge in the car for the final two races. The highly-talented ex-F1 driver found ovals a tough baptism, however, crashing late on at California and soldiering to 13th, and the last runner, at Texas.

Overall, after Unser's departure there was a sense of tick-over to Patrick's low-key operation. A link-up with Enge is planned for 2005, but it remains to be seen if this year was a holding season for a true all-out effort, or actually the dying embers of one of US open-wheel racing's longest standing teams.

20 AL UNSER JR.
Born: **April 19, 1962**
Hometown: **Albuquerque, N.M.**
Resides: **Henderson, Nev.**
Ht./Wt.: **5-11/170**
Previous INDY 500 starts: **16 (1983-94, 2000-03)**

20 JAQUES LAZIER
Born: **January 25, 1971**
Hometown: **Vail, Colo.**
Resides: **Alta Loma, Calif.**
Ht./Wt.: **5-11/170**
Previous INDY 500 starts: **3 (2000-01, 2003)**

20 JEFF SIMMONS
Born: **August 5, 1976**
Hometown: **Hartford, Conn.**
Resides: **East Granby, Conn.**
Ht./Wt.: **5-10/160**
Previous INDY 500 starts: **0**

20 TOMAS ENGE
Born: **September 11, 1976**
Hometown: **Liberec, Czech Republic**
Resides: **Monaco**
Ht./Wt.: **5-7/150**
Previous INDY 500 starts: **0**

NEWMAN/ HAAS RACING

BASE: Indianapolis, Ind.
DRIVER: Bruno Junqueira
SPONSORS: PacifiCare, Secure Horizons
EQUIPMENT: Panoz G Force/Honda/Firestone
BEST FINISH: 5th
BEST QUALIFYING: 4th
TOTAL POINTS: 30 – 28th

THE **MUCH-HERALDED RETURN OF CHAMP CAR KINGS**
Newman/Haas Racing to the Brickyard added a fascinating dimension to the 88th running of the great event. The squad's one-car effort for Brazilian ace Bruno Junqueira aimed to steal the greatest prize in racing from under the noses of the IndyCar regulars. Carl Haas came equipped to finally make an Indy 500 impact. He landed the only extra supply of the dominant new 3.0-liter Honda engines to mate to his Panoz G Force chassis, and hired legendary crew chief Jim McGee to run the operation. They so nearly did it.

Junqueira qualified fourth, but slipped out of the top ten until McGee rolled the tactical dice. On lap 133, with threatening rain clouds overhead, the field all made their regular pit stops – except for Junqueira. For 15 enthralling laps he led the field; if the heavens opened now, Newman/Haas had done it. The rain failed to materialise, however, and Junqueira had to pit, but still finished an impressive and well-deserved fifth.

BRUNO JUNQUEIRA
36
Born: **November 4, 1976**
Hometown: **Belo Horizonte, Brazil**
Resides: **Indianapolis, Ind.**
Ht./Wt.: **5-6/147**
Previous INDY 500 starts: **2 (2001-02)**

SAM SCHMIDT MOTORSPORTS

BASE: Indianapolis, Ind.
DRIVER: Richie Hearn
SPONSORS: Lucas Oil Products
EQUIPMENT: Panoz G Force/Toyota/Firestone
BEST FINISH: 20th
BEST QUALIFYING: 30th
TOTAL POINTS: 12 – 30th

LEADING **MENARDS INFINITI PRO SERIES TEAM SAM SCHMIDT**
Motorsports again ran a highly competent Indy 500-only effort for IndyCar veteran Richie Hearn, and earned a 20th-place finish.

The team, which ran American Hearn in the IndyCar Series full-time back in 2002 before stepping back to the Menards Infiniti Pro Series, repeated its move of last year by leasing out Marlboro Team Penske's spare Toyota-powered Panoz G Force chassis – now updated to a 2004 spec. The effort was not announced until the day before Bump Day – and fortunately, money-burning

practice was not necessary for a team and driver used to the challenges of the Brickyard, especially when only 33 cars were vying for the 33 starting spots.

Lucas Oils stepped in to fund the effort in its first appearance as an Indy sponsor, and Hearn duly planted the car in 30th place to make the show. In the race, Hearn quickly made up places to rise to 24th in the early stages, only falling off the lead lap after 50 laps. With more practice time the combination could no doubt have been more competitive, but Hearn kept going to the end to earn Schmidt a well-deserved $207,740 in prize money.

RICHIE HEARN
33
Born: **January 4, 1971**
Hometown: **Glendale, Calif.**
Resides: **Las Vegas, Nev.**
Ht./Wt.: **5-7/165**
Previous INDY 500 starts: **4 (1996, 2000, 2002-03)**

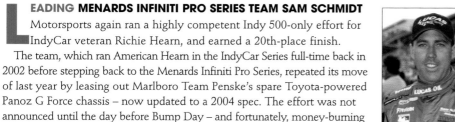

PDM RACING

BASE: Indianapolis, Ind.
DRIVER: Robby McGehee
SPONSOR: Burger King
EQUIPMENT: Dallara/Chevrolet/Firestone
BEST FINISH: 22nd
BEST QUALIFYING: 33rd
TOTAL POINTS: 12 – 32nd

PAUL **DIATLOVICH'S SQUAD WAS RESTRICTED TO A ONE-OFF** Indy 500 appearance for the first time in 2004. The team thought it had a multi-race program sewn up for its Dallara/Chevrolet with Briton Ben Collins, but when that deal fell through PDM was left bereft of an Indy program – with Diatlovich even announcing it would close its doors.

But four-time Indy 500 starter Robby McGehee combined with PDM to salvage an 11th-hour deal to enter the Brickyard classic with a car leased from Robby Gordon's team. It was the 33rd and final car to enter, thereby assuring the race maintained its tradition of a full 11 rows of machinery.

Without the threat of being bumped, McGehee could afford to just set up a comfortable car on Bump Day, and qualified last. A final-minute sponsorship deal with Burger King caught a few headlines, and then McGehee knuckled down to achieve his goal: getting a finish. In this he succeeded, taking the flag in 22nd place, three laps down and the last car still running.

18

ROBBY McGEHEE

Born: July 20, 1973
Hometown: St. Louis, Mo.
Resides: St. Louis, Mo.
Ht./Wt.: 6-2/175
Previous INDY 500 starts: 4 (1999-2001, 2003)

MARTY ROTH RACING

BASE: Indianapolis, Ind.
DRIVERS: Marty Roth (R)
SPONSORS: Roth Racing
EQUIPMENT: Dallara/Toyota/Firestone
BEST FINISH: 24th
BEST QUALIFYING: 32nd
TOTAL POINTS: 12 – 34th

GENTLEMAN **RACER MARTY ROTH SET HIMSELF A HUGE** challenge by turning a lifelong dream into reality and entering the Indianapolis 500. The 45-year-old Canadian, who had raced in the Menards Infiniti Pro Series for the past two years, elected to use his own team to run his Indy 500 effort – the first time a squad from the IRL's feeder series had made the step up. Roth unveiled his ambitious plans in March, having secured one of the few extra Toyota engine packages available to power his Dallara chassis. Roth's team, managed by the ex-PacWest Champ

Car engineer Mark Moore, hired Indy veteran Butch Winkle as chief mechanic for the car.

In practice, Roth ran more laps – totaling 1,500 miles – than any other driver. After several practice runs, he posted a speed on Bump Day – 11 mph off pole – that placed him 32nd on the grid. The squad's tireless persistence earned Winkle the Clint Brawner "Mechanical Excellence" award for his dedication.

In the race, Roth ran sensibly at the back until the car got away from him on lap 131 and he hit the wall at Turn Four. He plans to return in 2005.

25

MARTY ROTH

Born: December 15, 1958
Hometown: Toronto, Canada
Resides: Toronto, Canada
Ht./Wt.: 6-0/170
Previous INDY 500 starts: 0

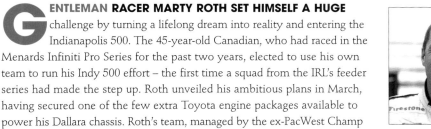

BECK MOTORSPORTS

BASE: Indianapolis, Ind.

DRIVER: P.J. Jones

SPONSORS: CURB Records

EQUIPMENT: Dallara/Chevrolet/Firestone

BEST FINISH: 28th

BEST QUALIFYING: 31st

TOTAL POINTS: 10 – 35th

to the Brickyard, and his sole attempt to qualify, in 2002, ended with him being knocked unconscious in an accident.

His father was at his side when the 2004 deal was announced, and the sense of history being repeated did not stop there: Beck landed backing from the Curb-Agajanian alliance – the original Agajanian team being the one with which Parnelli won his Borg-Warner Trophy. In deference, Jones's car was painted in the white and blue colors of "Old Calhoun," Parnelli's 1963-winning roadster.

Jones qualified on the inside of the back row and then ran well in the race, getting up to 24th until the car got away from him at Turn Two just before mid-distance and he hit the wall.

THE FIRST OF THE "MID-MONTH" DEALS TO BE STRUCK – a week after practice began – experienced IndyCar team boss Greg Beck's liaison with former Champ Car driver P.J. Jones was a bona fide effort to produce a strong Indy-only performance.

For Jones, the 35-year-old son of former 500 winner and Indy legend Parnelli, it was a chance to make his first start in the hallowed May Day event. His years in CART had come after the series had stopped coming

98 **P.J. JONES**

Born: **April 23, 1969**

Hometown: **Rolling Hills, Calif.**

Resides: **Scotsdale, Ariz.**

Ht./Wt.: **5-11/190**

Previous INDY 500 starts: **0**

ROBBY GORDON MOTORSPORTS

BASE: Indianapolis, Ind.

DRIVERS: Robby Gordon/Jaques Lazier

SPONSORS: Meijer, Coca-Cola

EQUIPMENT: Dallara/Chevrolet/Firestone

BEST FINISH: 29th

BEST QUALIFYING: 18th

TOTAL POINTS: 10 – 36th

IRREPRESSIBLE MAVERICK ROBBY Gordon tried for the third consecutive year to pull off the famous "double" by competing in both the Indy 500 and the Coca-Cola 600 NASCAR event at Charlotte in one day.

Engineer Thomas Knapp came on board as team manager and Gordon put together a well-

funded effort with a Dallara/Chevrolet package, but qualified a lowly 18th. Gordon's schedule required him to hop from his IndyCar straight onto a private jet, and as soon as rain delayed the Indy 500 by two hours, his hopes were dashed.

Still, he started the race and moved straight into the top ten by passing eight cars on the first lap. But when red flags were waved for rain after 27 laps, it was all over. Gordon left the track and Jaques Lazier was strapped into the car to become the first mid-race Indy 500 relief driver for 27 years.

Lazier was required to take the restart in last place, but rose to 23rd before an electrical problem dropped him from contention. Then, exiting the pits on lap 88, the halfshaft broke.

70 **ROBBY GORDON**

Born: **Jan 2, 1969**

Hometown: **Cerritos, Calif.**

Resides: **Orange, Ca. & Parker, Ariz.**

Ht./Wt.: **5-10/180**

Previous INDY 500 starts: **9 (93-95, 97, 99-03)**

70 **JAQUES LAZIER**

Born: **January 25, 1971**

Hometown: **Vail, Conn.**

Resides: **Alta Loma, Calif.**

Ht./Wt.: **5-11/170**

Previous INDY 500 starts: **3 (2000-01, 2003)**

TECHNICAL REVIEW

WORDS BY **ALEX SABINE**

ENGINES
HONDA

PRODUCTION BASE: Santa Clarita, Calif.
WINS: 14 (Kanaan 3, Wheldon 3, Rice 3, Fernandez 3, Franchitti 2)
POLES: 11 (Rice 5, Kanaan 2, Wheldon 2, Franchitti 1, Meira 1)
IRL MANUFACTURER'S POINTS: 154 – 1st

AFTER **A LOW-KEY MAIDEN IRL** IndyCar campaign in 2003 in which it mustered just two victories (the legacy in part of its late decision to join the series), Honda annihilated the competition in 2004, leaving slim pickings for Toyota and Chevrolet.

The statistics tell their own story: 14 wins in 16 races, achieved in an unbroken streak from Phoenix in April to Fontana in October; 11 pole positions; 74 percent of laps led. Such was Honda's dominance that it had sewn up the manufacturers' championship by Kentucky in mid-August, with five races still to run. At season's end Tony Kanaan headed a Honda one-two-three in the drivers' standings, with only three Toyota interlopers breaking into the top 10. Impressively, Kanaan completed all 3,305 racing laps, a testament to the HI4R motor's exemplary reliability.

Along the way, Honda laid to rest the ghosts of its ignominious past at the Indianapolis 500, where it had failed to qualify with Bobby Rahal in 1994 and then seen a probable victory slip away the following year when Scott Goodyear was penalized for jumping a late-race restart. This time, polesitter Buddy Rice overcame a botched pit stop to win the rain-curtailed Memorial Day classic and lead a Honda-powered sweep of the top seven finishing positions.

The Japanese manufacturer had already lifted a particularly tenacious monkey off its back by winning its home race at Twin Ring Motegi, the state-of-the-art facility it built in 1997 to bring American oval racing to the Land of the Rising Sun. In six previous attempts it had been upstaged in its own backyard, four times by Ford Cosworth and on the two most recent occasions – even more embarrassingly – by arch-rival Toyota. It fell to Dan Wheldon to set the record straight, to an almost audible sigh of relief from Honda's top brass.

Thus Honda accomplished all three of the goals it had set itself prior to the season – to win Motegi, the Indy 500 and the manufacturers' championship – and then some. Its success was especially praiseworthy in a year in which 11th-hour rule changes presented the engine manufacturers with unprecedented logistical challenges. Escalating speeds and safety concerns sparked by a pair of horrific accidents at the end of 2003, which left Kenny Bräck with serious injuries and tragically claimed the life of Tony Renna, prompted the IRL to modify its engine rules package one-third of the way into its planned three-year cycle.

For the first three events of 2004, the League mandated that a three-by-12 inch slot be cut into the cowling area behind the airbox intake in order to reduce horsepower by decreasing air pressure in the plenum, effectively canceling out performance gains made during the off-season (approximately 20hp).

More fundamental changes had to be implemented before the Indy 500 in May, when the existing 3.5-liter engines were downsized to 3.0 liters. The cylinder bore diameter and the essential engine block architecture remained unchanged, but the reduction in displacement necessitated a shorter crankshaft stroke and complementary alterations to connecting rods and pistons.

"We took an initial hit of over $1 million to make new pieces for the 3.0-liter engine," said Robert Clarke, vice-president and general manager of Honda Performance Development (HPD). "It was an extremely compressed timeline [less than five months from the announcement of the new regulations to the start of practice at Indy], and it was almost like starting a new season. When we first ran the new engine we were down 102hp. But as we moved toward Pole Day, we began to introduce development specs for the engine and software, and we started to claw that deficit back."

The manufacturers therefore had to press ahead with development of the 3.5-liter engines in the early part of the season whilst simultaneously scrambling to ready the 3.0-liter units for the season's showpiece event. It was a balancing act at which Honda proved remarkably adept, winning two of the three races held under the "old" rules (Phoenix and Motegi) and then the next 12 in succession following the adoption of the 3.0-liter formula.

"We spent last season playing catch-up as we didn't come in as strong as we had hoped," admitted Clarke. "In the off-season we made some dramatic changes to the product and, luckily, the improvements we found on the 3.5-liter engine were directly applicable to the 3.0-liter version."

As Clarke readily admits, one of the key advantages enjoyed by Honda was its technical partnership with Ilmor Engineering, which had two years' experience rebuilding GM Racing's IRL engines before affiliating with Honda in preparation for the latter's entry into the championship in 2003. Ilmor Engineering Inc., run by Paul Ray in Plymouth, Michigan, handled the lion's share of the rebuilding duties, while its sister company in Northampton, England assisted with development. The net result was that Honda was able to react faster and more effectively to the 2004 rule changes than either of its rivals.

"Thanks to our relationship with Ilmor we have a much stronger resource capability than our competitors," noted Clarke. "TRD [Toyota Racing Development] is basically all being done in the US as a single entity, and Chevy is from our point of view being done by Cosworth and limited to its resources."

In the past, the design and development of Honda's racing engines was largely the responsibility of its R&D center in Tochigi, Japan, while HPD confined itself to builds/rebuilds, trackside support and limited ancillary systems development. But the collaboration with Ilmor has allowed HPD to take on a more extensive role. Currently housed in Santa Clarita, California, the company is in the process of building a much larger (123,000sq.ft.) facility nearby, and the aim is that it will become fully autonomous by 2006.

"HPD is going through major changes," said Clarke. "Our decision was not just to leave CART to go to the IRL. We changed from being an engine supply, service and trackside support company to a company that can design, produce and race engines from a clean sheet of paper. In our CART days, the majority of our parts were from Japan; we made ten percent of our parts locally. Now we are manufacturing in-house, or outsourced but completely managed by HPD."

A crucial ingredient in Honda's banner season was the fact that its competing teams – most of which were recent Champ Car refugees, enticed by Honda to follow its lead and switch to the IRL – significantly raised their game in both numerical and performance terms compared to 2003. Andretti Green Racing expanded to a four-car stable, while Fernandez Racing and Rahal Letterman Racing also added cars as they switched their focus exclusively to the IRL. All three blossomed as the season progressed, with AGR assuming the mantle of Marlboro Team Penske as the series' powerhouse.

"As much as our engines have improved from last year, our teams have improved, too," acknowledged Clarke. "We started with transplanted teams from CART with zero IRL experience in 2003, and they have all stepped up in experience and performance."

TOYOTA

PRODUCTION BASE: Costa Mesa, Calif.,
Plymouth, Mich. and Brixworth, England

WINS: 2 (Hornish 1, Castroneves 1)

POLES: 5 (Castroneves 5)

IRL MANUFACTURER'S POINTS: 114 – 2nd

HOW **THE MIGHTY ARE FALLEN.**
Having swept all before it in its first
season of IRL IndyCar Series competition,
winning 11 races en route to the drivers' and
manufacturers' titles, Toyota suffered a retaliatory
drubbing of even more comprehensive proportions
at the hands of arch-rival Honda in 2004.

The season started according to plan, with Sam
Hornish out-dueling teammate Helio Castroneves
to win at Homestead on his debut for Marlboro
Team Penske. Little did anyone realize at the time,
but neither Penske nor Toyota would visit the
winner's circle again until the season finale at Texas
Motor Speedway in October, when Castroneves
narrowly (and controversially) prevailed over the
Honda-powered Andretti Green Racing machines
of Tony Kanaan and Dan Wheldon.

In the intervening seven-and-a-half months
Toyota's pride took a battering, as Honda piled
up the gongs with a remarkable streak of 14
consecutive victories. Among them were the two
that matter most to the Japanese automakers, their
home race at Motegi (which had eluded Honda
on six previous attempts) and, naturally, the
Indianapolis 500. In a mirror image of 2003, both
the drivers' championship and the manufacturers'
crown fell to Honda, although Toyota comfortably
saw off Chevrolet for the consolation prizes.

"It's been a pretty humbling season," admitted
Toyota's vice-president of motorsport Jim Aust,
before proffering one explanation for the
company's underperformance: "We learned in
CART that in order to succeed you've got to have
strength in teams and in numbers. Honda has eight
cars that are in the hunt every weekend and, all
things being equal, we have seven cars that don't
quite measure up."

Given that its standard-bearers were teams
of the caliber of Penske and Target Chip Ganassi
Racing, which between them had laid claim to
most of the trophies on offer in American open-
wheel racing over the previous decade, it might
seem curious for Toyota to cite shortcomings in
its customer base. But in fact it has a valid point,
for two reasons.

First, a numerical disadvantage meant that Toyota
simply had a lower probability of success in any
given race than Honda. While its five teams from
2003 all stayed on board, they accounted for a
mere seven cars – two fewer than in 2003 due to
Mo Nunn Racing and Kelley Racing downsizing
to one-car operations. Honda, meanwhile, made
a determined bid to boost its overall share of the
market, using financial inducements to persuade
Adrian Fernandez and Bobby Rahal to wind up
their Champ Car programs and focus exclusively

on the IRL. Combined with AGR's decision to
field a fourth car, that swelled Honda's numbers
from six in 2003 to nine in 2004. It amounted
to a decisive swing of the pendulum.

Toyota also lacked the strength in depth of its
main adversary, since just four of its cars (the Penske
and Ganassi entries) had a realistic shot at winning
races and only the Penske duo succeeded in
doing so. By contrast, all but one of the phalanx
of Hondas showed the pace to win at one stage
or another during the season, and five drivers
from three teams achieved the feat. From
Toyota's point of view, it was unfortunate that
Honda's three leading teams all simultaneously
upped the ante as they found their feet in the IRL
after recent transitions from the Champ Car
World Series.

But if Toyota possessed fewer and less potent
bullets in its chamber in terms of its competing
teams, equally it had no answer to Honda's
impressive parallel development of the two
engine formulae that the manufacturers had

to deal with in 2004. While Honda relentlessly fettled its soon-to-be-obsolete 3.5-liter powerplant in the early-season races (ensuring that it ran away with the high-stakes Motegi race), it also spared no effort or expense developing the new breed of 3.0-liter engines that saw the light of day at Indianapolis.

Toyota always seemed to be a half-step behind. By any ordinary yardstick its commitment – in terms of both human and financial resources – remained hard to gainsay. Inevitably, however, given its slide in performance and its burgeoning interest in NASCAR (whose Craftsman Truck division it had entered as a launchpad for a full-blown Nextel Cup assault in the near future), there were suspicions that it had taken its eye off the ball in the IRL arena. Implicitly at least, the Toyota hierarchy conceded that NASCAR was now vying for its attention.

"We had to make a choice – we couldn't continue to develop the 3.5-liter engine, build a 3.0-liter simultaneously, and undertake the challenges that faced us in NASCAR," Lee White, senior vice-president and general manager of Toyota Racing Development (TRD), said at Indy. "We had to focus on [which of the three projects] we perceived to be most important."

Notwithstanding the disparity in results, the performance differential between the Honda and Toyota engines was generally reckoned to be fairly small. The Penske and Ganassi drivers frequently mixed it with the leaders and Castroneves hit a purple patch in qualifying at the end of the season, chalking up four successive poles on tracks ranging from quirky, asymmetrical little Nazareth to the high-banked speedbowl of Texas. Clearly, there wasn't too much wrong with the late-season iterations of the motor.

Indeed, having wound up the year with something of a flourish, Toyota was at pains to reaffirm its commitment to the IRL – and its intent on regaining the upper hand over Honda. To that end, it indicated it was prepared to engage in a bidding war with its perennial foe to attract the best possible lineup of teams, if necessary by subsidizing chassis costs and drivers' salaries as well as by ramping up its technical support for chassis development and wind tunnel testing.

"You have to decide whether you want to be competitive or just be here," said Aust. "We came into this series to win so we're going to move forward, make changes and become competitive again. We've got to continue to develop our engine and shore up the possibilities of winning each week. We've got several teams and drivers we're looking at."

The announcement in November that Red Bull Cheever Racing will be switching from Chevrolet to Toyota power in 2005 has already bolstered TRD's numbers. A third Ganassi entry is also on its wish list to help combat the recent expansion of the Honda teams. Having been subjected to a Honda juggernaut in 2004, Toyota seems to have decided that it cannot stomach any further humiliation and is planning a concerted fightback.

CHEVROLET

PRODUCTION BASE: Torrance, Calif. and Northampton, England

WINS: 0

POLES: 0

IRL MANUFACTURER'S POINTS: 82 – 3rd

THE PAST TWO IRL INDYCAR SEASONS have been trying ones for General Motors, the most prolific and successful engine manufacturer in the history of American motorsport. One of the original IRL engine suppliers when the League first introduced its own equipment formula in 1997, GM enjoyed a six-year reign of supremacy during which it won every Indianapolis 500 and series championship, initially competing under the Oldsmobile Aurora banner before switching to Chevrolet branding in 2002.

But the arrival of Toyota and Honda in 2003 – coinciding with new rules that saw production-based engines replaced with smaller, lighter and more expensive purpose-built powerplants – changed all that. Chevy was not simply dethroned; for a time it was in danger of falling into oblivion. After its own design proved woefully uncompetitive in the first half of the season, GM turned to Ford-owned competition engine specialist Cosworth for help. The alliance immediately bore fruit; the new "Gen IV" motor introduced in the summer propelled Chevy standard-bearer Sam Hornish to three wins and hauled him up to a respectable fifth place in the points table.

Going into 2004, therefore, there appeared to be cause for optimism. Alas, it proved to be misplaced. Chevy endured a winless campaign for the first time since joining the IRL, and its highest-placed representative in the drivers' standings was Red Bull Cheever Racing's Alex Barron in 12th place. Barron also delivered the Bowtie Brigade's only podium finish (a fine third place at Texas in June) and its best qualifying performance (second at the Homestead season-opener). But the Californian's average starting and finishing positions (15.25 and 11.94 respectively) were more indicative of Chevy's place in the scheme of things, as was the statistic that it led a mere 40 of 3,305 racing laps.

"This season hasn't lived up to our expectations," admitted GM Racing's IRL program manager Joe Negri. "We felt we were competitive with the 3.5-liter engine at Homestead. At Motegi we were a little bit behind. Then when we debuted the 3.0-liter engine at Indy we found we weren't where the other manufacturers were. We worked hard

for the rest of the year, but once you're behind it's really tough to catch up."

In many ways, Homestead turned out to be the high-water mark, with Barron qualifying on the front row and both Panther Racing's Tomas Scheckter and Robbie Buhl in the unfancied Dreyer & Reinbold entry hanging in the lead pack with the best of the Toyotas and Hondas.

By Indianapolis it was clear that the Chevy teams were in for a long year. The Month of May yielded only a paltry 12th place for Barron as Honda swept the top seven finishing positions. The die was cast for the balance of the season: Chevy had simply fallen too far behind in the torrid development race to be able to get on terms with Toyota and, in particular, Honda.

It wasn't for the want of trying, and there were several occasions when GM threatened to break the Japanese duopoly. While Barron quietly put together a solid tally of decent results, including five top-ten finishes, Scheckter performed most of the heroics. Time and again the familiar yellow Pennzoil-sponsored car carved through the field on its trademark high line (pioneered by its previous incumbent, Hornish) only to be sidelined by contact, mechanical gremlins or a pit lane incident.

An uncanny knack of finding harm's way had been a feature of Scheckter's tumultuous IRL IndyCar career to date; but in 2004, more often than not the problems weren't of his making.

Michigan was a microcosm of his season. After starting 13th (appropriately), he made meteoric progress up the lap chart, cracking the top five within eight laps and climbing to second by lap 24 – only for Tora Takagi to run into him at his first pit stop and put him back to square one. Undeterred, Scheckter sliced through the field and was on the verge of regaining his lost lap when his fuel tank ran dry en route to the pits.

It was much the same story for Scheckter at Phoenix, Richmond, Kentucky, Pikes Peak, Chicagoland and Texas II – in each of the foregoing events, stirring early-race charges went unrewarded. In fact, fifth place at Homestead was all the South African had to show for a year of unstinting effort. But his pace at least gave some cheer to the Chevy

camp as it collected the wooden spoon in the manufacturers' contest for the second year running.

Hopes that it might end the year on a high note were raised when Scheckter qualified a season-high second for the Texas finale, armed with an upgraded engine specification that all of Chevy's customers agreed represented a significant step forward. However, both Panther Racing cars were subsequently relegated to the back of the grid after failing post-qualifying technical inspection. That in itself wasn't much of a hindrance to Scheckter, but another of his patented come-from-behind charges was cut short by mechanical failure while he was in contention for a podium finish.

The 24-year-old's catalog of woes meant that Chevy's results didn't do justice to the performance of the engine, which (in race conditions at least) was generally a reasonably competitive proposition, even at the fastest tracks like Michigan and Texas where top-end horsepower is all.

Nevertheless, the dearth of hard results did little to persuade senior GM executives that the company was getting a worthwhile return on its investment in the IRL, at a time when all its racing programs were under the microscope. Not unexpectedly, GM announced in early November that it would be pulling the plug on its IRL program at the end of 2005, citing escalating costs as the principal reason for its departure.

"We are proud of our long association with the Indy 500 and the IRL, but the investment didn't meet our business objectives any more," explained GM Racing director Doug Duchardt. "In the beginning we competed against Nissan with a certain model and that worked well. It's no secret that Honda and Toyota have driven the price up and we had to examine what we were spending and what we were getting out of it. We just found ourselves at a crossroads."

Ironically, the potential fallout from GM's withdrawal may jolt the IRL into returning to a production-based engine formula of the kind the Detroit-based automaker has always favored, in the interests of curbing costs. The League's founder and president Tony George admitted that a number of options were being considered for the next rules package, which will take effect in 2007 but needs to be in place by mid-2005 to give manufacturers enough lead time to prepare. GM sources indicated that a move back to production-based engines might persuade it to return to the IRL, possibly before it even gets a chance to leave.

CHASSIS
DALLARA AUTOMOBILI

PRODUCTION BASE: Varano Melegari, Italy

WINS: 10 (Kanaan 3, Wheldon 3, Franchitti 2, Hornish 1, Castroneves 1)

POLES: 10 (Castroneves 5, Kanaan 2, Wheldon 2, Franchitti 1)

IRL CHASSIS POINTS: 142 – 1st

WHILE **HONDA MADE MINCEMEAT** of the opposition on the engine front, the contest between chassis manufacturers in the 2004 IRL IndyCar Series proved much more evenly matched. As usual, it was a two-horse race between Dallara Automobili and Panoz G Force, with the Italian constructor ultimately prevailing in both the drivers' and manufacturers' championships – but G Force scooping the most coveted single prize, victory in the Indianapolis 500.

Dallara had the upper hand in 2003 as well, but despite claiming 11 wins in 16 races it contrived to let both Indy (where Gil de Ferran triumphed in a cameo appearance in a G Force) and the drivers' title (won by Scott Dixon) slip through its fingers, although it did emerge comfortably on top when the manufacturers' points were totted up. Tony Kanaan's well-deserved drivers' championship took care of one of those anomalies, and as the depth of competition from G Force was if anything stronger than a year ago – at least when mated to the formidable Honda engine – Dallara's tally of 10 victories was no mean feat.

The safety-related changes to the IRL's engine specifications for the 2004 season were accompanied by a parallel raft of modifications to the chassis rules. In part, these were designed to compensate for the reduced horsepower by cutting downforce by a corresponding amount, so as to prevent the cars from becoming too easy to drive on the faster tracks while also attempting to break up the "pack racing" that seemed constantly to betoken potential disaster. But a second, and even more pressing, objective was to address concerns about the IndyCars' basic aerodynamic stability, which had been brought into question the previous year by their alarming proclivity to become airborne in high-speed accidents.

A number of stopgap measures were taken for the first three races of the new season, before more significant modifications were implemented at Indianapolis. A quarter-inch vertical splitter or "spine" running down the length of the car was added, intended to disrupt airflow over the car should it get sideways and prevent low pressure from building up on one side. The purpose, explained IRL President and Chief Operating Officer Brian Barnhart, was to "increase the stability of the car when it is in yaw."

Kanaan said of the wicker, "It helps keep the front of the car down. As soon as it starts to lift, it will move somehow to the right or left, depending on how the wind is blowing or the car is lifting. The car won't do a flip, it will simply move one way or the other. I think it is very positive."

The IRL also mandated a quarter-inch "reverse wicker" on the underside of the rear wing main plane, as well as a curved skid plate that served the twin purposes of improving stability (by channeling air out of the other side of the car's belly rather than allowing it to build up and create lift) and reducing downforce (since it effectively raised the ride-height by 10mm).

The changes were the product of an exhaustive brainstorming process involving all the interested parties, and achieved their objectives almost to the letter. The pole speed at Indianapolis was down from 231.725 mph in 2003 to 222.024 mph, right on target, while the drivers pronounced themselves satisfied with the stability and drivability of the revised cars. The core features of the package – albeit with refinements to suit the various track configurations on the IndyCar schedule – were left in place for the balance of the season.

As with the engine rule changes, the chassis modifications were announced at extremely short notice and drove a coach and horses

through the manufacturers' planned update kits. The challenge from the engineers' standpoint became how to claw back the lost downforce within the new parameters. Judging by its mastery of the short ovals, Dallara was more successful at doing this than its rival, although Panoz G Force was at least a match for it at the larger tracks where minimizing drag remained the object of the exercise.

"The chassis are neck and neck," reckoned Dallara's US technical liaison Sam Garrett. "The rules are so tight that it's hard to get any sort of advantage. We can bias the car design to get a certain performance at a specific type of track but suffer on other tracks. There's a much greater difference between different teams using the same chassis than there is between the two chassis."

On that score, the odds were still stacked in Dallara's favor, since it outnumbered Panoz G Force 15-7 and, crucially, enjoyed the patronage of the mighty four-car Andretti Green Racing organization. The other five Honda-powered entries all campaigned Panoz G Force chassis, however, so the American constructor had plenty of firepower of its own.

Given Honda's dominance – and the near-parity between the chassis acknowledged by Garrett – the fluctuating fortunes of the two constructors essentially reflected which of the Honda-affiliated teams did a better job on a given weekend, and whether they were in the Dallara or Panoz G Force camp. While Rahal Letterman Racing and Fernandez Racing were certainly in the ascendancy, AGR was the class of the field, and Dallara duly prospered with it.

This does not, however, diminish the impressive achievements of the Italian marque, which has consistently set the benchmark in the modern IRL era. With the exception of 2003, Dallara-equipped drivers have won every IndyCar championship since 1998, as well as a clear majority of individual races.

AGR co-owner Michael Andretti, for one, sees no reason to tinker with a winning partnership. "The cars are fairly equal, and you've got to be careful not to get wrapped up in the equipment," he said. "I think the way the rules are, it's pretty tight and it's hard to gain an advantage. Besides, Dallara have been great to work with and really supportive of us. There's no reason to change."

PANOZ G FORCE

PRODUCTION BASE: Braselton, Ga.
WINS: 6 (Rice 3, Fernandez 3)
POLES: 6 (Rice 5, Meira 1)
IRL CHASSIS POINTS: 130 – 2nd

PANOZ **G FORCE'S 2004 IRL INDYCAR** season was like the proverbial curate's egg: good in parts. After being comprehensively outclassed by Dallara in the opening races, it bounced back in style at the Indianapolis 500, winning handsomely for the second year in a row thanks to a sterling drive from Buddy Rice. The gifted American spearheaded Panoz G Force's efforts through the summer before Adrian Fernandez picked up the baton and ran with it in the season's waning stages.

The net result was a respectable tally of six victories – one more than in 2003 – but defeat

past the post" basis rather than by aggregating every point scored by a manufacturer's representatives in the championship. In other words, since it was a two-way contest, if Panoz G Force had beaten Dallara more often than vice-versa it would have won. The Italian constructor's strength in numbers did give it better odds of success, however, as Panoz G Force's chief designer Simon Marshall readily admitted. "Statistically, one-third of the grid can be lost due to incidents, so we need more cars. And we need to make more money! In the last few races we've been talking to new teams [about 2005]."

The complexion of Panoz G Force's customer base had changed considerably over the winter due to the defection of Mo Nunn Racing to the Dallara camp and the arrival of Rahal Letterman Racing and Fernandez Racing, both of which were expanding to two-car operations. Unexpectedly, it was these two teams, rather than the more heralded Target Chip Ganassi Racing, that brought

in both the drivers' and manufacturers' championships. Ultimately, a lack of consistency, at least in comparison to the metronomic form of Dallara standard-bearer Andretti Green Racing, blunted Panoz G Force's challenge. There were occasions when Rice and Fernandez looked supreme (although rarely on the same day), but week in and week out no one could match AGR.

Founded in England in 1990, G Force was acquired by entrepreneur Don Panoz's Elan Motorsports Technologies company and relocated to Braselton, Georgia in 1999. It had supplied chassis to the IRL since the inception of the League's own equipment formula in 1997, since when it had won two Indy 500s but had generally been overshadowed by Dallara.

As in previous seasons, Panoz G Force was at a numerical disadvantage, supplying only seven of the 22 regular entrants. Although this was less than ideal from a sales point of view, it need not have been too much of a handicap in the manufacturers' championship, since points are awarded on a "first

home the bacon for Panoz G Force, partly because they "came of age" but mainly because they boasted Honda horsepower. Whatever the merits of the two chassis, the common denominator in most of their successes was the Honda engine.

"It was a huge stroke of good fortune when Fernandez and Rahal came on board," said Marshall. "Greg Ray led the way with the Honda installation in 2003. Honda seems to have been the engine of choice this year, and we're lucky to have these teams which have been so successful, particularly Fernandez who went through such a steep learning curve in a short time. Obviously we didn't win enough races this year to win the championship, but Buddy Rice came close."

Indeed, after midsummer victories at Kansas and Michigan, Rice seemed to be the man with the momentum. But he faded over the remaining six races – ironically just as Fernandez was getting into his stride, chalking up three wins in a five-race stretch (Kentucky through Fontana). Ganassi, meanwhile, struggled to make as effective use of

its Panoz G Force/Toyota combination as Marlboro Team Penske managed with its Dallara/Toyotas, and was often relegated to mid-pack status.

The Panoz G Force was in its element on the larger, faster tracks where speed "through the air" and minimal drag were the key requirements, as evidenced by the fact that all six of the marque's victories were achieved on tracks of 1.5 miles or longer. Conversely, its Achilles heel was the short ovals where it did not afford quite as much downforce as the Dallara.

"Most of our development has been on speedway setup and reducing drag, and we didn't concentrate on the short ovals," acknowledged Marshall. "Our focus was to win Indy, which we did, but it did involve sacrificing some of the other tracks. There are parts we can bolt onto the front wing for the short ovals, but there are some tendencies in the car's behavior that are 'hardwired' as a result of the choices you make in the design process."

The Dallara proved more versatile, winning on all types of tracks, and also seemed to have a larger handling "sweet spot." Dixon, in particular, found that it was difficult to arrive at an optimal balance on the G Force, while Fernandez allowed that it was "very sensitive sometimes." If teams could first find and then stay within that elusive sweet spot, the G Force was perhaps marginally quicker than the Dallara, but it was a fine line to tread.

"The G Force had a little less drag when it counted," noted Fernandez Racing co-owner Tom Anderson following Adrian's victory at Fontana. "We had problems learning the chassis at the beginning of the year, but the intensity generated by Adrian forced us to understand the relationship between changes we made to the car and the effects they had. You've got to understand the relationship between those changes and, with these cars, the ride-height, temperature changes and so many other factors are sensitive."

TIRES
FIRESTONE

PRODUCTION BASE: Nashville, Tenn. and Akron, Ohio

WINS: 16 (Kanaan 3, Wheldon 3, Rice 3, Fernandez 3, Franchitti 2, Hornish 1, Castroneves 1)

POLES: 16 (Rice 5, Castroneves 5, Kanaan 2, Wheldon 2, Franchitti 1, Meira 1)

BEING **THE EXCLUSIVE SUPPLIER IN** any auto racing series can be a mixed blessing. On the face of it, there is no downside – you are, after all, guaranteed to win every race, and the absence of competition obviates the need for extravagant development budgets and generally makes life easier. By the same token, however, the only way your company is likely to make the headlines is if something goes wrong. For a tire manufacturer there are numerous potential pitfalls, from unexpectedly high wear rates, "graining" and blisters due to excessive heat build-up, right through to full-scale delaminations (or, less euphemistically, blowouts).

Once again, Firestone's dedicated team of engineers and chemists, based in Akron, Ohio, came through with flying colors. The latest breed of Firestone Firehawk racing radials proved consistent, durable and reliable, with nary the hint of a problem during the entire 16-race season.

Consider the comments of Tony Kanaan after winning on a scorching spring day at Phoenix, which saw the air temperature nudging 100 degrees and track temperatures of more than 120 degrees: "The tires were very good all day. These were the worst conditions we could possibly have and still they held up really well. Obviously, after 65 laps everything can start to go away, not just the tires – but they worked perfectly all the way to the end. Firestone did a great job as usual; those guys are always on top of their game, and I appreciate all the effort they put into it."

That became a familiar refrain as the season progressed. As Bridgestone/Firestone Motorsports Director Al Speyer pointed out at Indianapolis, "Drivers and teams have relied on the Firestone tire consistency over the years to give them a constant baseline when setting up their cars. This year, with so many unknowns relating to car performance due to the engine and chassis changes, it's more important than ever for the Firehawks to deliver that stable feeling lap after lap, set after set, to enable the drivers to race wheel-to-wheel at over 200 mph."

Although the 15 tracks on the 2004 IRL IndyCar calendar might appear relatively homogenous to the untrained eye – all being ovals and many of them negotiated at full throttle all the way around – the reality is far more complex. Tiny, 0.75-mile Richmond International Raceway, where the laps are clicked off with a dizzying frequency, is a far cry from the wide open spaces of Michigan, while Nazareth, with its asymmetrical layout and

elevation changes, has been aptly described as a road course that just happens to turn left. Even the 1.5-mile "cookie-cutter" tracks have subtle differences of turn radii, surface and banking that require different solutions from engineers (if not necessarily drivers).

Indeed, Firestone produced no fewer than nine specifications of tire in the course of the season to cater for the full gamut of venues. These were drawn from two major categories: short oval and superspeedway. As a rule of thumb, the larger (and therefore usually faster) the track, the "harder" or more durable the rubber compound that was used. The sidewall construction also varied depending on the loads the tires were subjected to; at somewhere like Texas Motor Speedway, with its 24-degree banking and ultra-high speeds, they

took a real battering and a sturdier construction was required than for a slower, flatter track such as the Milwaukee Mile.

There were three different specifications of tire for the short ovals, where handling is more important than horsepower and "chemical grip" is paramount. The softest compound was used for Nazareth, a mid-range version for Phoenix and Richmond, and the most durable for Milwaukee and Pikes Peak. A larger degree of stagger – the difference in diameter between the right-rear and left-rear tires – was employed on the short ovals to help negotiate the comparatively tight corners (approximately 0.6 inches at Richmond compared to 0.35-0.45 inches at Indy).

In previous years, Firestone had divided its stock of IRL tires into an additional, intermediate

category, but the reconfiguration of Homestead (which dramatically increased the banking and made it much more like the other 1.5-mile ovals) and the abrasiveness of the concrete surface at Nashville led both tracks to be reclassified as superspeedways for tire purposes and the intermediates were left on the shelf.

A total of six distinct superspeedway specifications were pressed into service. An example of Firestone's attention to detail was the fact that it brought a different tire to the Texas season finale in October to that which had been used for the June race at TMS. There was no clamor to do so from the teams, but its engineers hadn't been entirely satisfied with the original version and developed an alternative combination (using the same compound as before but with the

construction employed for the Kansas spec) during the summer that subsequently worked a treat at both Chicagoland and Texas II.

In a nutshell, Firestone continued the tradition of excellence that has been its hallmark since it won the very first Indianapolis 500 in 1911, with Ray Harroun at the wheel. Buddy Rice's victory in the 2004 Memorial Day classic was the 55th by a Firestone-equipped driver – more than all the other tire manufacturers combined.

Having competed in every race since the IRL got off the ground in 1996 and been the sole tire supplier for the last five years, Firestone was proud to showcase its association with both the IMS and the League during the 2004 season. It produced a run of special-edition Firehawks for the Indy 500, featuring the Speedway's distinctive "wings and

wheel" emblem on the sidewalls alongside the Firestone name and logo – a nice touch that not only added to the pageantry of the occasion but, since it involved different color schemes on the right- and left-side tires, made it easier for pit crews to identify which tires they were handling!

Firestone also played a big part in the IRL's 100th event at Nazareth in late August, serving as title sponsor and celebrating the milestone with a commemorative decal on all the race tires.

"Firestone and the Indy Racing League have developed an incredible partnership over these nine seasons, and it is evident in the heavy involvement we have in this centennial event," declared Speyer. "We are proud to be a supplier and promotional partner with the IRL and hope to continue those relationships for years to come."

WORDS BY JOHN OREOVICZ

2004 INDYCAR® SERIES
SEASON REVIEW

HOMESTEAD

SAM HORNISH JR. ENSURED THE perfect start to his new career with Marlboro Team Penske by claiming an opportunistic victory in the Toyota Indy 300 at the newly reconfigured, more steeply banked Homestead-Miami Speedway. The two-time IndyCar Series champion also maintained a remarkable streak of success that had netted four victories and one second-place finish from his last six races.

Hornish and Helio Castroneves qualified only seventh and tenth respectively, but on race day they were clearly the men to beat. Nevertheless, in the closing stages they had to overcome Dan Wheldon, whose #26 Klein Tools/Jim Beam Dallara/Honda had vaulted into the lead following a calculated risk of saving a few precious seconds by eschewing a change of Firestone tires during his last scheduled pit stop.

The Englishman's advantage didn't last long, as the Penske tandem blew past on lap 188. Castroneves seemed to hold the upper hand, as he had for most of the afternoon, leading a race-high 85 laps, but Hornish wasn't done. Time and again he attempted to pass on the high side. On each occasion Castroneves clung resolutely to the lead. Then, on the very last lap, Hornish feinted once again to the outside in Turn One before abruptly ducking inside and sneaking the nose of his #6 Marlboro car alongside his rival in Turn Two.

The pair sped through the corner side by side but Hornish had the momentum and was ahead by a scant 0.0698 secs – one car's length – as they flashed beneath the waving checkered flags.

"It definitely was exciting," declared Hornish after snaring the record-extending 12th victory of his career. "It's just a great day to be able to come out here in my debut with Marlboro Team Penske and have a win."

"That was a great race," echoed Castroneves. "I've been in this situation before [dicing with Hornish], and this time I told myself he's not going to pass me on the outside. If I had let him go outside, I wouldn't have been able to sleep tonight. If he wanted to beat me, he was going to have to go on the inside. And unfortunately that's exactly what he did."

Wheldon couldn't hang on to the two red-and-white cars but his team's strategy still helped him

to a strong third ahead of Japanese veteran Tora Takagi's #12 Pioneer/Mo Nunn Racing Dallara/Toyota.

Tomas Scheckter, occupying the seat at Panther Racing that had been vacated during the off-season by Hornish, led 22 laps and finished fifth ahead of Darren Manning (Target Panoz G Force/Toyota) and pole-sitter Buddy Rice, whose Pioneer/Argent Mortgage Panoz G Force-Honda led the first 34 laps before losing time with a cut tire.

Notable retirements included defending series champion Scott Dixon, who lost control and crashed while making a routine pit stop on lap 88, outside front-row qualifier Alex Barron, who clashed with Manning on lap 127, and Dario Franchitti, who also hit the wall following contact with top rookie Kosuke Matsuura.

Facing page: Scheckter in the shade. Clockwise, from below right: Sam Hornish Jr. beats Helio Castroneves by a car's length; third placed Dan Wheldon; Hornish accepts his trophy.

IRL IndyCar® Series Race 1: Toyota Indy 300 at Homestead-Miami Speedway
Sunday, February 29, 2004

Place	Driver	Car	Nat.	Car Name	C/E/T	Laps Comp.	Running/ Reason Out	Q. Speed (mph)	Q. Time	Starting Position	IRL Pts.	Total IRL Pts.	IRL Standing	IRL Awards ($)	Designated Awards ($)	Total Awards ($)
1	Sam Hornish Jr.	6	USA	Marlboro Team Penske	D/T/F	200	Running	216.322	24.7132s	7	50	50	1	114,800	1,000	115,800
2	Helio Castroneves	3	BR	Marlboro Team Penske	D/T/F	200	Running	215.887	24.7630s	10	43	43	2	94,100	18,250	112,350
3	Dan Wheldon	26	GB	Klein Tools/Jim Beam	D/H/F	200	Running	215.017	24.8632s	14	35	35	3	78,500	0	78,500
4	Tora Takagi	12	J	Pioneer Mo Nunn Racing	D/T/F	200	Running	213.296	25.0638s	16	32	32	4	63,000	5,250	68,250
5	Tomas Scheckter	4	SA	Pennzoil Panther	D/C/F	200	Running	216.678	24.6726s	3	30	30	5	57,300	0	57,300
6	Darren Manning	10	GB	Target Chip Ganassi Racing	G/T/F	200	Running	215.070	24.8570s	13	28	28	6	50,200	0	50,200
7	Buddy Rice	15	USA	Pioneer/Argent Mortgage	G/H/F	200	Running	217.388*	24.5920s*	1	26	26	7	48,700	10,000	58,700
8	Tony Kanaan	11	BR	Team 7-Eleven	D/H/F	200	Running	215.976	24.7527s	8	24	24	8	47,400	0	47,400
9	Scott Sharp	8	USA	Delphi	D/T/F	200	Running	212.769	25.1258s	17	22	22	9	47,400	0	47,400
10	Robbie Buhl	24	USA	Team Purex/Dreyer & Reinbold	D/C/F	200	Running	215.774	24.7759s	11	20	20	10	45,900	0	45,900
11	Kosuke Matsuura (R)	55	J	Panasonic ARTA	G/H/F	200	Running	212.602	25.1456s	18	19	19	11	44,400	0	44,400
12	Ed Carpenter (R)	52	USA	Red Bull Cheever Racing	D/C/F	200	Running	215.924	24.7587s	9	18	18	12	43,100	0	43,100
13	Bryan Herta	7	USA	XM Satellite Radio	D/H/F	199	Running	216.545	24.6877s	5	17	17	13	41,800	0	41,800
14	Greg Ray	13	USA	Renovac	G/H/F	199	Running	214.593	24.9123s	15	16	16	14	40,200	750	40,950
15	A.J. Foyt IV	14	USA	Conseco/A.J. Foyt Racing	D/T/F	190	Engine	212.387	25.1710s	19	15	15	15	38,900	0	38,900
16	Alex Barron	51	USA	Red Bull Cheever Racing	D/C/F	126	Accident	216.904	24.6469s	2	14	14	16	37,500	0	37,500
17	Dario Franchitti	27	GB	ArcaEx	D/H/F	104	Accident	216.599	24.6815s	4	13	13	17	36,100	0	36,100
18	Scott Dixon	1	NZ	Target Chip Ganassi Racing	G/T/F	87	Accident	215.401	24.8188s	12	12	12	18	36,100	0	36,100
19	Mark Taylor (R)	2	GB	Menards/Johns Manville Racing	D/C/F	39	Accident	216.432	24.7006s	6	12	12	19	34,600	0	34,600
													Total:	1,000,000	35,250	1,035,250

* Track record (Previous record: March 1, 2003, Tony Kanaan, 203.560 mph, 26.5278s, qualifying).

Time of race: 1h 57m 56.3961s. Average speed: 151.094 mph. Margin of victory: 0.0698s.

Fastest lap: #6 Sam Hornish Jr. (Race lap 184, 216.593 mph, 24.6822s). Fastest leading lap: #3 Helio Castroneves (Race lap 180, 215.243 mph, 24.8370s).

MBNA Pole Award: #15 Buddy Rice (217.388 mph, 24.5920s). Marlboro Lap Leader Award. Firestone Leader at Lap 88 Award: #3 Helio Castroneves.

Caution flags: Laps 32-37, debris in T2; laps 41-47, #2 Taylor, accident T2; laps 89-101, #1 Dixon, accident pit entry; laps 105-114, #27 Franchitti, accident T4; laps 127-135, #51 Barron, accident T3. Total: 5 caution flags, 45 laps.

Lap leaders: Buddy Rice, 1-34; Sam Hornish Jr., 35; Helio Castroneves, 36-49; Scott Dixon, 50-52; Castroneves, 53-107; Rice, 108-122; Dan Wheldon, 123-131; Bryan Herta, 132-150; Tomas Scheckter, 151-172; Hornish, 173-175; Castroneves, 176-180; Darren Manning, 181-182; Wheldon, 183-187; Hornish, 188; Castroneves, 189-199; Hornish, 200. Total: 15 lead changes among 8 drivers.

Lap leader summary: Helio Castroneves, 4 times, 85 laps led; Buddy Rice, 2 times, 49 laps led; Tomas Scheckter, 1 time, 22 laps led; Bryan Herta, 1 time, 19 laps led; Dan Wheldon, 2 times, 14 laps led; Sam Hornish Jr., 4 times, 6 laps led; Scott Dixon, 1 time, 3 laps led; Darren Manning, 1 time, 2 laps led.

Legend: R – IndyCar Series Rookie. Chassis legend: D – Dallara (14); G – Panoz G Force (5). Engine legend: C – Chevrolet (5); H – Honda (7); T – Toyota (7). Tire legend: F – Firestone (19).

PHOENIX

ANDRETTI **GREEN RACING CLEARLY** took notice of the manner in which Marlboro Team Penske had underlined its powerhouse status in the opening race of the season. Undeterred, AGR unleashed its own brand of dominance in the Copper World Indy 200 at Phoenix International Raceway. Young Briton Dan Wheldon claimed the first pole of his

young career in the #26 Klein Tools/Jim Beam Dallara/Honda, whereupon Brazilian teammate Tony Kanaan turned the tables on race day, leading for 191 of the 200 laps in his similar Team 7-Eleven machine.

"This morning I felt I had the car to do it," said Kanaan following his second career victory and, coincidentally, his second at PIR. "It was just going to be a matter of taking the right opportunities at the right time, use the traffic to my advantage. I think we did that."

Kanaan lost no time in making his presence felt, swooping past Wheldon to take the lead on the opening lap. Indeed, the only time he relinquished his advantage was during the first round of scheduled pit stops, when Sam Hornish Jr. (Marlboro Team Penske Dallara/Toyota), Tomas Scheckter (Pennzoil Panther Dallara/Chevrolet) and Darren Manning (Target Chip Ganassi Racing Panoz G Force/Toyota) each took a brief turn out in front.

Hornish, after starting fourth, emerged as a serious challenger to Kanaan until a handling imbalance led to a rare error and a spin into the Turn Two wall.

"We had a real fast car today," noted Hornish. "The car had a little bit of push in Turn Two, and then it got loose after we put on our second set of tires. It caught me by surprise."

Hornish returned to competition after his crew made repairs to the Dallara's rear end, but by then he was out of contention for the win.

Hornish's mishap ensured the first of three caution periods. The others followed when Ed Carpenter crashed Eddie Cheever's #52 Red Bull Dallara/Chevrolet in Turn One, and when Robbie Buhl lost control of his Team Purex/Dreyer & Reinbold Dallara/Chevy in Turn Four. Ironically, when the yellow lights flashed on to warn of Buhl's impact, the ever-unfortunate Tomas Scheckter was rear-ended by Dario Franchitti who had been caught unawares. Exit two more contenders from the proceedings.

Facing page: Tony Kanaan celebrates his win.
This picture: Kanaan takes the checkered flag.
Below: AGR's Dan Wheldon.

"Nobody told me [on the radio] it had gone yellow," related Franchitti. "I tried to slow down but I took both of us out."

The final incident of the day led to a nine-lap dash to the checkered flag. Defending series champion Scott Dixon, having started fifth aboard Target Chip Ganassi's #1 Panoz G Force/Toyota, moved up to challenge Kanaan but was unable to get close enough to effect a pass. Still, after his embarrassing accident while entering the pits in Homestead, second place for Dixon ensured a useful points haul.

Wheldon struggled with a loose condition toward the end of each stint, so was relatively content with a third-place finish ahead of Alex Barron, who worked his way steadily forward in his Red Bull Cheever Racing Dallara/Chevrolet, after starting a lowly 17th.

IRL IndyCar® Series Race 2: Copper World Indy 200 at Phoenix International Raceway
Sunday, March 21, 2004

Place	Driver	Car	Nat.	Car Name	C/E/T	Laps Comp.	Running/ Reason Out	Q. Speed (mph)	Q. Time	Starting Position	IRL Pts.	Total IRL Pts.	IRL Standing	IRL Awards ($)	Designated Awards ($)	Total Awards ($)
1	Tony Kanaan	11	BR	Team 7-Eleven	D/H/F	200	Running	174.291	20.6551s	2	53	77	1	109,800	18,500	128,300
2	Scott Dixon	1	NZ	Target Chip Ganassi Racing	G/T/F	200	Running	173.367	20.7652s	5	40	52	7	90,200	750	90,950
3	Dan Wheldon	26	GB	Klein Tools/Jim Beam	D/H/F	200	Running	174.779	20.5974s	1	35	70	3	75,400	10,250	85,650
4	Alex Barron	51	USA	Red Bull Cheever Racing	D/C/F	200	Running	168.841	21.3218s	17	32	46	9	60,700	0	60,700
5	Darren Manning	10	GB	Target Chip Ganassi Racing	G/T/F	200	Running	172.995	20.8098s	6	30	58	5	55,300	0	55,300
6	Helio Castroneves	3	BR	Marlboro Team Penske	D/T/F	200	Running	174.168	20.6697s	3	28	71	2	48,600	0	48,600
7	Bryan Herta	7	USA	XM Satellite Radio	D/H/F	200	Running	172.062	20.9227s	9	26	43	11	47,200	0	47,200
8	Tora Takagi	12	J	Pioneer Mo Nunn Racing	D/T/F	199	Running	169.684	21.2159s	14	24	56	6	46,000	4,000	50,000
9	Buddy Rice	15	USA	Pioneer/Argent Mortgage	G/H/F	198	Running	169.834	21.1972s	12	22	48	8	46,000	0	46,000
10	Greg Ray	13	USA	Renovac	G/H/F	198	Running	170.485	21.1162s	11	20	36	14	44,600	0	44,600
11	Kosuke Matsuura (R)	55	J	Panasonic ARTA	G/H/F	198	Running	170.975	21.0557s	10	19	38	13	43,200	0	43,200
12	Mark Taylor (R)	2	GB	Menards/Johns Manville Racing	D/C/F	198	Running	169.555	21.2321s	15	18	30	17	41,900	0	41,900
13	Scott Sharp	8	USA	Delphi	D/T/F	197	Running	168.113	21.4142s	19	17	39	12	40,700	0	40,700
14	A.J. Foyt IV	14	USA	Conseco/A.J. Foyt Racing	D/T/F	197	Running	168.534	21.3607s	18	16	31	16	39,100	0	39,100
15	Sam Hornish Jr.	6	USA	Marlboro Team Penske	D/T/F	195	Running	173.945	20.6962s	4	15	65	4	37,900	0	37,900
16	Tomas Scheckter	4	SA	Pennzoil Panther	D/C/F	180	Accident	172.095	20.9187s	8	14	44	10	36,600	0	36,600
17	Dario Franchitti	27	GB	ArcaEx	D/H/F	180	Accident	172.887	20.8229s	7	13	26	19	35,200	0	35,200
18	Robbie Buhl	24	USA	Team Purex/Dreyer & Reinbold	D/C/F	177	Accident	165.182	21.7942s	20	12	32	15	35,200	0	35,200
19	Ed Carpenter (R)	52	USA	Red Bull Cheever Racing	D/C/F	132	Accident	169.120	21.2867s	16	12	30	17	33,800	0	33,800
20	Adrian Fernandez	5	MEX	Quaker State Telmex Tecate	G/H/F	0	Transmission	169.720	21.2114s	13	12	12	20	32,600	0	32,600
													Total	1,000,000	33,500	1,033,500

Time of race: **1h 33m 45.8490s.** Average speed: **127.981 mph.** Margin of victory: **0.5344s.**

Fastest lap: **#10 Darren Manning (Race lap 173, 161.433 mph, 22.3003s).** Fastest leading lap: **#11 Tony Kanaan (Race lap 4, 160.216 mph, 22.4696s).**

MBNA Pole Award: **#26 Dan Wheldon (174.779 mph, 20.5974s).** The Marlboro Lap Leader Award: **#11 Tony Kanaan.** Firestone Performance Award: **#11 Tony Kanaan.**

Caution flags: Laps **82-88,** #6 Hornish, light contact T2; laps **134-141,** #52 Carpenter, contact T2; laps **181-191,** #4 Scheckter, #24 Buhl and #27 Franchitti, contact T4. Total **3 caution flags, 26 laps.**

Lap leaders: **Tony Kanaan,** 1-67; **Sam Hornish Jr.,** 68-71; **Tomas Scheckter,** 72; **Darren Manning,** 73-76; **Kanaan,** 77-200. Total: **4 lead changes among 4 drivers.**

Lap leader summary: **Tony Kanaan,** 2 times, 191 laps led; **Darren Manning,** 1 time, 4 laps led; **Sam Hornish Jr.,** 1 time, 4 laps led; **Tomas Scheckter,** 1 time, 1 lap led.

Legend: **R – IndyCar Series Rookie.** Chassis legend: **D – Dallara (14); G – Panoz G Force (6).** Engine legend: **C – Chevrolet (5); H – Honda (8); T – Toyota (7).** Tire legend: **F – Firestone (20).**

MOTEGI

ANYTHING **YOU CAN DO, I CAN** do better seemed to be the gist of Dan Wheldon's bold statement to Andretti Green teammate Tony Kanaan as he drove to an accomplished maiden IndyCar Series victory in the Indy Japan 300 at Twin Ring Motegi. Kanaan, after all, had dominated the previous event at Phoenix, leading 191 of the 200 laps after passing pole-sitter Wheldon on the opening lap.

The 25-year-old Englishman not only snared his second straight pole behind the wheel of the #26 Klein Tools/Jim Beam Dallara/Honda, he then proceeded to lead 192 laps en route to a famous victory – Honda's first on home soil after having been thwarted in its six previous attempts.

Kanaan, after qualifying third, never once gave up the chase but finally wound up 1.4454 secs shy at the checkered flag.

"It's awesome for Honda and it's awesome for the team," enthused an overjoyed Wheldon. "I love being part of this team and it's just fantastic to win my first IndyCar Series race here for Honda."

Kanaan was thrilled for his young teammate – who took a narrow lead in the points chase, 123-117 – and was delighted to finish second.

"It was Andretti Green's day," said Kanaan. "I'm so happy for Dan, to get his first win. That's two wins in a row for the team."

Wheldon gave up the lead only briefly during the pit stop sequences. Aside from Kanaan, his only real challenge came from Helio Castroneves, who rocketed through the field after qualifying a disappointing 15th. Castroneves briefly vaulted to second place following his final pit stop, under caution on lap 171, but any hopes of victory were firmly dispelled when the green flags flew again on lap 176 and Kanaan immediately blew past. Still, a third-place finish enabled Castroneves to retain the number three spot in the points chase going into the 88th Indianapolis 500.

Teammate Sam Hornish Jr. wasn't quite so fortunate. The two-time IndyCar Series champ was running strongly among the top ten until he was caught up in traffic on lap 88. He made slight contact with Kosuke Matsuura before slamming heavily into the wall. Hornish was unhurt.

Local favorite Matsuura emerged unscathed from the melee and went on to claim his first top-ten finish; eighth aboard Super Aguri Fernandez Racing's Panasonic/ARTA Panoz G Force/Honda. Matsuura also maintained his 100 percent record as the top rookie finisher.

Target Chip Ganassi teammates Darren Manning and Scott Dixon finished fourth and fifth. The result was especially noteworthy for Dixon, who had crashed heavily during practice and sustained a hairline fracture in his left ankle.

Facing page: Dan Wheldon puckers up. Above: Wheldon takes the checkered flag, a first win on home soil for Honda. Left: Victory for Wheldon.

IRL IndyCar® Series Race 3: Indy Japan 300 at Twin Ring Motegi
Saturday, April 17, 2004

Place	Driver	Car	Nat.	Car Name	C/E/T	Laps Comp.	Running/ Reason Out	Q. Speed (mph)	Q. Time	Starting Position	IRL Pts.	Total IRL Pts.	IRL Standing	IRL Awards ($)	Designated Awards ($)	Total Awards ($)
1	Dan Wheldon	26	GB	Klein Tools/Jim Beam	D/H/F	200	Running	205.762	26.5938s	1	53	123	1	150,900	28,500	179,400
2	Tony Kanaan	11	BR	Team 7-Eleven	D/H/F	200	Running	205.690	26.6031s	3	40	117	2	124,300	750	125,050
3	Helio Castroneves	3	BR	Marlboro Team Penske	D/T/F	200	Running	203.281	26.9184s	15	35	106	3	104,400	250	104,650
4	Darren Manning	10	GB	Target Chip Ganassi Racing	G/T/F	200	Running	204.345	26.7783s	10	32	90	4	84,800	0	84,800
5	Scott Dixon	1	NZ	Target Chip Ganassi Racing	G/T/F	200	Running	204.985	26.6946s	6	30	82	5	77,400	0	77,400
6	Buddy Rice	15	USA	Pioneer/Argent Mortgage	G/H/F	200	Running	205.408	26.6397s	5	28	76	7	68,400	0	68,400
7	Dario Franchitti	27	GB	Alpine	D/H/F	199	Running	204.395	26.7717s	9	26	52	14	66,600	0	66,600
8	Kosuke Matsuura (R)	55	J	Panasonic ARTA	G/H/F	199	Running	205.629	26.6110s	4	24	62	10	64,900	0	64,900
9	Scott Sharp	8	USA	Delphi	D/T/F	199	Running	203.867	26.8410s	12	22	61	11	64,900	0	64,900
10	Tora Takagi	12	J	Pioneer Mo Nunn Racing	D/T/F	199	Running	195.054	28.0538s	21	20	76	7	63,000	2,000	65,000
11	Roger Yasukawa	16	USA	Sammy	G/H/F	198	Running	203.863	26.8415s	13	19	19	21	61,100	0	61,100
12	Alex Barron	51	USA	Red Bull Cheever Racing	D/C/F	196	Running	199.835*	27.3826s	22	18	64	9	59,400	0	59,400
13	Tomas Scheckter	4	SA	Pennzoil Panther	D/C/F	184	Running	202.952	26.9620s	16	17	61	11	57,800	0	57,800
14	Bryan Herta	7	USA	XM Satellite Radio	D/H/F	183	Radiator	204.015	26.8215s	11	16	59	13	55,700	0	55,700
15	A.J. Foyt IV	14	USA	Conseco/A.J. Foyt Racing	D/T/F	169	Running	202.055	27.0817s	17	15	46	16	54,000	0	54,000
16	Mark Taylor (R)	2	GB	Menards/Johns Manville Racing	D/C/F	167	Accident	203.787	26.8516s	14	14	44	17	52,300	0	52,300
17	Vitor Meira	17	BR	Rahal-Letterman BEA Systems	G/H/F	166	Clutch	204.631	26.7408s	8	13	13	22	50,400	0	50,400
18	Adrian Fernandez	5	MEX	Quaker State Telmex Tecate	G/H/F	153	Mechanical	201.649	27.1362s	18	12	24	20	50,400	0	50,400
19	Sam Hornish Jr.	6	USA	Marlboro Team Penske	D/T/F	87	Accident	204.890	26.7070s	7	12	77	6	48,600	0	48,600
20	Greg Ray	13	USA	Renovac	G/H/F	55	Suspension	205.722	26.5990s	2	12	48	15	46,900	0	46,900
21	Robbie Buhl	24	USA	Team Purex Dreyer & Reinbold	D/C/F	38	Handling	195.358	28.0101s	20	12	44	17	46,900	0	46,900
22	Ed Carpenter (R)	52	USA	Red Bull Cheever Racing	D/C/F	38	Mechanical	195.454	27.9963s	19	12	42	19	46,900	0	46,900
* Changed engines following qualifying												Total:		1,500,000	31,500	1,531,500

Time of race: 1h 49m 48.2611s. Average speed: 166.114 mph. Margin of victory: 1.4454s.

Fastest lap/Fastest leading lap: #26 Dan Wheldon (Race lap 4, 201.165 mph, 27.2016s).

MBNA Pole Award: #26 Dan Wheldon (205.762 mph, 26.5938s). Marlboro Lap Leader Award: #26 Dan Wheldon. Firestone Performance Award: #26 Dan Wheldon.

Caution flags: Laps 78-84, debris T3; laps 88-95, #6 Hornish, contact T1; laps 169-176, #2 Taylor, contact T2. Total: 3 caution flags, 23 laps.

Lap leaders: Dan Wheldon, 1-47; Scott Sharp, 48-49; Wheldon, 50-136; Darren Manning, 137-138; Helio Castroneves, 139-142; Wheldon, 142-200. Total: 5 lead changes among 4 drivers.

Lap leader summary: Dan Wheldon, 3 times, 192 laps led; Helio Castroneves, 1 time, 4 laps led; Darren Manning, 1 time, 2 laps led; Scott Sharp, 1 time, 2 laps led.

Legend: R – IndyCar Series Rookie. Chassis legend: D – Dallara (14); G – Panoz G Force (8). Engine legend: C – Chevrolet (5); H – Honda (10); T – Toyota (7). Tire legend: F – Firestone (22).

WORDS BY JOHN OREOVICZ

INDIANAPOLIS

500

SUNDAY MAY 9
PRACTICE SESSION – **OPENING DAY**

UNSEASONABLY **HOT AND HUMID** weather greeted competitors for the 88th Indianapolis 500 when they arrived at the Indianapolis Motor Speedway for the first day of official practice, with temperatures climbing to the mid-80s. In honor of Mothers' Day, Reba Fisher waved the green flag to kick off the Month of May, and appropriately her daughter Sarah won the race to be first driver on the track.

Sarah Fisher admitted that her month had got off to an otherwise difficult start and confirmed that her Bryant Heating & Cooling/Cure Autism Now Dallara/Toyota didn't feel anywhere near as good as it had in the Indianapolis open test a fortnight earlier. But her mom was clearly on cloud nine.

"Waving that green flag for Sarah meant the world to me and made this the greatest Mothers' Day any mom could ask for," said Reba. "The toughest part was holding back the tears in front of everyone."

With more than 40 hours of practice time available prior to Pole Day qualifying on May 15, most of the teams used Opening Day primarily as a systems check. Not so for defending IRL IndyCar Series champion Scott Dixon, who quickly got down to business and paced the day's action with a 219.760 mph lap in his Target Panoz G Force/Toyota.

"Today we were just getting up to speed," remarked the New Zealander. "It was pretty windy but we were surprised how much grip the car had. Toyota has made some great gains in the engine and we're still expecting more from that, so it's looking pretty decent."

Two-time Indy winner Helio Castroneves's month got off to a solid start as well, with the Brazilian ace joining Dixon as the only drivers over 219 mph.

"The car seemed to be handling with no problems," he reported after clocking a best lap of 219.752 mph in his Marlboro Team Penske Dallara/Toyota. "We spent a lot of time in the pits because we were waiting for more guys to get on the track. But everyone knows Indy is like two races: one is for qualifying and the next one is the race."

Adrian Fernandez was pleased to end the day third fastest after his first laps at Indianapolis since 1995. The Mexican was putting the first miles

Clockwise from main: Scott Dixon takes a corner; Sarah Fisher in the pits before rejoining practice; Sarah's mom Reba waves the green flag; Helio Castroneves was one of only two drivers to top 219 mph on the first day of practice.

on a brand new Honda-powered Panoz G Force chassis and ended with a best lap of 218.342 mph.

"The car felt a lot more comfortable than at the Open test and I did my best lap without a tow, so that's good," said Fernandez.

Tomas Scheckter was fourth fastest in his Pennzoil Dallara/Chevrolet, putting all three of the IRL engine manufacturers among the day's top four runners. Dan Wheldon (Klein Tools/Jim Beam Dallara/Honda) was fifth, while rookie Mark Taylor made it a good day for the Panther Racing operation by running the sixth quickest lap in his Menards/Johns Manville Dallara/Chevrolet.

A total of 25 drivers turned laps on the day in 33 cars. Notable by his absence was Marlboro Team Penske's Sam Hornish Jr., who sat out with an upper respiratory infection.

MONDAY MAY 10
PRACTICE SESSION – 2

AFTER **THE POMP AND CIRCUMSTANCE** of opening day, many drivers and teams treated Monday as the real first day of work. For Helio Castroneves, that meant spending his 29th birthday in his Marlboro Dallara/Toyota, but the Brazilian didn't mind. In fact, he was the first driver out of the pits when defending race champion Gil de Ferran waved the green flag to start the day's action.

De Ferran, of course, retired on a victorious note at the end of the 2003 IndyCar season. The Brazilian spent most of the Month of May 2004 as a television commentator for ESPN and ABC and he admitted that he was still having to adapt to his new lifestyle, which also includes writing a monthly column for RACER magazine.

"It was a funny sensation driving into the track today thinking that it has already been a year," said de Ferran. "It will always be an incredible feeling to be part of the history here."

Sam Hornish Jr., who stepped in as de Ferran's replacement at Marlboro Team Penske, was back in action on Monday. But the two-time IRL series champion still didn't feel up to par and was happy when rain interrupted the proceedings for three hours and 35 minutes in the afternoon.

"I'm not back to 100 percent yet and it was a good thing the rain came because I was starting to feel a bit of sinus pressure," said the American.

When practice resumed at 4:42pm, Scott Dixon's 219.373 mph lap was the speed to beat. But the yellow soon flew for the month's first spin, by rookie Marty Roth. The Canadian's Dallara/Toyota was undamaged.

"I needed to get that out of the way," said the 45-year old from Toronto. "That's the way to spin at Indy – to touch nothing."

Robby Gordon wasn't so lucky. The versatile racer was starting a simulated qualifying run when he lost control of his Meijer Dallara/Chevrolet between Turns One and Two at 5:44pm. After

a half-spin, Gordon kept the car off the inside wall, but it veered up the track and clouted the SAFER Barrier on the outside with the left side wheels, causing moderate damage.

"The car compressed in the corner and the rear got a bit sideways," related Gordon. "When I tried to save it, it hooked back the other way and spun around."

The track went green with only six minutes remaining and Castroneves celebrated his birthday in style by clocking the first 220 mph lap of the month, a 220.300 mph flyer. "We're looking good, but we can't celebrate anything other than my birthday yet," grinned Castroneves.

Dixon improved to 219.569 mph, while Tony Kanaan ran third at 219.553 mph, just edging Hornish's 219.357 mph effort. Technical partners Adrian Fernandez and Kosuke Matsuura as well as Dario Franchitti also topped 219 mph, while eighth placed Tomas Scheckter was Chevrolet's top runner at 218.893 mph.

TUESDAY MAY 11
PRACTICE SESSION – 3

WITH **RAIN FORECAST FOR LATER** in the week, Tuesday turned out to be the busiest day of the month, with 1,711 laps completed under ideal conditions. As teams turned their attention toward determining a qualifying set-up, speeds were on the rise, topped by impressive rookie Kosuke Matsuura's 221.857 mph lap in Super Aguri Fernandez Racing's Panasonic/ARTA Panoz G Force/Honda.

Making it an even better day for flagship team Fernandez Racing, owner/driver Adrian Fernandez was second fastest clocking 221.705 mph in his Quaker State/Telmex/Tecate car.

Fernandez had taken Matsuura out to Turn Three in a golf cart so the 23-year-old rookie could see what 220 mph looked like from the outside. Kosuke responded by turning the fastest lap of the month at 4:27pm.

"I put on new tires and after two laps I had the quickest time," Matsuura explained. "I could have made a better lap but it wasn't necessary. I think in qualifying we could have 222 or 223 mph."

Matsuura had never driven on an oval prior to joining the IndyCar Series in 2004, but his learning curve was made easier when Fernandez made a late decision to leave the Champ Car

World Series to focus on the IRL. It took the 40-year-old Mexican a couple of races to get the hang of IRL machinery, but by the time the Month of May rolled around he was fully adapted to his new surroundings.

"A fantastic day for the team," bubbled Fernandez. "The engineers [John Dick, John Ward and Chris Finch] and the team are doing a great job. We just have to keep up the momentum because we are still in the early stages."

Andretti Green Racing teammates Tony Kanaan (third at 220.855 mph) and Bryan Herta (fifth at 219.909 mph) gave Honda four of the day's top five speeds, while Marlboro Team Penske's Helio Castroneves and Sam Hornish Jr. ran fourth and sixth for Toyota. Tomas Scheckter, ninth at 219.172 mph, was once again the top Chevrolet runner.

Rookie Marty Roth again managed to spin without hitting anything, but he continued to struggle for speed, achieving a best lap of 204.040 mph. Roth was luckier than Felipe Giaffone, who caused moderate damage to the right front corner of Dreyer & Reinbold Racing's Purex Dallara/Chevrolet when he crashed in Turn Four two minutes into "Happy Hour."

From top: Adrian Fernandez ready for take off; rookie Kosuke Matsuura; Matsuura logged the fastest lap of the day at 221.857 mph.

Main picture and inset: Brazilian Tony Kanaan produced the best lap of the day at 222.668 mph.

WEDNESDAY MAY 12

PRACTICE SESSION – 4

ANOTHER **PERFECT DAY FOR SPEED.** Cloudy skies and temperatures in the low 80s produced the first 222 mph laps of the month. Just 49 minutes into practice, Tony Kanaan turned a 222.605 mph lap, immediately followed by the 222.668 mph flyer that stood as the best lap of the day. But the Brazilian cautioned to view the impressive speed with a pinch of salt.

"I had a *big* tow," said the diminutive Brazilian. "I got Bruno Junqueira coming out of the pits and when he pulled in, [teammate] Bryan [Herta] pulled me around for two laps. I wish I could have done it myself, but that's not the reality.

"It's Wednesday so it doesn't matter who is fastest now," he added. "I'm sure all three engine manufacturers have more to come because the real war is Saturday."

Rahal Letterman Racing's Roger Yasukawa (third fastest at 221.248 mph) was a new face on the leaderboard, while Scott Dixon reminded all that he was the League's defending champion by posting the fifth quickest lap at 220.941 mph in the Target Panoz G Force/Toyota.

Dixon was the lone exception as Honda powered six of the top seven drivers, with Rahal Letterman Racing's Buddy Rice last in that group at 220.530 mph. But Rice agreed with Kanaan that many speeds on the board were achieved with a draft.

"It's easy to get caught up in Happy Hour and get caught in drafting, trying to put up a big number," said the American. "I don't get too concerned about our speed because I know we haven't shown everything yet."

The consistent Adrian Fernandez was fourth fastest but he maintained that practice speeds really didn't mean anything.

"We'll see on Saturday," commented Fernandez. "Honda is looking strong right now but I'm sure

the other manufacturers are going to respond. We won't know for sure until Pole Day."

By this stage of the week, after more than 13,000 miles of running, most doubts about the supply and reliability of the new 3.0-liter engines had been eliminated, and the manufacturers intensified their quest for the pole.

"Most people won't put qualifying engines into a car until this afternoon or tomorrow so it's really difficult to tell," remarked Joe Negri, GM's IRL project manager. "I think we're fifth quick on laps without a tow and we're within three-quarters of a mile-per-hour of the best Honda lap without a tow. I'll be very surprised if we don't see a Chevrolet on the front row."

Toyota Racing Development's IRL program manager John Faivre was also confident about his powerplant's chances on Pole Day. "Obviously, everyone will bring out their best available engines for qualifying on Saturday, but I think you'll continue to see new development throughout the month," Faivre said. "I don't know that we've ever had this rapid a rate of in-season development."

Above from top: Defending IndyCar Series champion Scott Dixon; Tony Kanaan signs autographs for the crowd. Below: Roger Yasukawa was third-fastest. Left: Yasukawa takes some time out.

THURSDAY MAY 13
PRACTICE SESSION – 5

MOTHER **NATURE THREW A WRENCH** into the plans of many teams by moving into central Indiana on Wednesday night for what was predicted to be a two-day visit. The start of Thursday practice was delayed until 2:55pm, with Scott Sharp first on track in Kelley Racing's Delphi Dallara/Toyota.

The 1996 IRL co-champion also earned the dubious distinction of bringing the day's action to an end seven minutes early by spinning and pounding the wall backwards in Turn One. After struggling all week for speed with a best lap of 217.975 mph, Sharp lost control unusually early in the turn, but the SAFER Barrier minimized what would have been a major impact for the American and he stepped out of the car uninjured.

"Bam! It just snapped and I was sideways," he stated. "I don't even know what happened."

With cooler temperatures and a green track, speeds dropped. Helio Castroneves set the pace in the Marlboro Dallara/Toyota at 221.156 mph, but the Brazilian wasn't thrilled.

"Unfortunately, I did have a draft," he said. "It was important to test today to have a little bit of an understanding going from the hot weather to not so hot."

The top ten drivers all topped 220 mph, with Dario Franchitti (Andretti Green Racing ArcaEx Dallara/Honda) right behind at 219.999 mph. Roger Yasukawa was second overall in Rahal Letterman Racing's Sammy Panoz G Force/Honda at 221.093 mph, while Castroneves's teammate Sam Hornish Jr. lurked in third at 220.956 mph ahead of five consecutive Honda-powered drivers.

Darren Manning earned the wrath of his team and his teammate by damaging the right side suspension of Scott Dixon's #1T Panoz G Force/Toyota when he brushed the Turn One wall. "I got a little loose coming out of Turn One and got out of the groove and white-walled the right rear a little bit," said the Englishman with typical honesty. Manning's best lap came in at 219.519 mph.

Clockwise from top: Scott Sharp's practice finished early with a crash on Turn One; Darren Manning clipped the Turn One wall; Scott Sharp; Helio Castroneves.

FRIDAY MAY 14
PRACTICE SESSION – **6**

FAST **FRIDAY NEVER GOT THE CHANCE** to live up to its name as rain ground the practice proceedings to a halt after four minutes. Only nine laps were run as a front settled in over Indianapolis.

Sarah Fisher, who along with Kelley Racing teammate Scott Sharp had struggled for speed all week, was first on track getting up to 212 mph in her five laps. "We're dealing with the rain the best we can and trying to restrategize and work on a different game plan," she remarked. "You can't have too many laps here, especially after being out of a car for seven months."

The rain penalized those teams that elected to put off work on their qualifying setup until late in the week. Dario Franchitti and Bryan Herta of Andretti Green Racing were in that predicament, but they knew they could rely on the information gleaned by teammates Tony Kanaan and Dan Wheldon during the week's dry running.

"The rain today hurt us a little bit," Herta acknowledged. "We spent most of the week working on a race set-up and Thursday was the only day we worked on a qualifying package. But then again, sometimes if you run too much, you get lost and the weather may have kept us from doing that today."

With steady rain falling, the garage area became a social scene for those who felt fully prepared for qualifying. "It was fun to hang out with Kosuke [teammate Matsuura] and everyone in the garage and the pits, just seeing a lot of good friends," noted Adrian Fernandez.

Patrick Racing took the opportunity to announce Stacker 2 as an associate sponsor for its #20 Dallara/Chevrolet driven by Al Unser Jr. The two-time Indy winner remained upbeat despite struggling for speed.

"We definitely could have used more practice time," Unser said. "Each day we got another mile an hour out of the car and we'll keep working on it. It's twice as tough as it used to be."

With little else to talk about until the Friday evening qualifying draw, attention turned toward predicting the pole speed. Most guesses came in the 222 mph range.

"High 221s or low 222s," reckoned Marlboro Team Penske's Sam Hornish Jr. "I would have thought it would be a bit faster coming out of the Open Test, but speeds have been slower over the last few days."

"I think it will be around 221.5 mph if conditions don't improve in the afternoon," said Buddy Rice. "A 222 is possible later in the day."

His words would prove remarkably prescient.

Top: Kosuke Matsuura idles in the pits as rain stops activity. Above: Sam Hornish Jr. predicted pole speeds just edging 222 mph.

POLE DAY

SATURDAY, MAY 15

ON POLE DAY, THE WEATHER FORCED everyone to basically start again from scratch. Rain continued overnight until 9:30am and at 12:23pm REO Speedwagon lead vocalist Kevin Cronin finally waved the green flag for the practice session that was supposed to have started at 8pm.

And it was cold – barely 60 degrees. Having practiced in 80-degree heat all week, with track temperatures almost always above 110 degrees, the teams and drivers were confronted with completely different conditions – similar, actually, to the late-April Open Test.

Demonstrating their professionalism, the IndyCar teams adapted quickly. After just 13 minutes of practice, Roger Yasukawa turned the fastest lap of the month at 222.990 mph in the Sammy Panoz G Force/Honda. When the second group of cars took to the track for their 30 minutes of final practice, Tony Kanaan upped the ante to 223.224 mph in his 7-Eleven Dallara/Honda.

The practice sessions weren't smooth sailing for everyone. Mark Taylor spun at the pit entrance but didn't hit anything in the Menards/Johns Manville Dallara/Chevrolet, while Robby Gordon's Meijer-sponsored car

required gearbox work. A.J. Foyt IV missed the session entirely after a small fire broke out in a wiring loom, requiring a Toyota engine change in his Conseco Dallara.

At 2:19pm, Yasukawa turned in the first qualifying run, but the second-year American driver of Japanese descent was disappointed with his 220.030 mph average. "I guess being first out, you don't know what to expect," commented Yasukawa. "The car was very solid but the 221s didn't come."

Sam Hornish Jr. upped the target, posting a time of 220.180 mph in the Marlboro

Left: Dan Wheldon sets the early target with a brave 221.524 mph run. Right: Bryan Herta. Below: Rahal Letterman Racing crew members attend to Roger Yasukawa's ride.

Dallara/Toyota, but Gordon was not happy with his 216.522 mph run in his repaired Meijer Dallara/Chevrolet. He couldn't wave it off, however, because he was set to start that night's NASCAR Nextel Cup race from sixth on the grid at Richmond International Raceway.

At 2:45pm, Bryan Herta suffered a nasty crash as he hurtled into Turn One to start his qualifying run. Herta backed his XM Satellite Radio Dallara/Honda into the Turn One SAFER Barrier, emerging with abrasions to his right leg. "We tried to free the car up and I think we went a little too far," understated the American ace.

Herta's Andretti Green Racing teammate Dan Wheldon was the next driver to qualify, and he turned in a 221.524 mph run under what had to have been enormous pressure. Wheldon's gutsy run set the early benchmark. "I was a little bit apprehensive," admitted the Englishman. "I had gotten loose on my last lap of practice and then I saw what happened to Bryan. It's more difficult when you're so close to somebody and they crash."

Twenty minutes after Wheldon's run, Felipe Giaffone had his second incident of the week in the Purex Dallara/Chevrolet. The Brazilian lost control later in the turn than Herta before

smacking the wall flush with the left side of the car. Much later in the day (at 5:33pm), Alex Barron also crashed in Turn One, causing heavy damage to the left side of Cheever Racing's Red Bull Dallara/Chevrolet.

Just after 4pm, Wheldon's effort came under fire when Bruno Junqueira recovered from a big Turn One moment on his first qualifying lap to post a 221.379 mph average. "That's as sideways as I have ever been at this place," said Junqueira.

Buddy Rice started his qualifying run at 4:14pm, and suddenly a new contender for the MBNA Pole Award emerged. Rice dropped jaws with his 222.113 mph opening lap, and he improved to 222.224 mph on his second tour of the IMS oval. His third and fourth laps clocked in at 221.9 mph and 221.8 mph, leaving the Phoenix native with a 222.024 mph average and an agonizing wait to see if anyone could beat it.

The chief threat seemingly came from Kanaan. But the Brazilian waved off a run at 4:38pm after opening with laps of 221.0 mph and 220.4 mph, heading back to the garage for more setup work. Helio Castroneves failed to repeat his 2003 Indianapolis pole, accepting a 220.882 mph average in the Marlboro Dallara/Toyota at 4:55pm, after waving off an earlier run, while practice pacesetter Adrian Fernandez wasn't thrilled with his 220.999 mph average.

Dario Franchitti's opening lap of 220.768 mph didn't look that special, but the Scotsman posted three more laps in the 221.7 mph range during his 5:11pm run for a four-lap average of 221.471 mph; third best so far. But teammate Kanaan still had one more bullet in his gun.

The Brazilian drove onto the track at 5:27pm and the crowd was as excited as it had been all day. But Kanaan failed to wrest the top spot from Rice, turning in a 221.200 mph run that ended up fifth fastest.

"Obviously I am a bit disappointed because I thought we had a shot for the pole," he related. "The conditions were different and I think we produced too much downforce in the end."

At the end of the day, 22 drivers had qualified for the 88th Indianapolis 500, with the tail brought up by the two A.J. Foyt Racing Dallara/Toyotas driven by A.J. Foyt IV and Larry Foyt. Larry's 213.277 mph stood as the projected bump speed.

Meanwhile at the front of the pack, Buddy Rice had secured his second pole of the 2004 season – and by far the biggest one of his racing career. "It's just an unbelievable feeling right now," he said. "I don't think what happened today has completely sunk in. It's a huge accomplishment for myself and for the Rahal Letterman team to expand to three cars and be as competitive as we are. Obviously, in this weather some of [the competition] dropped off and our car maybe picked up. It's just about doing your homework. People kind of said we were under the radar all week, but we knew where we stood."

Rice's qualifying run impressed Rahal Letterman Racing Chief Operating Officer Scott Roembke. "I don't think anybody has hung it out like that for a long time," Roembke grinned. "That was a thrill ride. But you're not going to sit on the pole at Indy playing defense. You have to go after it."

Beyond Rice's pole, the big story of Pole Day was Honda's total dominance as the Japanese manufacturer swept the top seven positions on the starting grid. Those who speculated that Honda's desire to win at Twin Ring Motegi in Japan in the IRL IndyCar Series' last outing using 3.5-liter engines would cause the company's 3.0-liter engine to lag in development were proven dramatically wrong. If anything, the Honda 3.0-liter engine displayed a bigger advantage over its Toyota and Chevrolet competition than the 3.5-liter version had.

Left: Roger Yasukawa, who turned in the day's first qualifying run. Right: Rahal Letterman Racing team-mates Dan Wheldon and Bryan Herta. Below: sparks fly as Bryan Herta makes contact with the wall at Turn One.

"First through seventh is a big achievement," remarked a delighted Yoshihiro Wada, president of Honda Performance Development. "But it is not just the engine; the teams did a very good job. Last year, Andretti Green Racing did well but we did not have a second strong team. Now Fernandez is doing very well and Rahal is doing a wonderful job. Until yesterday, we were worried about Newman/Haas, but today Bruno did great and managed to qualify on the inside of the second row."

Wada confirmed that many of the developments that Honda perfected for the outgoing 3.5-liter engine produced similar gains in the de-stroked 3.0-liter mill. "We knew it was the end of the 3.5-liter program but we put a lot of effort on it because of Motegi," he said. "But we believed some of the new technology we developed for the 3.5 would also work for the 3.0-liter. It is also benefiting and clearly today it was quick, though I personally expected to see a 223 mph pole speed."

SUNDAY MAY 16
QUALIFICATION SESSION

A MUCH MORE PLEASANT INDIANA spring day greeted the competitors, but only four drivers made qualification runs, bringing the total number of qualified cars to 26. By far the most significant were the efforts of Bryan Herta and Alex Barron, coming a day after both men suffered big crashes in Turn One. Herta claimed the $25,000 prize for being the fastest second-day qualifier with a 219.871 mph average in the XM Satellite Radio Dallara/Honda out of the Andretti Green Racing stable, while Barron posted a 218.836 mph average in his spare Red Bull Dallara/Chevrolet.

"I knew that it would take a couple of laps this morning to get the feeling back and put yesterday out of my mind," Herta admitted. "I just asked my engineer [Eddie Jones] to give me a comfortable car to start with and he did that. We didn't need a 220 mph car today, but we nearly had one. We just wanted to get in comfortable and move

on to the next phase of the week, which was working on race setup with my teammates."

"It was a long night last night," Barron added. "You can't help but replay the whole scenario in your head and analyze everything, but I'm lucky to have a great group of engineers and a great crew that sticks by me. They put together a good car today and we had a solid run. It's a relief to be in the field and focus only on the race."

Continuing the theme of coming back strongly after wall contact, Felipe Giaffone found 216.259 mph in the Purex Dallara/Chevrolet run by Dreyer & Reinbold Racing. Tora Takagi was the day's final qualifier, running 214.364 mph in Mo Nunn's Pioneer/Denso Dallara/Toyota.

"All the guys were a little concerned, and we wanted to get qualifying done today so at least we did it," Giaffone said. "We pretty much ran race downforce and the car was all right but not perfect."

With only four qualification attempts between noon and 6pm, there was plenty of track time available for practice. While many teams took the day off, others including Penske Racing, Andretti Green Racing and Newman/Haas Racing worked on their race setups. With a Champ Car race at Monterrey, Mexico, looming, NHR's Bruno Junqueira ran 137 practice laps, knowing that this would be the last time he would be at Indianapolis until Carburetion Day. "We learned a few things today, but I was hoping for more traffic to run in," said Junqueira. "I was alone on the track a lot today and it would have been good to have a teammate to work together with, to get a car that runs good in traffic."

Off the track, a new car/driver combination was announced as Beck Motorsports named P.J. Jones to drive its #98 Dallara/Chevrolet. The Curb Records-sponsored car was painted up similar to the car that Jones' father, Parnelli, drove to victory in the 1963 Indianapolis 500.

"It's great to have an opportunity like this, and we're going to work as hard as we can to get where we need to be on race day," said P.J., who crashed in practice in 2002 in his only previous Indianapolis appearance.

Left: Tora Takagi, the day's final qualifier at 214.364 mph. Below: The green flag starts practice on the second day of qualifying. Bottom: Felipe Giaffone logged 216.259 mph.

Main picture: Kosuke Matsuura running with full tanks.
Below: Dario Franchitti celebrates his 31st birthday.

WEDNESDAY MAY 19
PRACTICE SESSION – 7

AFTER A MUCH APPRECIATED TWO-day break, on-track activity resumed at the Indianapolis Motor Speedway. The day started on a light-hearted note when Dario Franchitti got a surprise 31st birthday gift in the form of a ride around the Brickyard in the IRL Experience two-seater driven by team boss Michael Andretti.

"I was terrified not being in control," Dario admitted. "If it hadn't been Michael, I'd have never done it – though I'd probably ride with Mario [Andretti] too. It must be a heck of an experience for somebody who's never done it before."

Mark Taylor's difficult rookie season with Panther Racing got a little bit worse shortly after 1pm when the Englishman had a minor accident after spinning his back-up car in Turn One. Taylor almost kept the #2T Menards/Johns Manville Dallara/Chevrolet off the wall before just tapping the SAFER Barrier at the entry to Turn Two with the rear of the car.

"We were just working on race stuff, trying to run with other cars, and we hadn't got quite enough downforce in the car yet," Taylor explained. "It was only a light brush with the wall so it shouldn't take too long to fix."

All but three of the 24 qualified drivers ran their spare cars as Scott Dixon's 220.576 mph lap in the Target/Ganassi Panoz G Force/Toyota topped the timesheets. The New Zealander was the only pilot to crest 220 mph on the day.

"We ran some back-to-back stuff close to the qualifying set-up to see if we had sort of stepped on ourselves there," Dixon said. "We didn't find much and we still have some issues with the rear of the car. Toyota is working extremely hard to have something a little better for the race."

Kosuke Matsuura (Panasonic ARTA Panoz G Force/Honda) led three Honda pilots in the 219 mph bracket. But three Honda cars – specifically those driven by Adrian Fernandez, Bryan Herta and Dan Wheldon – stopped trackside with apparent engine problems.

"This was the first time I ran with full tanks, and at the beginning my car had a big push in almost every corner," Matsuura reflected. "We ended up with a completely different setup and the car had a good balance."

THURSDAY MAY 20
PRACTICE SESSION – **8**

ANOTHER **PERFECT DAY FOR PRACTICE,** with sunny skies and temperatures in the mid-80s. Yet oddly, only one not-yet-qualified driver took to the track, and Marty Roth was barely able to top 212 mph. However, two more car/driver combinations were confirmed and set to begin practice in the days ahead. Ron Hemelgarn announced he had reached a deal to run 1996 Indianapolis 500 winner (and 2000 IRL champion) Buddy Lazier in a second Dreyer & Reinbold Racing entry alongside Felipe Giaffone. It would mark Hemelgarn's 28th year of involvement at the IMS.

"We began discussing this idea of working together a few weeks ago and the further we delved into it, the more it made sense," remarked D&R co-owner Dennis Reinbold. Added Hemelgarn: "We first ran Buddy in 1991 and it was important to us to help him get a good ride.

"I thought it was very, very important for Buddy to be in the Indy 500."

Later in the day, PDM Racing owner Paul Diatlovich revealed that he had secured the finance and the Chevrolet engine necessary to field an entry for 1999 Indianapolis Rookie of the Year Robby McGehee. "I certainly would have preferred to get on the track earlier," McGehee acknowledged. "Our major sponsor backed out just before Opening Day, but now we are ready to race."

Target Chip Ganassi Racing's Scott Dixon and Darren Manning were the first drivers to take to the track when the green flag was waved at

12:15pm, following the Menards Infiniti Pro Series practice, and Manning went on to claim the day's "Ironman" tag by completing 146 laps. But the Yorkshireman was well down the speed charts in 15th place with a best lap of 215.112 mph. Dixon managed 218.121 mph to run sixth on the day.

Again the quickest laps came out of the Fernandez Racing stable, with Kosuke Matsuura pacing the action with a lap of 220.784 mph in his Super Aguri Fernandez Racing entry. Owner/driver Adrian Fernandez was right

behind at 220.077 mph, while two-time 500 winner Helio Castroneves was third on the day at 218.676 mph.

"We had another good day, but even though we are the fastest two guys, it doesn't mean anything," Fernandez said. "There are two or three other cars that also look strong and in race trim we are still not as fast as we would like to be."

A.J. Foyt IV produced the only wall contact of the day, spinning the Conseco Dallara/Toyota exiting Turn Three at mid-afternoon before bumping the inner wall with the rear wing. Damage was light.

"I was just starting to get on it and the car just stepped out on me a little bit," related Foyt. "Any time you spin here and you don't tear up the car real bad, you have to consider yourself lucky."

Main picture: Scott Dixon powers through a turn. Clockwise from above: team owner/driver Adrian Fernandez and crew; Sam Hornish Jr. and Marlboro Team Penske get some pit stop practice; Marty Roth was the only not-yet-qualified driver on the track.

FRIDAY MAY 21
PRACTICE SESSION – **9**

THE LAZIER BROTHERS HEADED THE day's storylines as Buddy and younger sibling Jaques took to the Indianapolis Motor Speedway for the first time in 2004. Buddy's #24T Dallara/Chevrolet was one of the first cars on the track, while late in the day, four-time Indianapolis winner A.J. Foyt Jr. asked Jaques to shake down the #14T Dallara/Toyota. But the Indy legend said he was unlikely to run a third car along those driven by family members A.J. IV and Larry.

"I've got two cars in the race and I don't need three," reckoned the elder Foyt. "I set the car up pretty soft for Anthony, and I just wanted to see what [Lazier's] feelings were on the car to give me some feedback. I was using it as a test car, mainly. I really don't have three crews to run another car properly, and if I do something, I like to do it proper. I wouldn't want to cheat him."

Jaques Lazier managed 212.340 mph during his ten-lap run, while brother Buddy was the day's fastest non-qualifier at 215.513 mph after running 66 laps.

"I enjoyed the day and I'll be comfortable going forward," Lazier said. "The car is excellent. We worked all day on race setups and we went just as fast on old tires as we did on new ones."

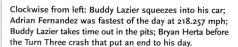

Clockwise from left: Buddy Lazier squeezes into his car; Adrian Fernandez was fastest of the day at 218.257 mph; Buddy Lazier takes time out in the pits; Bryan Herta before the Turn Three crash that put an end to his day.

IRL newcomer Adrian Fernandez was once again fastest, his speed limited to 218.257 mph by temperatures that were pushing the 90 degree mark. The Mexican was one of four drivers who completed more than 100 laps on the day, led by Vitor Meira, who ran 120 orbits in his teammate Roger Yasukawa's spare #16 T Panoz G Force/Honda. "We're more confident than we were yesterday," Fernandez commented. "My car was much more consistent in traffic today, even when it got windier towards the end of the day."

While Honda powered the fastest driver, the top ten on the day included five Toyotas and Tomas Scheckter's Chevrolet. However, it wasn't a perfect day for the Honda camp because a mechanical failure at the right rear of his car sent Bryan Herta hard into the Turn Three wall. The XM Satellite Radio Dallara/Honda sustained heavy left-side damage, but the Californian was uninjured after his second substantial crash of the month.

"I tried to save it and thought I could for a second," Herta related. "Then I thought I'd let the car brush up against the wall, but it whipped around and we took the hit."

Pole winner Buddy Rice had a much less stressful day, spending his morning doing the rounds of media interviews before taking batting practice with the Indianapolis Indians AAA-League baseball team.

"I actually hit the ball better than I thought I would," said Rice, who played baseball for his high school team. "I guess I had a day out of the car but not a day off."

SATURDAY MAY 22
PRACTICE SESSION – **10**

THE HOTTEST DAY OF THE MONTH greeted the drivers vying for the seven remaining spots in the Indianapolis 500 field. By noon, the ambient temperature reached 90 degrees and Firestone engineers reported a track temperature over 120 degrees.

The prospect of filling the 33-car field looked more likely after two more drivers were nominated to previously entered cars. Jeff Simmons parlayed a second-place finish in the Futaba Freedom 100 Menards Infiniti Pro Series

support race into a ride in Mo Nunn's #12 T Dallara/Toyota, while Sam Schmidt Motorsports leased a Panoz G Force/Toyota from Penske Racing for Richie Hearn to drive.

"It's really tough on your psyche to walk around here all month without a ride, but if I only get limited practice I'll deal with it," Hearn said after reaching 212.617 mph. "With only a day-and-a-half on the track, we don't have time to mess around. I've done this a few times, so I know how hard to push and what needs to be done

to make the car comfortable without scaring myself or over-stepping the boundaries."

Unlike the experienced Hearn, Simmons jumped into the IndyCar as a raw rookie. "I was taking my time to try to build everything up, just trying to go about it very professionally," he said after reaching 209.982 mph. "I think everyone was satisfied with what we did at the end of the day. It goes to show that the IndyCar Series team owners are watching the Pro Series races and looking for new talent."

Buddy Lazier was fastest of the not-yet-qualified drivers at 214.414 mph, while P.J. Jones (208.342 mph) and Robby McGehee (shakedown) turned their first laps of the month. "This was the first time the car had run and we're not really worried about the speed right now," Jones stated.

Clockwise from left: Adrian Fernandez delivered the fastest lap at 218.495 mph; seasoned veteran Richie Hearn gets psyched up for the race ahead; Hearn lowers himself into his car; 45-year-old rookie Marty Roth hit 213 mph for the first time.

"We just want to find a balance and get me going a little bit. I felt like I was getting the rust off and I'm excited to qualify tomorrow."

Marty Roth, meanwhile, edged over 213 mph for the first time. "At this place, you have to put your time in," said the 45-year old rookie. "I know how hard it is to get to the 213 mph mark. You don't just put a car on the track and go fast."

Unless, of course, you are with Fernandez Racing, which again set the outright pace. Adrian Fernandez locked down the top spot at 218.495 mph despite running only 19 laps, while Kosuke Matsuura was right behind at 218.300 mph. Fernandez also ran 60 laps in his backup car, reaching 217.755 mph.

"Another great day and now we are finished!" exclaimed Fernandez. "We are ready."

BUMP DAY

SUNDAY, **MAY 23**

When qualifications started at noon, P.J. Jones was first out, logging four laps in the 213 mph bracket for an average speed of 213.355 mph. The oldest son of 1963 Indy winner Parnelli Jones had suffered a broken back when he crashed in practice in 2002 in his only other IMS appearance. "Those were the four best and the most comfortable, easy laps since I've been here," said P.J.

"It's a little emotional, especially after [younger son] Page getting hurt [in a mid-'90s sprint car accident]," admitted the elder Jones. "I'm just delighted he's in the race. He probably had maybe 30 or 35 hot laps. I think he has a lot of talent and he's a good race driver."

Marty Roth (211.974 mph) was the next qualifier, followed by Buddy Lazier (215.110 mph) and Jeff Simmons (214.783 mph), leaving three spots open in the field. Nobody else was in the qualifying line, though nearly six hours remained. "It was a whirlwind 24 hours," Simmons said. "I haven't had a moment to stop yet. It's just been tremendous, getting the car in the show solidly, and now we're ready to focus on next weekend."

The 1999 IRL champion Greg Ray took to the track for the first time all month at 12:35pm in his #13 Panoz G Force/Honda. Within a handful of laps, Ray was running nearly 217 mph and ready to qualify.

When qualifying resumed, Richie Hearn ran 213.715 mph in the re-numbered #33 Sam Schmidt Motorsports car, followed half an hour later by Robby McGehee's 211.631 mph run. When Ray turned in a four-lap average of 216.641 mph at 1:40pm to claim the prize for being the day's fastest qualifier, the field was filled. While most of the field had nearly 70 hours of practice throughout the week, Ray logged a mere 65 minutes of track time.

"It wasn't the optimal situation to just jump in the car," admitted Ray, winner of five races and 13 poles in his IRL career. "It's been nerve-wracking the last two weeks. I've been working from sun-up to sundown to create a better future for our team. We could have gone faster, but we wouldn't have qualified any higher up, and every time you push the boundaries you take on additional risks. We just needed to get it safely in the show."

Just when it appeared the day's excitement had peaked, a sideshow emerged in the form of 1997 IRL champion (and current NASCAR Nextel Cup star) Tony Stewart. The Hoosier racer hung out in his pal A.J. Foyt's garage throughout the day and created a media frenzy when he donned a plain white driving suit for a seat fitting late in

116

Facing page, from top: Greg Ray and crew take to the track; Tony Stewart causes a media stir. Clockwise from left: Ray takes a stroll down Gasoline Alley; Bump Day qualifier P.J. Jones; Ray posted the day's fastest qualifier run; Stewart gets a seat fitting in the Foyt garage and then suits up for the cameras.

the afternoon. But contractual obligations to Chevrolet prevented Stewart from driving Foyt's Toyota-powered IndyCar.

"I want to be in that car more than you can imagine," Stewart noted. "When A.J. called me this morning, I thought he was joking, but I soon noticed he was pretty serious. I think it started out as a joke but when we got talking about it, we got our hopes up."

"We were still working on it with less than an hour to go," confirmed Stewart's manager, Cary Agajanian. "Fifty years ago, driving the car was the only thing you concerned yourself with, but that's not the case anymore."

The 33-car field included 22 Dallara and 11 Panoz G Force chassis, powered by 12 Toyotas, 11 Hondas and 10 Chevrolets. Eighteen of the 33 drivers were American, and the field included four former Indianapolis winners and eight rookies. The field average was 217.821 mph.

CARBURETION DAY

WORDS BY JOHN OREOVICZ

CARBURETION **DAY HAS BECOME** the second biggest draw during the Month of May at the Indianapolis Motor Speedway, a day when Hoosiers play hooky from work or school to party at the Brickyard. As usual, there was much more reason to attend than the two-hour final practice for the IndyCar Series drivers and teams prior to the Indianapolis 500, highlighted by a concert in the infield that featured an opening set by injured driver Kenny Bräck and his band the Subwoofers prior to the main act, alternative rock band Live.

There was also business to take care of prior to the cars taking to the track. Patrick Racing announced that the Subway chain of restaurants would serve as an associate sponsor on Al Unser Jr.'s #20 Dallara/Chevrolet, while Greg Ray revealed a new paint scheme for his #13 Access

Main picture and inset: Scott Dixon was third fastest of the day in his Toyota, averaging 217.391 mph.

Motorsports Panoz G Force/Honda along with sponsorship from Rent-A-Center and University Loft Co. Finally, Robby Gordon nominated Jaques Lazier as his relief driver in case of any weather delays on race day at Indianapolis that would affect his commitment to compete in the NASCAR Nextel Cup Coca-Cola 600 at Lowe's Motor Speedway in Charlotte that same evening.

"The one thing I don't control is the weather," Gordon said. "Jaques is a friend of mine and he obviously has a lot of experience in these cars. He'll spot for me today and race day and will be available to drive just in case."

Conditions were 15 degrees cooler than when most of the competitors last took to the 2.5 mile oval, and even cooler weather in the 60s was forecast for race day. As such, most of the field chose to utilize the early portion of their two

Clockwise from above: Adrian Fernandez; Kenny Bräck takes the stage; Kosuke Matsuura logged the day's fastest lap; TV "Survivor" Rupert Boneham gets the flag-waving honors.

finish at the Champ Car race in Monterrey, Mexico. The 2002 Indianapolis pole winner quickly got reacquainted with IRL machinery and ran eighth fastest at 215.861 mph.

"I'm quite happy with the car," he reported. "Maybe I had a little more understeer than I needed, but conditions will be different on race day so we developed some things to help out in different situations."

Junqueira ran 37 laps, a total exceeded only by Greg Ray (41) and Robby McGehee.

"This was our first time on full tanks – I just wish we had been able to do this earlier," said McGehee, who ran 40 laps in the PDM Racing Dallara/Chevrolet. "We learned a lot about the car."

The only mechanical drama of the day centred on P.J. Jones, who waited nearly an hour-and-a-half while an oil leak was repaired on his Beck Motorsports Dallara/Chevrolet. Jones completed 17 laps with a best speed of 211.170 mph.

hours of track time for their final pre-race tune-up before the day heated up, and there wasn't much activity for the final half-hour. It was the first day all month that 33 drivers practiced on the same day.

Japanese rookie Kosuke Matsuura continued to demonstrate how quickly he was picking up oval racing by running convincingly fast in his Super Aguri Fernandez Racing Panoz G Force/Honda. He lapped the Brickyard at 219.226 mph, almost 1.2 mph clear of the next fastest driver – Adrian Fernandez, owner of sister team Fernandez Racing. "We basically just did a few laps, making sure that we did what we have been doing all month," said a satisfied Fernandez. "We had a great day. The cars are good and that's it. We're ready to race."

"The car is fast, and for drafting has a very good balance," added Matsuura. "Everything is perfect."

Once again, the timing screens were dominated at the top by Honda-powered cars. Seven of the top ten speeds on Carburetion Day were achieved with Honda engines. Third-placed Scott Dixon (Target/Ganassi Panoz G Force) was the top Toyota driver at 217.391 mph. The best Chevy was Gordon, down in 13th place and nearly 5 mph off Matsuura's pace.

Despite his competitive performance, Dixon sounded like a man ready for a change of scenery after four weeks in Indianapolis. "It would be good if the race was tomorrow," he said. "It just needs to be over and done with."

In a much happier frame of mind were Rahal Letterman Racing drivers Vitor Meira and Roger Yasukawa, who ran fourth and fifth respectively. "The car feels better than I expected," said Meira of his Centrix Panoz G Force/Honda. "I've always heard that the Month of May is like a puzzle and that you want to put all of the pieces together on Carb Day. Today we have done that."

Ten days had elapsed since Bruno Junqueira last sat in his PacifiCare Panoz G Force/Honda as the Brazilian, along with his Newman/Haas Racing pit crew, was away earning a second-place

CHECKERS/RALLY'S
PIT STOP CHALLENGE

WORDS BY **JOHN OREOVICZ**

PART **OF THE CARBURETION DAY** tradition at the Indianapolis Motor Speedway is the finals of the annual Pit Stop Challenge. This year's 28th edition of the competition was sponsored by Checkers/Rallys restaurants, with a total of $80,000 in prize money up for grabs.

On Wednesday, May 19, the teams of Bryan Herta (XM Satellite Radio Dallara/Honda) and Kosuke Matsuura (Panasonic/ARTA Panoz G Force/Honda) qualified in a run-off for the final two spots in the 12-team field. But both were eliminated in Round One of the finals. Matsuura's crew succumbed to Helio Castroneves and Marlboro Team Penske, who turned in a blistering 8.424-second stop, while Red Bull Cheever Racing's Alex Barron knocked out Herta's hustlers with a 9.204-second stop that was just 0.2 secs faster than Andretti Green Racing could manage.

Top: A loose lug nut sees Dan Wheldon edged out of the competition. Above: the Malboro Team Penske crew put in another blistering effort.

Also advancing was the Andretti Green crew of Tony Kanaan (9.115 secs, beating Scott Sharp and Kelley Racing), and Sam Hornish Jr., whose Penske crew was even quicker than Castroneves' with an 8.422-second effort, besting Scott Dixon and Target/Ganassi Racing.

Castroneves' team had a close call in the quarter-finals with a 10.238-second stop that shaded Dario Franchitti and Andretti Green, who managed 10.404 secs. However, Franchitti's Andretti Green teammates Kanaan and Dan Wheldon advanced, with the 7-Eleven team defeating the Target/Ganassi crew of Darren Manning with an 8.835-second service. Wheldon's Jim Beam/Klein Tools men eliminated Alex Barron, warming up with a 9.438-second stop. Meanwhile Buddy Rice and Rahal Letterman Racing entered the fray and won by default when Hornish stalled and his engine wouldn't refire.

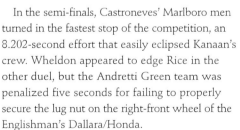

In the semi-finals, Castroneves' Marlboro men turned in the fastest stop of the competition, an 8.202-second effort that easily eclipsed Kanaan's crew. Wheldon appeared to edge Rice in the other duel, but the Andretti Green team was penalized five seconds for failing to properly secure the lug nut on the right-front wheel of the Englishman's Dallara/Honda.

The finals pitted Rice and Rahal Letterman against Castroneves and Penske. Neither crew turned in their best stop, but when the Argent/ Pioneer car left the pit box after 12.337 secs, it was quick enough for an easy victory and the $30,000 first prize. Castroneves ran over an air hose for a ten-second penalty on top of his 14.53-second stop.

It was the second year in a row that Rice was behind the wheel of the Pit Stop Challenge-winning car, though in 2003 he was with Red Bull Cheever Racing. Rahal-Hogan Racing was the contest winner back in 1992.

"These guys have never given up," Rice enthused of his Ricardo Nault-led crew. "They have done an excellent job the whole time. So this is huge for them. This is their deal and their time to shine, and they did what they are supposed to.

"We're starting on the pole and have been working hard all month," added the Phoenix native. "This is just icing on the cake for them. Now we have to go and focus on Sunday and hope we can win the big one."

Rice's magical Month of May therefore continued in grand style. Earlier on Carburetion Day, team boss Bobby Rahal publicly confirmed that Rice, who had been hired as a substitute until injured regular driver Kenny Bräck was fit to return, had earned the Pioneer/Argent seat for the rest of the 2004 season. "Two out of three so far," said a smiling Rahal. "Now we'll go for the trifecta."

Clockwise from above: Alex Barron in his #51 Dallara/Chevrolet; Buddy Rice; and the Rahal Letterman crew after completing another pit stop.

WORDS BY JOHN OREOVICZ

LEADER OF THE PACK

Facing page: Actor Morgan Freeman gets acquainted with the pace car, a Chevrolet Corvette convertible. Clockwise, from top: the Corvette sets the pace; the Corvette features a special Americana paint job; Freeman gets a ride in the Indy Racing Experience two-seater.

GENERAL **MOTORS HAS BEEN A** strong supporter of the Indy Racing League since the League's inception, so it came as no surprise when the Chevrolet Corvette convertible was selected as the official pace car for the 88th Indianapolis 500. GM products have paced the Indianapolis field every year since 1995, and this year's race marked the record sixth time that Chevrolet's flagship sports car would play an integral role in the Memorial Weekend Classic. It was also the third year in succession that the honor went to the Chevrolet brand.

"The Indianapolis 500 and Chevrolet have had a long relationship," said Indianapolis Motor Speedway president and CEO Tony George. "It's an honor to have Corvette lead the field and also to have the Chevy Indy V8 competing for the win on May 30."

Chevrolet products have served as the official pace car at the Indianapolis 500 15 times since 1948, the most appearances by any brand. Company founder Louis Chevrolet competed in the famous May event four times, and since then Chevy Indy V8 engines have won 103 open-wheel races, including seven Indianapolis 500 victories.

"We are proud that this year's Memorial Day classic will showcase America's favorite sports car at the 'Greatest Spectacle in Racing,'"

stated Brent Dewar, Chevrolet general manager. "As the 2004 model year is the last of Corvette's current design, pacing the Indy 500 acknowledges the significance the vehicle has played in American culture."

The 2004 Indy 500 pace car was virtually identical to the Convertibles available through any local Chevrolet dealership. The C5 series of Corvettes debuted in 1997 and a revised version

of the platform known as the C6 went on sale in autumn 2004. The C5 Corvette also paced the Indianapolis 500 in 1998.

As a genuine 150 mph sports car, very few modifications were necessary to prepare the stock Corvette for its role as official pace car. Heavy-duty transmission, power steering coolers and a lower restriction exhaust system were installed in the vehicle, as well as four-point, racing-type seat belt harnesses and a safety strobe light system. The car's distinctive white-and-blue, two-tone paint treatment incorporated Americana-themed graphics, tying into Chevrolet's new "American Revolution" marketing theme, which attempted to capture Chevrolet's pride and passion for innovation.

Renowned actor Morgan Freeman was tabbed to drive the Corvette pace car on race day. The 67-year-old, three-time Academy Award nominee said the experience was a highlight of his life: "This is one of those times in your life when you realize you're involved in something just a little bit bigger than awesome. Since I got off the plane [there] was one very nice, pleasant, exciting experience after another.

"This is my first time on a racetrack with 350,000 people there, and with an extraordinary amount of excitement surrounding the event," he added. "You're not a spectator, you're part of it. It's just an incredible amount of excitement."

Another race fan prepares for the ride of a lifetime with the Indy Racing Experience.

PAGEANTRY, POMP AND
CIRCUMSTANCE

WORDS BY **JOHN OREOVICZ**

THE **MONTH OF MAY IN INDIANAPOLIS** is naturally dominated by on-track activity at the Indianapolis Motor Speedway. But an ever-evolving series of social events in the weeks leading up to the Indianapolis 500 comprise an important element of the tradition that is the Indianapolis 500. Since 1957, the 500 Festival, a not-for-profit volunteer group, has organized the civic events that celebrate the greatest race in the world, and in 2004 nearly 425,000 Hoosiers and visitors participated in festival activities with the theme "Lights, Camera, Traction!"

Activities kicked off on Saturday, May 8, when a record 30,000 runners participated in the Indianapolis Life 500 Festival Mini Marathon, the largest half-marathon in the nation. Several competitors suffered in the humid conditions, causing the race to be red-flagged. Reuben Chebii, a 21-year-old Kenyan, won the men's

division in 1:04:56 while Albina Ivanova of Russia repeated as women's champion with a time of 1:12:36.

Presented by WIBC-AM, the flagship station of the Indianapolis Motor Speedway Radio Network, the May 12 Toro Fast Track lunch on Monument Circle featured a number of Indy 500-themed attractions, including the Indy Racing Fan Experience, Indy 500 show cars, vintage race cars , and culminating in a Toro tractor race around the Circle with the WIBC morning team versus WIBC personality (and IMS Radio Network commentator) Dave "The King" Wilson.

The IRL Fan Experience, which travels to domestic IndyCar Series races with the League and has no admission fee, includes areas such as "Indy Racing Challenge," "Indy Racing Kids," and "Indy Racing Pit Stop Challenge." The Fan Experience was open to fans at the IMS grounds for 18 days during the Month of May.

Vintage race cars could be seen on the track during the May activities. Top: A youngster takes a leisurely spin.

Want to get even closer to the real thing? The Indy Racing Experience, a two-seat version of an Indy-style race car, offered fans a chance to ride around the Brickyard at speeds of up to 185 mph. Just $1,000 got you your own chauffeur-driven, four-lap simulated qualifying run on May 17, 18, 24 and 25.

The annual "Racing to Recovery Gala," a benefit for the Sam Schmidt Paralysis Foundation and the Rehabilitation Hospital of Indiana, was held Sunday, May 16 at Eddie Merlot's Restaurant. Former IMS Radio Network and Public Address announcer Bob Jenkins served as emcee. More than $100,000 was raised, added to more than $1 million generated in past years.

On Friday, May 21, the 38th Louis Schwitzer Award was presented to Honda for its HI4R-A Honda Indy V-8 engine used in the IndyCar Series. Honda Performance Development General Manager Robert Clarke accepted the award, which also earned the recipients $5,000. The Schwitzer Award is presented by the Indiana Section of the Society of Automotive Engineers in recognition of individuals with the "courage and conviction to explore and develop new concepts in auto racing technology."

Saturday, May 22 started with the annual Mayor's Breakfast, established in 1958. An estimated 1,000 patrons joined 55 Indiana mayors including host, Indianapolis Mayor Bart Peterson at the IMS Plaza Pavilion to hear remarks by keynote speaker Roger Penske. Defending Indianapolis 500 champion Gil de Ferran then crowned Indiana University student Jennifer McConnell of Indianapolis as 500 Festival Queen. Lauren Petticrew of Zionsville and Margaret Kleinhenn of Noblesville were named Princesses to the Queen's court.

Later in the day, Indianapolis Motor Speedway President and CEO Tony George received the Louis Meyer Award during the annual Hall of Fame/500 Oldtimers Banquet. George Brattain, president of the 500 Oldtimers Club, presented the top honor handed out by the club, named for the first three-time winner of the Indianapolis 500. Later in the program, George introduced the five new members inducted into the Auto Racing Hall of Fame at the Indianapolis Motor Speedway: Indy 500-winning drivers Mark Donohue, Emerson Fittipaldi and Tom Sneva, and team owners Lindsey Hopkins and John Zink.

The second-annual "Women in the Winner's Circle" luncheon, a benefit for the Lyn St. James Foundation, took place Monday, May 24 at the Schwitzer Student Center on the campus of the University of Indianapolis. Mike King, lead announcer for the IMS Radio Network, served as emcee.

Honoring opposite ends of the Indianapolis 500 grid, The Front Row party was held Tuesday, May 25 at popular Broad Ripple district club Rock Lobster, while the Indianapolis Press Club staged the 32nd annual Last Row Party on Thursday, May 27 at the Brickyard Crossing

Clockwise from top left: The Rahal Letterman team takes some time out; Jessica Simpson performs the National Anthem; Community Day fun and games.

and Resort Pavilion. Bob Jenkins oversaw the proceedings as P.J. Jones, Marty Roth and Robby McGehee were presented with jackets and checks totaling $0.96.

500 Festival Community Day on May 26 offered fans the chance to drive their personal cars around the Indianapolis Motor Speedway for a lap before an Indy Racing League driver autograph session. Two days later, NBC Nightly News anchor Tom Brokaw delivered the keynote address for the 500 Festival's 46th annual Memorial Service at Monument Circle, where Indiana Governor Joe Kernan and Indianapolis Mayor Bart Peterson also took part in the ceremonies. It was then a short walk to the annual CARA Charities Fashion Show at the Westin Hotel Grand Ballroom.

A large crowd attended the Drivers' Meeting at 11am on Saturday, May 29 in front of the Bombardier Pagoda. Seating was available in Tower Terrace as the 33-driver field gathered to receive final race instructions from Chief Steward Brian Barnhart and pre-race awards.

The meeting was immediately preceded by another driver autograph session.

The annual 500 Festival Parade, the nation's largest motor racing parade, wound through downtown Indianapolis on May 29, while the eve of the race was highlighted by the 500 Festival Snakepit Ball at the Indiana Roof Ballroom. The Oscar night-like gala, in keeping with the 2004 500 Festival theme of "Lights, Camera, Traction!" featured entertainment by The Spinners and a host of celebrities in town for the race including Morgan Freeman and Jane Pauley.

Race Day itself brought its share of celebrities to Indianapolis. Vying for most popular honors were Jessica Simpson, who performed the National Anthem, and Indianapolis resident Rupert Boneham, the popular veteran of CBS's "Survivor" shows.

The Month of May concluded with the Indianapolis 500 Victory Celebration on Monday, May 31 at the IMS Plaza Pavilion. Race winner Buddy Rice was the toast of the evening, taking home $1,761,740 from the record $10,250,580 purse.

Excitement mounts as cars and drivers are started.
Below left: Country singer Lee Ann Womack gets a spin
in the pace car. Below right: Star of MTV's *Newlyweds*,
singer Nick Lachey waves the green flag on Race Day.

WORDS BY **JOHN OREOVICZ**

88TH INDIANAPOLIS 500

AFTER **SPENDING A MONTH IN INDIANAPOLIS, THE LAST** thing anyone wants is to have the Greatest Spectacle in Racing delayed. Yet that has happened five times in the last eight years, and sure enough, rain began blanketing the Indianapolis Motor Speedway at about 6:00am on Race Day morning. The precipitation continued off and on before finally relenting at about 10:30am, just half an hour before the scheduled start. The festivities and razzmatazz that traditionally precede the Indianapolis 500 would have to wait until a fleet of service vehicles and jet dryers got the 2.5-mile oval into racing shape.

The man most affected by the delay was Robby Gordon, who needed to leave Indianapolis by 2:40pm in order to make the start of the NASCAR Nextel Cup race in Charlotte later that same evening. Relief driver Jaques Lazier stood by ready to take over.

"I was hoping that we would have an on-time start," Gordon remarked while he waited. "My best-case scenario, and I hate to say this to all the Indy 500 fans, is that it rains here in Indy and we'll come back and do this tomorrow."

Alas, Gordon didn't get his wish, and at 1:02pm, after a delay of 2 hours, 11 minutes, Indianapolis Motor Speedway Chairman Mari Hulman George gave the time-honored command, "Lady and Gentlemen, Start Your Engines!" Finally, after three parade laps, pole man Buddy Rice led the

field across the yard of bricks under Bryan Howard's waving green flag to begin the 88th Indianapolis 500. From the outside of the front row, Dario Franchitti pulled ahead of Andretti Green Racing teammate Dan Wheldon to slot into second place. An obviously pumped Gordon made the biggest gain at the start, jumping from 17th on the grid to end the first lap in tenth place.

At the front of the field, Rice pulled away with apparent ease, running a 215 mph pace to build a 3.3-sec lead over Franchitti by the tenth lap. But then A.J. Foyt IV spun and crashed in Turn One after brushing the wall exiting Turn Four just a few moments earlier. Damage to the Conseco Dallara/Toyota was moderate, but Anthony's day was seemingly done.

"I thought everything was OK after I hit the wall coming out of Turn Four," Foyt said. "But when I got into One, I found out it wasn't. It was pretty stupid on my part."

On the 13th lap, 30 of the remaining 32 runners made their first pit stops under caution. Alex Barron (Red Bull Cheever Racing Dallara/Chevrolet) and Bryan Herta (XM Satellite Radio Dallara/Honda) stayed out and Barron briefly led the field when racing resumed on the 16th lap. Herta led one lap before ceding the lead to teammate Wheldon, whose crew won the initial battle in the pits. But the yellow flag again greeted the field at the end

The pace car leads the field around the famous oval. Below: marching to the beat of the "world's largest" drum. Facing page, from top: Alex Barron awaits the start of the action; pre-race entertainment in full swing; and they're off.

of the 22nd lap with reports of rain falling on parts of the Speedway.

The race was red-flagged after 28 laps with Wheldon leading Helio Castroneves, who had slotted past both Tony Kanaan and Rice with a nifty move on lap 17. Sam Hornish Jr.'s Marlboro Team Penske Dallara/Toyota ran fifth when the race was halted, followed by Herta and Franchitti, then top rookie Kosuke Matsuura (Panasonic/ ARTA Dallara/Honda) and teammate Adrian Fernandez (Quaker State/Telmex/Tecate Dallara/ Honda). The best-placed Chevrolet runner,

"AT 3:29PM, IMS PUBLIC ADDRESS LEGEND TOM CARNEGIE CALLED 33 ENGINES BACK TO LIFE"

Tomas Scheckter, rounded out the top ten in the Pennzoil Panther team's Dallara.

Within half an hour, Gordon departed in an IMS helicopter to begin his journey to Charlotte, handing his car to Lazier in 14th place after a slow pit stop. The Meijer Dallara/Chevrolet was dropped to the tail of the field, as was Greg Ray's Rent-A-

Center Panoz G Force/Honda. Having already lost a lap while an ECU was replaced during a lap 13 pit stop, the Access crew took the #13 machine back to the garage for additional diagnosis during what turned out to be a 1 hour, 47-minute rain delay.

At 3:29pm, IMS Public Address legend Tom Carnegie called 33 engines back to life, the Foyt crew having made repairs to send its driver back into the fray 14 laps down. Following a lap behind the Chevrolet Corvette Pace Car, Wheldon brought the field back up to speed but lost the lead to Rice in Turn Two on the 33rd tour.

A new challenger now appeared in the form of Hornish. The Ohio native gained three places on the track during the seven laps of racing between caution periods, and he continued his march forward after the rain delay. On the 34th lap, Hornish passed his teammate Castroneves for third place, and then took second from Wheldon on lap 46. When leader Rice encountered heavy traffic, Hornish made an opportune move and seized the lead on the main straight starting the 50th lap. Amazingly, it was the first time the two-time Indy Racing League champion had ever led at Indianapolis and he quickly moved out to a 4.7-sec advantage over Rice.

The Foyt team again slowed the proceedings on lap 56, this time when Larry Foyt scraped the Turn Two wall. "I just got up in the marbles," said the converted stock car driver. "My car was

128

bad all day and it got under me in Turn Two and took me into the fence."

The Rahal Letterman Racing crew regained the lead for Rice when the field pitted on lap 58 under yellow. Wheldon still held third ahead of Herta, who benefited from being able to refuel during the race stoppage. Then came Kanaan, Vitor Meira, Castroneves (who was badly balked in traffic, losing three positions just before the pit stops) and Franchitti. Lapped cars were also giving the Scotsman fits and he dropped as low as tenth place.

"We just kept going backwards all day and it was pretty frustrating," Franchitti said. "Traffic was tough. One guy would go by you, and it seems two or three would line up and get you afterward. That's what we were fighting all day."

A much bigger accident brought out the yellow flag again after a single lap of green flag racing. Ed Carpenter (Red Bull Cheever Dallara/Chevrolet) and Mark Taylor (Menards/Johns Manville Dallara/Chevrolet) touched going into Turn Three, with both cars slamming into the SAFER Barrier.

"I got a good run off Two on Alex [Barron] and Mark," reported Carpenter. "Alex about ran me into the grass so I gave way and Mark and I went in two-wide. You just can't have two-wide at Indy. The guy on the outside has to give the guy on the inside some room."

It was Rice, Wheldon and Hornish when the field was again released on lap 70. Three laps later, Kanaan passed his AGR teammate Herta for fourth, while Darren Manning (Target Ganassi Panoz G Force/Toyota) charged up to sixth place before claiming fifth from Herta on the 89th lap.

Wheldon peeled off from third place to begin the next round of pit stops on lap 94 and the Englishman was lucky that he didn't lose a lap immediately due to P.J. Jones's riding the Turn Two SAFER Barrier. The leaders promptly pitted under caution on lap 97, with Wheldon assuming the lead from Kanaan and Hornish. But the Penske driver had to return to the pits twice more under caution to rectify a sticking fuel vent. Manning was another driver to lose out in this pit stop exchange, dropping from third to 16th.

The real scare was in the Rahal Letterman pit, where Rice stalled his engine after routine service. The Pioneer/Argent crew refired the Honda engine and the Phoenix native resumed, albeit back in eighth place.

On the lap 103 restart, Kanaan took the lead from Wheldon, and Herta took third place from Castroneves, briefly creating a one-two-three for Andretti Green Racing. But Castroneves got right back past the Californian, only for all hell to break lose in Turn Four in the day's most spectacular incident. Ray, running six laps down after fixing his electrical problems, got racy and made a move on Manning. But the front end of Ray's Panoz G Force/Honda washed out into Manning's similar Panoz G Force/Toyota, and as the two cars

The action resumed on lap 137 and Junqueira, running 20 laps lighter on fuel, edged away in the PacifiCare Panoz G Force/Honda. "We didn't have the best car in traffic, but we had a good car to run by ourselves," the Brazilian noted. "Running a different strategy helped us lead some laps."

Rice lost fifth place to defending IndyCar Series champion Scott Dixon on the restart, but reclaimed the position on lap 140. He passed Herta for fourth place three laps later before demoting Wheldon to third three laps after that. Almost simultaneously as Junqueira pitted on lap 151, Rice zipped inside Kanaan for the lead entering Turn One. It wrapped up a superb stint for Rice.

"It was kind of a late pass, but I needed to make it to give myself a barrier. Tony got bottled up so bad that I couldn't see him in the mirror and that cushion helped us get back to conserving fuel."

"I think it was clear that Buddy was by far the fastest car out there," observed team owner Bobby Rahal. "You could see he had the pace and could pass people, I won't say at will, because I'm sure it took some effort. When he passed Kanaan there to get back the lead it was a key moment."

Once back in front, Rice put down the hammer and pulled out a 3-second gap. This time Kanaan kicked off what was set to be the final round of pit stops, coming in on lap 164. With rain imminent, picking the right time to pit was a huge gamble.

"Everyone started to sequence through their pit stops, and I could very much see somebody winning who wasn't in the hunt all day," Rahal recalled. "I was gnashing my teeth thinking about all that because that would have been immensely dissatisfying if the 500 had been decided in that manner."

One by one, the leaders followed Kanaan into the pits: Wheldon on lap 165, Rice on lap 167, Herta on lap 169. Now light rain began to fall. Adrian Fernandez, long known for his fuel-stretching ability, made it all the way until lap 171 before stopping. That cycled Rice back into the lead, followed by Andretti Green triplets Kanaan, Wheldon and Herta. And then it started to rain much harder.

Out came the Pace Car to lead the field through laps 174-179, when the white flag was shown to Rice. After averaging just 67.5 mph for his final lap, Rice then received the red and checkered flags at the end of 450 miles. He had won the Indianapolis 500 on his second attempt. It was the first rain-shortened race at Indianapolis since the 1976 race was rained out after 255 miles.

With heavy rain falling, the Victory Lane celebration was moved into the base of the Bombardier Pagoda. There, Rice was able to begin savoring the biggest day of his life, starting with a messy swig of the traditional milk that goes to the Indianapolis 500 champion.

speared to the inside of the track, they collected Hornish's Dallara/Toyota. The trio of out-of-control machines slid into the pit entrance, with Manning's car T-boning the end of the pit wall. Thankfully, there were no injuries to the drivers but Hornish and Manning were rightfully upset. IMS safety worker David Stout suffered an injured foot.

"There were a bunch of guys stacked up," Hornish reported. "Darren was on the outside of Greg, and Greg just ran right up into him. I was right behind and there was nowhere to go. It's not very fun when two guys get together in front of you, especially when one of them is seven [sic] laps down."

"I don't know what was up with Greg," Manning added. "He just kept coming up the track and clipped my left rear. But I guess it was my fault for running back there anyway. I had been up in third place, but I missed my marks in the pits and dropped right back. I guess that's what Indy is all about – the highs and the lows. It bit me today, that's for sure."

Ray, whose shoestring team certainly didn't need the cost of another wrecked car, refused to take the blame for the wreck. "I wasn't being aggressive in traffic," he retorted. "I gave [Manning] room at the wall, I could see him and my spotter told me he was there. But he got into my left rear. Just wrong time, wrong place for us all."

In a reversal of the previous restart, Wheldon passed Kanaan on the outside into Turn One on lap 117. But the Brazilian fought back three laps later. With rain clouds again building on the southwest horizon, things were getting serious now; but again a caution spoiled the flow of the race, this time when rookie Marty Roth shaved the outside SAFER Barrier exiting Turn Four before veering back across the track to clout the inner wall.

Roth's crash interrupted an intense inter-team duel between Kanaan and Wheldon. "I never had so much fun in my life with a teammate

Top and above: A.J. Foyt IV crashes in spectacular style. Facing page, from top: Bryan Herta makes a successful pit stop; Buddy Rice builds up an early lead.

like I had with Dan today," Kanaan later recalled. "When you can fight that hard between each other and get out of the car and laugh about it, to me, that's priceless."

"Like Tony said, that was probably my most enjoyable race ever from driving," Wheldon noted. "I could race like that every day of the week, 365 days a year."

Lap 133 saw the leaders pit under yellow, with Wheldon, Kanaan, Herta and Rice leading the way. Out front was Bruno Junqueira, who was one of a handful of drivers who had pitted during the caution for the Hornish-Manning-Ray crash. Having last stopped on lap 114, Junqueira and the Newman/Haas Racing crew hoped their alternate pit stop sequence might put them out front if the rain returned.

"This is pretty unbelievable," he exclaimed. "I had to fill in for Kenny Bräck and that's not the way you want to come into a ride. To get all the support he's given is pretty cool. It's great for my family and everybody who really helped me out. We knew we had it all month. We were strong and we knew it. We had to go through some diversions – we had an issue with one of the pit stops, but hey, these guys have been fighting all year."

Team co-owner David Letterman, an Indianapolis native, was overcome by emotion. "My god, what a job Buddy did today," he gushed. "He just kept coming after it and coming after it. It's just a thrill to be a part of this and I just want to thank everybody with the organization for the hard work they have done since I was a part of this team."

Rice led five times for 91 of the 180 laps. He averaged 138.518 mph. "We knew there was going to be a lot of fuel strategy," he said. "Pit stops were going to be crucial and whoever made the fewest mistakes was probably going to win. With the way it's so close now from top to bottom, you knew that was coming.

"Stalling in the pits wasn't part of the plan, but there was no need to panic," Rice related. "Maybe if there were 20 or 30 laps to go, but we were only halfway through the race and we knew we had another couple of stops before any weather was coming. Scott Roembke made all the right calls on fuel strategy and we did what we needed to do."

The victory was particularly sweet for Roembke, who, like Letterman, is an Indianapolis native. "We always thought Buddy had talent and that he could win races," Roembke said. "He's a veteran driver and he's calm in the race car. But he knows when he has to push the button. Watch his qualifying run – I don't think anybody has hung it out like that for a long time. But he did it when he needed to do it.

"This is a long race, and sometimes you can get away with making a mistake and some years you can't," he added. "We stalled and went to the back, but circumstances allowed us to come back today. I think it was quite obvious we had the fastest car and we won the race with Mother Nature today."

Rahal was awarded a second Indianapolis 500 ring to go with the one he earned for driving the winning car in 1986. Rahal's other cars, driven by Vitor Meira and Roger Yasukawa, finished seventh and 10th respectively.

"Obviously it's very sweet," Rahal commented. "People have asked me if it's sweeter than doing it as a driver, and all I can say is that it's different. There's nothing like crossing the yard of bricks when you're driving a racing car and yet by the same token, this has been just a great achievement for our team."

While Rahal brought out a huge cheer when he turned his cap backward to mimic the style that Rice favors, Andretti Green Racing quietly mulled over a two-three-four finish. "Buddy had too much car at the end for us," said team owner Michael Andretti, whose best run at Indy came in

"BUDDY HAD THE FASTEST CAR AND HE WON. THAT'S THE WAY THE INDY 500 IS SUPPOSED TO BE"

1991 when he finished second to Rick Mears. "It's a little disappointing, but we'll take second, third and fourth. We were competitive; we just weren't quick enough."

"Let's not get greedy – the right guy won today," remarked Herta after his fourth-place finish. "Buddy had the fastest car and he won the race. That's the way the Indy 500 is supposed to be. We just have to work a little harder, but after the month I had [marked by two accidents], this feels like a win."

"Buddy was much stronger," agreed Tony Kanaan, who led 28 laps but officially fell 0.156 secs short in his bid for victory. "I don't think I had the car to pass him. He was much faster

and he had a better car today, so he deserves it. I did my best."

A third-place finish kept Wheldon in the IndyCar Series point lead. "When you work so hard and miss by so little, it's disappointing in a way," said the Englishman. "But Buddy had a really strong month and other than somebody on our team, you couldn't have had a better winner. You've got to hang it out to win, and Buddy certainly did that today."

MATSUURA CLAIMS TOP ROOKIE HONORS

Kosuke Matsuura followed Tora Takagi as the second consecutive Japanese driver to win Bank One Rookie of the Year honors. The 24-year-old from Aichi qualified ninth and finished 11th in the Panasonic/ARTA Panoz G Force/Honda operated out of the Super Aguri Fernandez Racing stable.

Clockwise from top left: Roger Yasukawa gets some pre-race support; Sam Hornish Jr.'s wrecked car is cleared from the track; David Letterman enjoys the rush of Race Day.

Remarkably, Matsuura had never driven on an oval prior to his first test with the Super Aguri team in November 2003. The task of learning the uniquely American style of racing was made easier for the Japanese driver – a veteran of Formula 3 and Formula Renault V6 competition in Europe – when team co-owner Adrian Fernandez departed from the Champ Car series into IndyCars in early March. Though he was much more experienced, Fernandez was in many ways also facing a steep learning curve, but once the team gained an understanding of what the Panoz G Force chassis required, Matsuura and Fernandez ran very quickly in practice at Indianapolis.

Matsuura, furthermore, had never driven in a race longer than 100 miles heading into 2004, so the Indianapolis 500 represented his sternest test yet. But he passed it with flying colors, never getting into trouble on the track while learning about the inevitable ups and downs of oval racing.

"I knew if I didn't make a crash, I would finish among the top rookies," said Matsuura, who won a $25,000 bonus along with a trophy as the top rookie. "I was quite competitive at the beginning and passed three or four cars. But when the temperature was lower, others were quicker than us and that was difficult.

"I'm happy, but I am also disappointed because I could have finished in the top five," he added. "I overtook a lot of cars on the track but I lost a lot of positions to a couple of mistakes in the pits. But tomorrow I will be happy because I got a lot of prize money!"

NO INDY CHEER FOR HORNISH

Sam Hornish Jr. dominated Indy Racing League competition in 2001 and 2002, but his least competitive race was always the

Indianapolis 500. The Defiance, Ohio native's best Indianapolis finish was 14th place in 2001 and he had never qualified higher than seventh.

Hornish thought that moving to Marlboro Team Penske – the most successful team in Indianapolis history – would improve his chances of scoring a victory in the Memorial Day Classic. But he once again failed to complete the race he most wants to win, this time through no fault of his own.

Hornish was always among the quickest Toyota runners in practice and he qualified 12th, second only to his teammate Helio Castroneves in terms of Toyota-powered drivers. But in the first third of the rain-interrupted race, Sam had one of the quickest cars on the track, and he confidently moved to the front to take the lead at the 50-lap mark. Remarkably, the nine laps Hornish led prior to full-field pit stops were his first ever at the front of the Indianapolis field.

Hornish exchanged second with Dan Wheldon during the next stint, but the Penske team had a problem with the Dallara/Toyota's fuel vent mechanism during the next round of pit stops, necessitating two extra calls to the pits – fortunately while the field ran behind the Pace Car. However, the delay put Hornish deep in the pack and he was swept into the Turn Four accident between Darren Manning and Greg Ray on lap 106. Ray was running six laps down at the time.

"FOR TWO GUYS TO GET TOGETHER IN FRONT OF ME, WHEN ONE OF THEM IS SEVEN LAPS DOWN, IT'S NOT FUN"

"Greg and Darren got together, and I really didn't have anywhere to go," Hornish said when he emerged from the Trackside Medical Center.

"It was not the greatest thing that could have happened at that point in time," he added, with more than a hint of sarcasm. "We were up at the front doing everything we could to stay out of trouble, and we had a problem that was nobody's fault. We came in, fixed it, went back out and were moving back up through the field.

"For two guys to get together in front of me, when one of them is seven laps down, it's not very fun," he concluded. "But we'll move on, wait for the next time, and see if we can win one of these days."

HERTA'S INDY PAYBACK

Bryan Herta's Indianapolis career has featured its share of highs and lows. After debuting with a solid ninth-place finish in 1994, Herta suffered a massive crash in practice while driving for Ganassi Racing a year later, leaving him with a concussion.

After joining the Indy Racing League with Andretti Green Racing in 2003, Herta claimed a victory at Kansas Speedway that demonstrated his ability to win on ovals. But the 34-year-old Californian suffered a punishing Month of May 2004 before it all came good in the form of a fourth-place finish when it counted on Race Day.

Herta's troubles started on the rainy Pole Day when he tried a radical setup that didn't work. The result was a jarring crash at Turn One. Yet the next day, Herta returned to the IMS oval in his spare XM Satellite Radio Dallara/Honda to claim the $25,000 prize as the fastest Day Two qualifier.

However, Herta's troubles weren't over yet. On May 21, a mechanical failure at the right rear of his car sent him hard into the Turn Three wall. He was uninjured, but the car was badly damaged.

In the race, Herta and Team Manager George Klotz made their own luck. When the rest of the field pitted under yellow on lap 13, Herta and Alex Barron remained on track. When the red flag came out during a rainstorm, Herta was able to re-fuel his car (like everyone else) at a time when his tank was nearly dry. From that point on, he never ran outside the top six.

"With the month I've had this feels like a win for the XM Satellite Radio team," Herta remarked. "I went into the wall hard on Pole Day and then a second time during practice. But during the race it all came right. We caught a break out there with the red flag today. George made a gutsy call to not pit under the first caution and then we were able to add fuel and put new tires on without making a pit stop."

"It was an all-around great team effort and I can't say enough about this XM Satellite Radio team," Klotz added.

MR. EFFICIENT

Vitor Meira put together a quietly effective month than ended with a sixth-place finish in the Indianapolis 500. Combining with winner Buddy Rice and tenth-place finisher Roger Yasukawa, Rahal Letterman Racing put three cars in the top ten, a result that delighted team owners Bobby Rahal and David Letterman. But Meira thought it would have been much better had he not been penalized for driving over an air hose during a lap-60 pit stop.

"I think we made up 27 positions from that point until the end of the race," said the ever-smiling Brazilian. "We had the quickest lap of the race for Rahal Letterman, so we really couldn't ask for more."

"This has just been a great achievement for our team," said Rahal. "Three in the top ten! I mean, I can't be happier. Buddy drove the wheels off that thing and Roger did a great job."

RLR chief operating officer Scott Roembke was impressed by Meira's performance. "We brought in Vitor in the second car and that was a breath of fresh air because he's such a nice guy and he drives hard," Roembke said. "He could have won a couple of races and it's been a very satisfying year on that side of the team."

TAKING ON THE BIG BOYS

Part of the charm of the Indianapolis 500 has been the notion that the "little guy" can compete for one of the 33 spots in the starting field. In an age dominated by manufacturer-backed superteams, the "little guy" has almost been pushed completely aside, but Marty Roth and his small band of helpers exhibited the proper spirit.

Roth, a 46-year old rookie from Toronto, hadn't raced seriously in more than a decade. He ran 13 Menards Infiniti Pro Series races in 2002 and 2003 as a tune-up to Indy before entering an unsponsored Dallara/Toyota in the Indianapolis 500. The car was run by a small crew led by ex-PacWest Racing chiefs Mark Moore and Butch Winkle.

"The goal from the start of joining the Menards Infiniti Pro Series was to move up," Roth said. "That's been the ultimate mission, to get into the 500 and bring the team up to the IndyCar Series level. We're on track."

Roth found running competitive speeds in an IndyCar was more difficult than he'd anticipated. He endured two spins without damaging his lone Dallara before finally qualifying with the second slowest speed in the field.

"It's been a huge learning curve as a driver and a team owner and just about everything," he said. "We thought we knew how to set

Facing page: Buddy Rice takes the checkered flag. This page: Rice shares the moment with Bobby Rahal, winner in 1986. Below: The famous Borg-Warner trophy.

these cars up but I think this was a humbling experience for us. We thought we could do a better job of it."

Roth kept his nose clean in the early stages of the race but ultimately found the Turn Four SAFER Barrier after completing 128 laps. "I got caught in Robby McGehee's wash and pushed into the wall," he noted after finishing 24th. "This was

a great experience. It was an awesome first IRL race for us, and I look forward to our next."

SUPER SUB

Buddy Rice entered the 2004 season as a substitute driver, filling in for the injured Kenny Bräck at Rahal Letterman Racing. By the time the Month of May rolled around, Rice already knew he'd secured the Pioneer/Argent seat for the rest of the season. And though he couldn't drive, the rehabilitating Bräck, a former 500 winner, was a constant presence in the Rahal pit and engineering room, playing his own part in Rice's Indy 500 win.

"I had to fill in for Kenny and that's not the best way to come in, especially after what happened to him," Rice reflected. "So all the support and help he's given me has been pretty cool."

Team boss Bobby Rahal saw Bräck's contributions first-hand. "Kenny and Buddy and I talked a lot before the race about how to win Indy," Rahal said. "Kenny instilled in Buddy that even if you have a little glitch like we did with the stall during the pit stop, he must not overdrive it and get desperate and impatient. He just calmly and methodically picked them off one by one, and I think he gained some of that perspective from Kenny and me."

The last driver who actually won the Indy 500 in a substitute role? That would be Al Unser in 1987, taking over at Penske Racing from an injured Danny Ongais…

FACTS AND FIGURES
88TH INDIANAPOLIS 500-MILE RACE

Practice Session 1 (May 9) Results

Rank	Car	Driver	C/E/T	Time	Speed (mph)	Best Lap	Total Laps
1	1	Scott Dixon	G/T/F	40.9537s	219.760	21	22
2	3	Helio Castroneves	D/T/F	40.9552s	219.752	28	39
3	5	Adrian Fernandez	G/H/F	41.2197s	218.342	32	34
4	4	Tomas Scheckter	D/C/F	41.2261s	218.308	35	39
5	26	Dan Wheldon	D/H/F	41.2831s	218.007	9	10
6	2	Mark Taylor	D/C/F	41.3578s	217.613	49	50
7	52T	Ed Carpenter	D/C/F	41.3973s	217.405	65	66
8	36	Bruno Junqueira	G/H/F	41.4127s	217.325	36	38
9	11	Tony Kanaan	D/H/F	41.4233s	217.269	12	14
10	10	Darren Manning	G/T/F	41.4330s	217.218	29	31
11	7	Bryan Herta	D/H/F	41.4521s	217.118	5	11
12	1T	Scott Dixon	G/T/F	41.4689s	217.030	6	7
13	24	Felipe Giaffone	D/C/F	41.5200s	216.763	33	46
14	55	Kosuke Matsuura	G/H/F	41.5331s	216.695	12	23
15	51T	Alex Barron	D/C/F	41.5353s	216.683	35	48
16	3T	Helio Castroneves	D/T/F	41.6655s	216.006	3	5
17	8	Scott Sharp	D/T/F	41.7369s	215.637	6	72
18	39	Sarah Fisher	D/T/F	41.7908s	215.358	57	63
19	20	Al Unser Jr.	D/C/F	41.7947s	215.338	35	57
20	70	Robby Gordon	D/C/F	41.7989s	215.317	4	6
21	7T	Bryan Herta	D/H/F	41.8572s	215.017	10	15
22	26T	Dan Wheldon	D/H/F	41.9154s	214.718	5	6
23	17	Vitor Meira	G/H/F	41.9665s	214.457	21	29
24	16	Roger Yasukawa	G/H/F	41.9999s	214.286	9	10
25	27T	Dario Franchitti	D/H/F	42.0483s	214.040	15	22
26	12T	Tora Takagi	D/T/F	42.0754s	213.902	13	15
27	11T	Tony Kanaan	D/H/F	42.0985s	213.784	5	9
28	12	Tora Takagi	D/T/F	42.6347s	211.096	14	30
29	25	Marty Roth	D/T/F	42.6697s	210.923	41	55
30	10T	Darren Manning	G/T/F	42.8099s	210.232	19	20
31	70T	Robby Gordon	D/C/F	42.9118s	209.733	10	11
32	15T	Buddy Rice	G/H/F	43.9989s	204.551	5	6
33	14	A.J. Foyt IV	D/T/F	73.3210s	122.748	3	4
					Total laps in session:		913

Chassis legend: **D** – Dallara, **G** – Panoz G Force
Engine legend: **C** – Chevrolet, **H** – Honda, **T** – Toyota
Tire legend: **F** – Firestone

Practice Session 2 (May 10) Results

Rank	Car	Driver	C/E/T	Time	Speed (mph)	Best Lap	Total Laps
1	3	Helio Castroneves	D/T/F	40.8533s	220.300	26	28
2	1	Scott Dixon	G/T/F	40.9894s	219.569	31	32
3	11	Tony Kanaan	D/H/F	40.9923s	219.553	43	46
4	6	Sam Hornish Jr.	D/T/F	41.0290s	219.357	30	32
5	5	Adrian Fernandez	G/H/F	41.0737s	219.118	28	55
6	55	Kosuke Matsuura	G/H/F	41.0895s	219.034	49	53
7	27	Dario Franchitti	D/H/F	41.0911s	219.026	40	43
8	4T	Tomas Scheckter	D/C/F	41.1160s	218.893	30	41
9	8	Scott Sharp	D/T/F	41.1788s	218.559	55	57
10	70	Robby Gordon	D/C/F	41.2002s	218.446	22	23
11	17	Vitor Meira	G/H/F	41.2002s	218.446	10	36
12	10	Darren Manning	G/T/F	41.2103s	218.392	25	60
13	26	Dan Wheldon	D/H/F	41.2145s	218.370	10	17
14	7	Bryan Herta	D/H/F	41.2422s	218.223	39	41
15	52T	Ed Carpenter	D/C/F	41.2558s	218.151	88	90
16	16	Roger Yasukawa	G/H/F	41.3406s	217.704	11	17
17	51T	Alex Barron	D/C/F	41.3650s	217.575	25	37
18	36	Bruno Junqueira	G/H/F	41.4593s	217.080	20	56
19	15	Buddy Rice	G/H/F	41.5096s	216.817	17	22
20	24	Felipe Giaffone	D/C/F	41.5826s	216.437	7	57
21	2T	Mark Taylor	D/C/F	41.6139s	216.274	40	42
22	6T	Sam Hornish Jr.	D/T/F	41.6898s	215.880	10	13
23	12T	Tora Takagi	D/T/F	41.7491s	215.574	21	43
24	20	Al Unser Jr.	D/C/F	41.8262s	215.176	44	45
25	16T	Roger Yasukawa	G/H/F	41.8264s	215.175	6	7
26	14	A.J. Foyt IV	D/T/F	41.8499s	215.054	30	34
27	39	Sarah Fisher	D/T/F	41.8596s	215.004	55	62
28	41	Larry Foyt	D/T/F	43.2729s	207.982	7	12
29	25	Marty Roth	D/T/F	44.0802s	204.173	16	17
30	12	Tora Takagi	D/T/F	45.1998s	199.116	1	4
					Total laps in session:		1122

Chassis legend: **D** – Dallara, **G** – Panoz G Force
Engine legend: **C** – Chevrolet, **H** – Honda, **T** – Toyota
Tire legend: **F** – Firestone

From top: Marty Roth gets focussed; a relaxed Vitor Meira on the first day of practice; Meira's Rahal Letterman team-mate Roger Yasukawa. Facing page: Scott Sharp.

Practice Session 3 (May 11) Results

Rank	Car	Driver	C/E/T	Time	Speed (mph)	Best Lap	Total Laps
1	55	Kosuke Matsuura	G/H/F	40.5666s	221.857	53	55
2	5	Adrian Fernandez	G/H/F	40.5944s	221.705	33	61
3	11	Tony Kanaan	D/H/F	40.7507s	220.855	20	25
4	3	Helio Castroneves	D/T/F	40.9208s	219.937	78	79
5	7	Bryan Herta	D/H/F	40.9261s	219.909	55	91
6	6	Sam Hornish Jr.	D/T/F	40.9444s	219.810	53	67
7	15	Buddy Rice	G/H/F	40.9501s	219.780	26	76
8	26	Dan Wheldon	D/H/F	40.9807s	219.616	59	61
9	4T	Tomas Scheckter	D/C/F	41.0636s	219.172	46	48
10	1T	Scott Dixon	G/T/F	41.0871s	219.047	17	18
11	36	Bruno Junqueira	G/H/F	41.0961s	218.999	19	66
12	16	Roger Yasukawa	G/H/F	41.1147s	218.900	5	71
13	10	Darren Manning	G/T/F	41.1719s	218.596	69	102
14	27	Dario Franchitti	D/H/F	41.1747s	218.581	52	54
15	52T	Ed Carpenter	D/C/F	41.1897s	218.501	39	65
16	51	Alex Barron	D/C/F	41.2840s	218.002	31	38
17	17	Vitor Meira	G/H/F	41.3424s	217.694	56	94
18	2	Mark Taylor	D/C/F	41.3641s	217.580	18	115
19	8	Scott Sharp	D/T/F	41.5155s	216.787	41	49
20	24	Felipe Giaffone	D/C/F	41.5439s	216.638	19	20
21	1	Scott Dixon	G/T/F	41.5963s	216.365	3	19
22	20	Al Unser Jr.	D/C/F	41.6341s	216.169	71	83
23	39	Sarah Fisher	D/T/F	41.6533s	216.069	48	79
24	24T	Felipe Giaffone	D/C/F	41.7222s	215.712	19	20
25	12T	Tora Takagi	D/T/F	41.8056s	215.282	23	61
26	14	A.J. Foyt IV	D/T/F	41.8999s	214.798	42	46
27	70T	Robby Gordon	D/C/F	42.0269s	214.149	9	21
28	8T	Scott Sharp	D/T/F	42.0882s	213.837	20	43
29	41	Larry Foyt	G/T/F	42.2279s	213.129	25	53
30	25	Marty Roth	D/T/F	44.1089s	204.040	25	26
31	6T	Sam Hornish Jr.	D/T/F	50.9239s	176.734	4	5
				Total laps in session:			1711

Chassis legend: **D – Dallara, G – Panoz G Force**
Engine legend: **C – Chevrolet, H – Honda, T – Toyota**
Tire legend: **F – Firestone**

Practice Session 4 (May 12) Results

Rank	Car	Driver	C/E/T	Time	Speed (mph)	Best Lap	Total Laps
1	11	Tony Kanaan	D/H/F	40.4189s	222.668	20	29
2	26	Dan Wheldon	D/H/F	40.5491s	221.953	53	55
3	16	Roger Yasukawa	G/H/F	40.6783s	221.248	47	55
4	5	Adrian Fernandez	G/H/F	40.6881s	221.195	39	40
5	1	Scott Dixon	G/T/F	40.7348s	220.941	57	64
6	55	Kosuke Matsuura	G/H/F	40.7969s	220.605	5	62
7	15	Buddy Rice	G/H/F	40.8107s	220.530	39	43
8	4T	Tomas Scheckter	D/C/F	40.8285s	220.434	20	32
9	6	Sam Hornish Jr.	D/T/F	40.8668s	220.228	20	99
10	3	Helio Castroneves	D/T/F	40.9231s	219.925	19	62
11	51T	Alex Barron	D/C/F	41.0308s	219.347	32	34
12	52T	Ed Carpenter	D/C/F	41.0601s	219.191	59	66
13	70T	Robby Gordon	D/C/F	41.0895s	219.034	41	43
14	51	Alex Barron	D/C/F	41.1031s	218.962	4	53
15	36T	Bruno Junqueira	G/H/F	41.1042s	218.956	6	27
16	10	Darren Manning	G/T/F	41.1258s	218.841	24	32
17	2T	Mark Taylor	D/C/F	41.1563s	218.679	51	59
18	10T	Darren Manning	G/T/F	41.2749s	218.050	14	15
19	8	Scott Sharp	D/T/F	41.2892s	217.975	27	60
20	17	Vitor Meira	G/H/F	41.3250s	217.786	40	41
21	24	Felipe Giaffone	D/C/F	41.3829s	217.481	40	58
22	27	Dario Franchitti	D/H/F	41.3857s	217.466	29	79
23	20	Al Unser Jr.	D/C/F	41.4376s	217.194	74	75
24	7T	Bryan Herta	D/H/F	41.4810s	216.967	4	57
25	12T	Tora Takagi	D/T/F	41.7387s	215.627	69	85
26	36	Bruno Junqueira	G/H/F	41.8742s	214.929	16	45
27	39	Sarah Fisher	D/T/F	42.1208s	213.671	26	32
28	25	Marty Roth	D/T/F	42.3825s	212.352	125	128
29	39T	Sarah Fisher	D/T/F	43.0096s	209.256	31	37
				Total laps in session:			1567

Chassis legend: **D – Dallara, G – Panoz G Force**
Engine legend: **C – Chevrolet, H – Honda, T – Toyota**
Tire legend: **F – Firestone**

Practice Session 5 (May 13) Results

Rank	Car	Driver	C/E/T	Time	Speed (mph)	Best Lap	Total Laps
1	3	Helio Castroneves	D/T/F	40.6952s	221.156	39	44
2	16	Roger Yasukawa	G/H/F	40.7068s	221.093	27	29
3	6	Sam Hornish Jr.	D/T/F	40.7320s	220.956	45	49
4	15	Buddy Rice	G/H/F	40.7649s	220.778	11	13
5	11	Tony Kanaan	D/H/F	40.7732s	220.733	17	19
6	17	Meira Vitor	G/H/F	40.7857s	220.666	28	33
7	55T	Kosuke Matsuura	G/H/F	40.7893s	220.646	39	40
8	5T	Adrian Fernandez	G/H/F	40.7925s	220.629	12	14
9	4T	Tomas Scheckter	D/C/F	40.8479s	220.330	17	21
10	5	Adrian Fernandez	G/H/F	40.8646s	220.240	11	19
11	27	Dario Franchitti	D/H/F	40.9092s	219.999	23	25
12	7	Bryan Herta	D/H/F	40.9309s	219.883	30	33
13	2T	Mark Taylor	D/C/F	40.9901s	219.565	12	32
14	1T	Darren Manning	G/T/F	40.9988s	219.519	22	38
15	51	Alex Barron	D/C/F	41.1010s	218.973	14	21
16	51T	Alex Barron	D/C/F	41.1101s	218.924	12	26
17	24	Felipe Giaffone	D/C/F	41.1758s	218.575	23	24
18	52T	Ed Carpenter	D/C/F	41.2327s	218.273	19	21
19	20	Al Unser Jr.	D/C/F	41.2921s	217.959	41	68
20	36	Bruno Junqueira	G/H/F	41.2962s	217.938	22	80
21	8	Scott Sharp	D/T/F	41.4397s	217.183	35	64
22	27T	Dario Franchitti	D/H/F	41.5375s	216.672	7	9
23	12	Tora Takagi	D/T/F	41.5423s	216.647	17	28
24	14	A.J. Foyt IV	D/T/F	41.6641s	216.013	43	46
25	41	Larry Foyt	G/T/F	41.9199s	214.695	30	47
26	12T	Tora Takagi	D/T/F	42.0475s	214.044	26	27
27	25	Marty Roth	D/T/F	42.7689s	210.433	23	61
28	39	Sarah Fisher	D/T/F	43.1309s	208.667	6	12
29	26T	Dan Wheldon	D/H/F	44.1144s	204.015	1	3
30	55	Kosuke Matsuura	G/H/F	70.2454s	128.122	1	1
				Total laps in session:			947

Chassis legend: **D – Dallara, G – Panoz G Force**
Engine legend: **C – Chevrolet, H – Honda, T – Toyota**
Tire legend: **F – Firestone**

Practice Session 6 (May 14) Results

Rank	Car	Driver	C/E/T	Time	Speed (mph)	Best Lap	Total Laps
1	39	Sarah Fisher	D/T/F	42.3298s	212.616	2	5
2	14	A.J. Foyt IV	D/T/F	46.4662s	193.689	2	2
3	36	Bruno Junqueira	G/H/F	69.7141s	129.099	1	1
4	15	Buddy Rice	G/H/F	86.2108s	104.395	1	1
				Total laps in session:			9

Chassis legend: **D – Dallara, G – Panoz G Force**
Engine legend: **C – Chevrolet, H – Honda, T – Toyota**
Tire legend: **F – Firestone**

Practice Session 7 (May 15) Results

Rank	Car	Driver	C/E/T	Time	Speed (mph)	Best Lap	Total Laps
1	11	Tony Kanaan	D/H/F	40.3182s	223.224	6	30
2	16	Roger Yasukawa	G/H/F	40.3606s	222.990	11	26
3	5	Adrian Fernandez	G/H/F	40.3891s	222.832	19	32
4	36	Bruno Junqueira	G/H/F	40.4357s	222.576	10	20
5	55	Kosuke Matsuura	G/H/F	40.4638s	222.421	14	29
6	15	Buddy Rice	G/H/F	40.4997s	222.224	29	31
7	17	Vitor Meira	G/H/F	40.5143s	222.144	20	28
8	26	Dan Wheldon	D/H/F	40.5636s	221.874	24	25
9	27	Dario Franchitti	D/H/F	40.5857s	221.753	33	35
10	4	Tomas Scheckter	D/C/F	40.6496s	221.404	10	27
11	7	Bryan Herta	D/H/F	40.6634s	221.329	13	20
12	3	Helio Castroneves	D/T/F	40.6759s	221.261	11	26
13	6	Sam Hornish Jr.	D/T/F	40.6831s	221.222	19	34
14	1	Scott Dixon	G/T/F	40.7281s	220.978	12	27
15	52T	Ed Carpenter	D/C/F	40.9074s	220.009	22	27
16	2	Mark Taylor	D/C/F	40.9540s	219.759	20	26
17	10	Darren Manning	G/T/F	40.9925s	219.552	23	25
18	51	Alex Barron	D/C/F	41.1315s	218.810	14	25
19	24	Felipe Giaffone	D/C/F	41.1562s	218.679	22	23
20	20	Al Unser Jr	D/C/F	41.2330s	218.272	16	29
21	70T	Robby Gordon	D/C/F	41.2381s	218.245	14	21
22	8T	Scott Sharp	D/T/F	41.4412s	217.175	23	28
23	39	Sarah Fisher	D/T/F	41.6914s	215.872	34	34
24	12	Tora Takagi	D/T/F	41.8529s	215.039	14	29
25	14	A.J. Foyt IV	D/T/F	41.9764s	214.406	4	4
26	41	Larry Foyt	G/T/F	42.1300s	213.624	21	29
27	25	Marty Roth	D/T/F	42.3245s	212.643	20	21
				Total laps in session:			711

Chassis legend: **D – Dallara, G – Panoz G Force**
Engine legend: **C – Chevrolet, H – Honda, T – Toyota**
Tire legend: **F – Firestone**

Practice Session 8 (May 16) Results

Rank	Car	Driver	C/E/T	Time	Speed (mph)	Best Lap	Total Laps
1	7T	Bryan Herta	D/H/F	40.8956s	220.073	21	22
2	11T	Tony Kanaan	D/H/F	40.9564s	219.746	13	55
3	51T	Alex Barron	D/C/F	41.1049s	218.952	15	18
4	36T	Bruno Junqueira	G/H/F	41.3149s	217.839	36	137
5	3T	Helio Castroneves	D/T/F	41.3489s	217.660	36	85
6	6T	Sam Hornish Jr.	D/T/F	41.3940s	217.423	63	84
7	26T	Dan Wheldon	D/H/F	41.4515s	217.121	43	53
8	27T	Dario Franchitti	D/H/F	41.4894s	216.923	59	65
9	24	Felipe Giaffone	D/C/F	41.5383s	216.668	29	29
10	12	Tora Takagi	D/T/F	41.6907s	215.875	35	48
11	20	Al Unser Jr.	D/C/F	41.7674s	215.479	64	66
12	14	A.J. Foyt IV	D/T/F	41.7720s	215.455	37	42
13	12T	Tora Takagi	D/T/F	41.8573s	215.016	27	47
14	41	Larry Foyt	G/T/F	41.9974s	214.299	39	44
15	25	Marty Roth	D/T/F	42.3433s	212.548	93	93
				Total laps in session:			888

Chassis legend: **D – Dallara, G – Panoz G Force**
Engine legend: **C – Chevrolet, H – Honda, T – Toyota**
Tire legend: **F – Firestone**

Top right: Kosuke Matsuura, having nailed the day's top spot on Practice Session 10. Above from top: British driver Mark Taylor; Felipe Giaffone loses control in Turn One on Pole Day; Tomas Sheckter prepares to record Practice Session 1's fastest Chevrolet time, placing fourth.

Practice Session 9 (May 19) Results

Rank	Car	Driver	C/E/T	Time	Speed (mph)	Best Lap	Total Laps
1	1T	Scott Dixon	G/T/F	40.8022s	220.576	13	85
2	55T	Kosuke Matsuura	G/H/F	41.0178s	219.417	109	111
3	16T	Roger Yasukawa	G/H/F	41.0634s	219.173	6	91
4	5T	Adrian Fernandez	G/H/F	41.0638s	219.171	21	62
5	3T	Helio Castroneves	D/T/F	41.1512s	218.706	46	75
6	6T	Sam Hornish Jr.	D/T/F	41.1671s	218.621	27	88
7	11T	Tony Kanaan	D/H/F	41.1816s	218.544	40	103
8	15T	Buddy Rice	G/H/F	41.2013s	218.440	65	96
9	26T	Dan Wheldon	D/H/F	41.2493s	218.186	68	85
10	10T	Darren Manning	G/T/F	41.2985s	217.926	76	107
11	51T	Alex Barron	D/C/F	41.3292s	217.764	10	55
12	52	Ed Carpenter	D/C/F	41.3773s	217.511	9	127
13	7T	Bryan Herta	D/H/F	41.3976s	217.404	41	62
14	4T	Tomas Scheckter	D/T/F	41.4212s	217.280	8	66
15	27T	Dario Franchitti	D/H/F	41.4330s	217.218	71	76
16	2T	Mark Taylor	D/C/F	41.4764s	216.991	24	40
17	8T	Scott Sharp	D/T/F	41.6541s	216.065	27	64
18	70	Robby Gordon	D/C/F	41.7597s	215.519	8	46
19	41	Larry Foyt	G/T/F	41.7699s	215.466	41	60
20	20T	Al Unser Jr.	D/C/F	41.8613s	214.996	23	67
21	24T	Felipe Giaffone	D/C/F	42.0420s	214.072	16	16
22	14T	A.J. Foyt IV	D/T/F	42.0856s	213.850	41	47
23	39T	Sarah Fisher	D/T/F	42.1207s	213.672	66	78
24	25	Marty Roth	D/T/F	42.2257s	213.140	40	60
25	12T	Tora Takagi	D/T/F	42.6267s	211.135	20	45
				Total laps in session:			1812

Chassis legend: **D – Dallara, G – Panoz G Force**
Engine legend: **C – Chevrolet, H – Honda, T – Toyota**
Tire legend: **F – Firestone**

Practice Session 10 (May 20) Results

Rank	Car	Driver	C/E/T	Time	Speed (mph)	Best Lap	Total Laps
1	55T	Kosuke Matsuura	G/H/F	40.7638s	220.784	96	101
2	5T	Adrian Fernandez	G/H/F	40.9077s	220.007	10	85
3	3T	Helio Castroneves	D/T/F	41.1567s	218.676	43	98
4	15T	Vitor Meira	G/H/F	41.1678s	218.617	27	44
5	11T	Tony Kanaan	D/H/F	41.1928s	218.485	19	95
6	1T	Scott Dixon	G/T/F	41.2615s	218.121	21	102
7	16T	Roger Yasukawa	G/H/F	41.3795s	217.499	27	103
8	27T	Dario Franchitti	D/H/F	41.4503s	217.127	47	68
9	6T	Sam Hornish Jr.	D/T/F	41.4569s	217.093	14	78
10	52	Ed Carpenter	D/C/F	41.5326s	216.697	72	87
11	70	Robby Gordon	D/C/F	41.5865s	216.416	20	101
12	26T	Dan Wheldon	D/H/F	41.5880s	216.409	9	94
13	7T	Bryan Herta	D/H/F	41.7037s	215.808	51	78
14	4T	Tomas Scheckter	D/C/F	41.8352s	215.130	61	74
15	10T	Darren Manning	G/T/F	41.8386s	215.112	100	146
16	24T	Felipe Giaffone	D/C/F	41.8408s	215.101	49	107
17	8T	Scott Sharp	D/T/F	41.8871s	214.863	21	118
18	12T	Tora Takagi	D/T/F	41.9747s	214.415	17	75
19	2	Mark Taylor	D/C/F	42.0013s	214.279	25	49
20	14T	A.J. Foyt IV	D/T/F	42.0530s	214.016	31	31
21	51T	Alex Barron	D/C/F	42.0703s	213.928	14	63
22	41	Larry Foyt	G/T/F	42.1149s	213.701	24	49
23	20T	Al Unser Jr.	D/C/F	42.1972s	213.284	7	56
24	25	Marty Roth	D/T/F	42.3824s	212.352	7	47
25	39T	Sarah Fisher	D/T/F	42.4468s	212.030	32	78
				Total laps in session:			2027

Chassis legend: **D – Dallara, G – Panoz G Force**
Engine legend: **C – Chevrolet, H – Honda, T – Toyota**
Tire legend: **F – Firestone**

Practice Session 11 (May 21) Results

Rank	Car	Driver	C/E/T	Time	Speed (mph)	Best Lap	Total Laps
1	5T	Adrian Fernandez	G/H/F	41.2358s	218.257	13	111
2	3T	Helio Castroneves	D/T/F	41.2769s	218.040	45	74
3	1T	Scott Dixon	G/T/F	41.3527s	217.640	7	8
4	55T	Kosuke Matsuura	G/H/F	41.3755s	217.520	89	98
5	15T	Buddy Rice	G/H/F	41.4271s	217.249	18	100
6	10T	Darren Manning	G/T/F	41.5538s	216.587	10	65
7	6T	Sam Hornish Jr.	D/T/F	41.5784s	216.459	47	54
8	10	Darren Manning	G/T/F	41.6252s	216.215	9	26
9	16T	Vitor Meira	G/H/F	41.6542s	216.065	8	120
10	4	Tomas Scheckter	D/C/F	41.6630s	216.019	28	41
11	52	Ed Carpenter	D/C/F	41.7015s	215.820	77	102
12	11T	Tony Kanaan	D/H/F	41.7242s	215.702	24	40
13	26T	Dan Wheldon	D/H/F	41.7406s	215.617	6	18
14	51T	Alex Barron	D/C/F	41.7455s	215.592	68	79
15	24T	Buddy Lazier	D/C/F	41.7609s	215.513	13	66
16	27T	Dario Franchitti	D/H/F	41.8011s	215.305	4	41
17	14T	A.J. Foyt IV	D/T/F	41.8187s	215.215	7	29
18	1	Scott Dixon	G/T/F	41.8267s	215.174	7	16
19	7T	Bryan Herta	D/H/F	41.8937s	214.829	45	46
20	8T	Scott Sharp	D/T/F	41.9616s	214.482	58	78
21	2	Mark Taylor	D/C/F	42.1553s	213.496	12	33
22	20T	Al Unser Jr.	D/C/F	42.2587s	212.974	67	78
23	14	A.J. Foyt IV	D/T/F	42.2742s	212.896	20	21
24	41	Larry Foyt	G/T/F	42.2984s	212.774	9	43
25	39T	Sarah Fisher	D/T/F	42.3256s	212.637	6	48
26	14T	Jaques Lazier	D/T/F	42.3849s	212.340	10	10
27	12T	Tora Takagi	D/T/F	42.7204s	210.672	57	73
					Total laps in session:		1518

Chassis legend: **D – Dallara, G – Panoz G Force**
Engine legend: **C – Chevrolet, H – Honda, T – Toyota**
Tire legend: **F – Firestone**

Practice Session 12 (May 22) Results

Rank	Car	Driver	C/E/T	Time	Speed (mph)	Best Lap	Total Laps
1	5	Adrian Fernandez	G/H/F	41.1908s	218.495	15	19
2	55T	Kosuke Matsuura	G/H/F	41.2276s	218.300	23	76
3	6T	Sam Hornish Jr.	D/T/F	41.2663s	218.096	24	103
4	11T	Tony Kanaan	D/H/F	41.2720s	218.066	22	41
5	26T	Dan Wheldon	D/H/F	41.3004s	217.916	20	44
6	5T	Adrian Fernandez	G/H/F	41.3309s	217.755	32	60
7	3T	Helio Castroneves	D/T/F	41.4319s	217.224	44	107
8	27T	Dario Franchitti	D/H/F	41.6109s	216.289	27	44
9	6	Sam Hornish Jr.	D/T/F	41.6500s	216.086	12	16
10	51T	Alex Barron	D/C/F	41.6548s	216.062	76	97
11	70T	Robby Gordon	D/C/F	41.7148s	215.751	20	43
12	52	Ed Carpenter	D/C/F	41.7240s	215.703	65	112
13	24T	Felipe Giaffone	D/C/F	41.7315s	215.664	22	35
14	20T	Al Unser Jr.	D/C/F	41.7429s	215.606	109	128
15	14T	A.J. Foyt IV	D/T/F	41.9390s	214.597	36	36
16	91	Buddy Lazier	D/C/F	41.9748s	214.414	25	60
17	8T	Scott Sharp	D/T/F	42.1022s	213.766	23	66
18	41	Larry Foyt	G/T/F	42.1832s	213.355	20	20
19	39T	Sarah Fisher	D/T/F	42.2073s	213.233	91	94
20	25	Marty Roth	D/T/F	42.2342s	213.097	39	39
21	33	Richie Hearn	G/T/F	42.3296s	212.617	26	48
22	12T	Tora Takagi	D/T/F	42.4485s	212.022	27	54
23	3	Helio Castroneves	D/T/F	42.5807s	211.363	6	10
24	12T	Jeff Simmons	D/T/F	42.8939s	209.820	20	21
25	98	P.J. Jones	D/C/F	43.1981s	208.342	31	36
26	18	Robby McGehee	D/C/F	51.1556s	175.934	5	5
					Total laps in session:		1414

Chassis legend: **D – Dallara, G – Panoz G Force**
Engine legend: **C – Chevrolet, H – Honda, T – Toyota**
Tire legend: **F – Firestone**

Practice Session 13 (May 23) Results

Rank	Car	Driver	C/E/T	Time	Speed (mph)	Best Lap	Total Laps
1	55T	Kosuke Matsuura	G/H/F	41.1538s	218.692	7	9
2	55	Kosuke Matsuura	G/H/F	41.2780s	218.034	9	10
3	91	Buddy Lazier	D/C/F	41.4038s	217.371	18	25
4	13	Greg Ray	G/H/F	41.4794s	216.975	16	20
5	12T	Jeff Simmons	D/T/F	41.7362s	215.640	35	81
6	4	Tomas Scheckter	D/C/F	41.8984s	214.805	7	52
7	33	Richie Hearn	G/T/F	41.9906s	214.334	26	69
8	8T	Scott Sharp	D/T/F	42.0750s	213.904	44	47
9	25	Marty Roth	D/T/F	42.1226s	213.662	21	37
10	98	P.J. Jones	D/C/F	42.1667s	213.439	18	55
11	3	Helio Castroneves	D/T/F	42.1765s	213.389	3	18
12	14T	A.J. Foyt IV	D/T/F	42.2043s	213.248	12	43
13	18	Robby McGehee	D/C/F	42.3202s	212.664	42	46
14	41	Larry Foyt	G/T/F	42.5725s	211.404	28	41
15	3T	Helio Castroneves	D/T/F	62.8275s	143.249	11	12
					Total laps in session:		565

Chassis legend: **D – Dallara, G – Panoz G Force**
Engine legend: **C – Chevrolet, H – Honda, T – Toyota**
Tire legend: **F – Firestone**

Above: Marlboro Team Penske's Sam Hornish Jr. gets attended to in front of Indy's famous Bombardier Pagoda tower. Below: 2003 IndyCar Series champ Scott Dixon keeps Toyota in contention on May 12; Buddy Lazier gets a word of advice on Bump Day.

Final Practice Session (May 27) Results

Rank	Car	Driver	C/E/T	Time	Speed (mph)	Best Lap	Total Laps
1	55	Kosuke Matsuura	G/H/F	41.0536s	219.226	11	17
2	5	Adrian Fernandez	G/H/F	41.2719s	218.066	5	11
3	1	Scott Dixon	G/T/F	41.4000s	217.391	7	8
4	17	Vitor Meira	G/H/F	41.4419s	217.172	14	17
5	16	Roger Yasukawa	G/H/F	41.4519s	217.119	5	13
6	11	Tony Kanaan	D/H/F	41.6337s	216.171	11	20
7	13	Greg Ray	G/H/F	41.6845s	215.908	24	41
8	36	Bruno Junqueira	G/H/F	41.6935s	215.861	10	18
9	6	Sam Hornish Jr.	D/T/F	41.7939s	215.342	8	12
10	10	Darren Manning	G/T/F	41.8001s	215.310	8	16
11	15	Buddy Rice	G/H/F	41.8739s	214.931	5	14
12	26	Dan Wheldon	D/H/F	41.9105s	214.743	9	15
13	70	Robby Gordon	D/C/F	41.9326s	214.630	20	20
14	3	Helio Castroneves	D/T/F	41.9700s	214.439	6	16
15	91	Buddy Lazier	D/C/F	41.9903s	214.335	6	15
16	27	Dario Franchitti	D/H/F	42.0674s	213.942	7	22
17	7	Bryan Herta	D/H/F	42.0819s	213.869	10	19
18	2	Mark Taylor	D/C/F	42.0948s	213.803	17	19
19	4	Tomas Scheckter	D/C/F	42.1143s	213.704	16	16
20	20	Al Unser Jr.	D/C/F	42.3113s	212.709	18	19
21	51	Alex Barron	D/C/F	42.3327s	212.602	13	15
22	21	Jeff Simmons	D/T/F	42.3524s	212.503	16	25
23	24	Felipe Giaffone	D/C/F	42.4382s	212.073	17	18
24	41	Larry Foyt	G/T/F	42.4572s	211.978	21	22
25	8	Scott Sharp	D/T/F	42.5170s	211.680	14	19
26	52	Ed Carpenter	D/C/F	42.5378s	211.577	13	18
27	12	Tora Takagi	D/T/F	42.5404s	211.564	15	19
28	98	P.J. Jones	D/C/F	42.6196s	211.170	14	17
29	14	A.J. Foyt IV	D/T/F	42.8704s	209.935	8	24
30	18	Robby McGehee	D/C/F	42.9801s	209.399	17	40
31	25	Marty Roth	D/T/F	43.0088s	209.260	19	21
32	39	Sarah Fisher	D/T/F	43.0909s	208.861	11	19
33	33	Richie Hearn	G/T/F	43.1859s	208.401	11	19
					Total laps in session:		624

Chassis legend: **D – Dallara, G – Panoz G Force**
Engine legend: **C – Chevrolet, H – Honda, T – Toyota**
Tire legend: **F – Firestone**

Combined Practice Sessions Results

Rank	Car	Driver	C/E/T	Time	Speed (mph)	Session	Total Laps
1	11	Tony Kanaan	D/H/F	40.3182s	223.224	May 15	183
2	16	Roger Yasukawa	G/H/F	40.3606s	222.990	May 15	221
3	5	Adrian Fernandez	G/H/F	40.3891s	222.832	May 15	271
4	36	Bruno Junqueira	G/H/F	40.4357s	222.576	May 15	324
5	55	Kosuke Matsuura	G/H/F	40.4638s	222.421	May 15	250
6	15	Buddy Rice	G/H/F	40.4997s	222.224	May 15	200
7	17	Vitor Meira	G/H/F	40.5143s	222.144	May 15	278
8	26	Dan Wheldon	D/H/F	40.5491s	221.953	May 12	183
9	27	Dario Franchitti	D/H/F	40.5857s	221.753	May 15	258
10	4	Tomas Scheckter	D/C/F	40.6496s	221.404	May 15	175
11	7	Bryan Herta	D/H/F	40.6634s	221.329	May 15	196
12	3	Helio Castroneves	D/T/F	40.6759s	221.261	May 15	322
13	6	Sam Hornish Jr.	D/T/F	40.6831s	221.222	May 15	309
14	1	Scott Dixon	G/T/F	40.7281s	220.978	May 15	188
15	55T	Kosuke Matsuura	G/H/F	40.7638s	220.784	May 20	435
16	5T	Adrian Fernandez	G/H/F	40.7925s	220.629	May 13	332
17	1T	Scott Dixon	G/T/F	40.8022s	220.576	May 19	220
18	4T	Tomas Scheckter	D/C/F	40.8285s	220.434	May 12	282
19	7T	Bryan Herta	D/H/F	40.8956s	220.073	May 16	280
20	52T	Ed Carpenter	D/C/F	40.9074s	220.009	May 15	353
21	2	Mark Taylor	D/C/F	40.9540s	219.759	May 15	177
22	11T	Tony Kanaan	D/H/F	40.9564s	219.746	May 16	343
23	2T	Mark Taylor	D/C/F	40.9901s	219.565	May 13	288
24	10	Darren Manning	G/T/F	40.9925s	219.552	May 15	292
25	1T	Darren Manning	G/T/F	40.9988s	219.519	May 13	38
26	51T	Alex Barron	D/C/F	41.0308s	219.347	May 12	472
27	16T	Roger Yasukawa	G/H/F	41.0634s	219.173	May 19	201
28	70T	Robby Gordon	D/C/F	41.0895s	219.034	May 12	159
29	51	Alex Barron	D/C/F	41.1010s	218.973	May 13	137
30	36T	Bruno Junqueira	G/H/F	41.1042s	218.956	May 12	164
31	3T	Helio Castroneves	D/T/F	41.1512s	218.706	May 19	456
32	24	Felipe Giaffone	D/C/F	41.1562s	218.679	May 15	275
33	6T	Sam Hornish Jr.	D/T/F	41.1671s	218.621	May 19	425
34	15T	Vitor Meira	G/H/F	41.1678s	218.617	May 20	44
35	8	Scott Sharp	D/T/F	41.1788s	218.559	May 10	302
36	70	Robby Gordon	D/C/F	41.2002s	218.446	May 10	176
37	15T	Buddy Rice	G/H/F	41.2013s	218.440	May 19	202
38	20	Al Unser Jr.	D/C/F	41.2330s	218.272	May 15	442
39	26T	Dan Wheldon	D/H/F	41.2493s	218.186	May 19	303
40	10T	Darren Manning	G/T/F	41.2749s	218.050	May 12	353
41	52	Ed Carpenter	D/C/F	41.3773s	217.511	May 19	428
42	91	Buddy Lazier	D/C/F	41.4038s	217.371	May 23	85
43	27T	Dario Franchitti	D/H/F	41.4330s	217.218	May 19	325
44	8T	Scott Sharp	D/T/F	41.4412s	217.175	May 15	463
45	13	Greg Ray	G/H/F	41.4794s	216.975	May 23	61
46	12	Tora Takagi	D/T/F	41.5423s	216.647	May 13	158
47	39	Sarah Fisher	D/T/F	41.6533s	216.069	May 11	306
48	16T	Vitor Meira	G/H/F	41.6542s	216.065	May 21	120
49	14	A.J. Foyt IV	D/T/F	41.6641s	216.013	May 13	223
50	24T	Felipe Giaffone	D/C/F	41.7222s	215.712	May 11	178
51	21	Jeff Simmons	D/T/F	41.7362s	215.640	May 23	127
52	12T	Tora Takagi	D/T/F	41.7387s	215.627	May 12	525
53	20T	Al Unser Jr.	D/C/F	41.7429s	215.606	May 22	329
54	91	Buddy Lazier	D/C/F	41.7609s	215.513	May 21	81
55	41	Larry Foyt	G/T/F	41.7699s	215.466	May 19	420
56	14T	A.J. Foyt IV	D/T/F	41.8187s	215.215	May 21	186
57	33	Richie Hearn	G/T/F	41.9906s	214.334	May 23	136
58	7	Bryan Herta	D/H/F	42.0819s	213.869	May 27	19
59	39T	Sarah Fisher	D/T/F	42.1207s	213.672	May 19	335
60	25	Marty Roth	D/T/F	42.1226s	213.662	May 23	605
61	98	P.J. Jones	D/C/F	42.1667s	213.439	May 23	108
62	18	Robby McGehee	D/C/F	42.3202s	212.664	May 23	91
63	14T	Jaques Lazier	D/T/F	42.3849s	212.340	May 21	10
						Total combined session laps:	15,828

Chassis legend: **D – Dallara, G – Panoz G Force**
Engine legend: **C – Chevrolet, H – Honda, T – Toyota**
Tire legend: **F – Firestone**

MBNA Pole winner Buddy Rice.

Qualification Attempts

SP	Date	Car	Driver	Lap 1	Lap 2	Lap 3	Lap 4	Total Time	Average (mph)
1	Pole Day	15	Buddy Rice	40.5634s	40.5614s	40.4997s	40.5200s	02m 42.1445s	222.024
2	Pole Day	26	Dan Wheldon	40.5910s	40.5636s	40.6465s	40.7092s	02m 42.5103s	221.524
3	Pole Day	27	Dario Franchitti	40.5927s	40.6042s	40.5857s	40.7667s	02m 42.5493s	221.471
4	Pole Day	36	Bruno Junqueira	40.5877s	40.6229s	40.6243s	40.7824s	02m 42.6173s	221.379
5	Pole Day	11	Tony Kanaan	40.7879s	40.6948s	40.6383s	40.6278s	02m 42.7488s	221.200
6	Pole Day	5	Adrian Fernandez	40.6906s	40.7798s	40.7112s	40.7153s	02m 42.8969s	220.999
7	Pole Day	17	Vitor Meira	40.6836s	40.7421s	40.7424s	40.7588s	02m 42.9269s	220.958
8	Pole Day	3	Helio Castroneves	40.7826s	40.7594s	40.7305s	40.7105s	02m 42.9830s	220.882
9	Pole Day	55	Kosuke Matsuura	40.7499s	40.7785s	40.7825s	40.7769s	02m 43.0878s	220.740
10	Pole Day	4	Tomas Scheckter	40.8464s	40.8296s	40.8149s	40.8362s	02m 43.3271s	220.417
11	Pole Day	6	Sam Hornish Jr.	40.9586s	40.9130s	40.8706s	40.7601s	02m 43.5023s	220.180
12	Pole Day	16	Roger Yasukawa	40.9853s	40.9153s	40.8738s	40.8394s	02m 43.6138s	220.030
13	Pole Day	1	Scott Dixon	41.0386s	41.0729s	40.9983s	41.0349s	02m 44.1447s	219.319
14	Pole Day	2	Mark Taylor	41.0519s	41.0428s	41.0287s	41.0490s	02m 44.1724s	219.282
15	Pole Day	10	Darren Manning	41.0703s	41.0272s	40.9925s	41.0904s	02m 44.1804s	219.271
16	Pole Day	52T	Ed Carpenter	41.1783s	41.1390s	41.1903s	41.1845s	02m 44.6921s	218.590
17	Pole Day	20	Al Unser Jr.	41.2825s	41.2951s	41.2883s	41.2974s	02m 45.1633s	217.966
18	Pole Day	70T	Robby Gordon	41.7777s	41.5512s	41.4806s	41.4553s	02m 46.2648s	216.522
19	Pole Day	39	Sarah Fisher	41.6914s	41.7077s	41.7518s	41.6928s	02m 46.8437s	215.771
20	Pole Day	8T	Scott Sharp	41.6428s	41.6506s	41.7976s	41.8575s	02m 46.9485s	215.635
21	Pole Day	14	A.J. Foyt IV	41.9764s	42.0002s	42.0174s	42.0295s	02m 48.0235s	214.256
22	Pole Day	41	Larry Foyt	42.2267s	42.2052s	42.1879s	42.1746s	02m 48.7944s	213.277
23	Second Day	7T	Bryan Herta	40.8956s	40.9278s	40.9377s	40.9711s	02m 43.7322s	219.871
24	Second Day	51T	Alex Barron	41.1276s	41.1408s	41.1335s	41.1049s	02m 44.5068s	218.836
25	Second Day	24	Felipe Giaffone	41.5383s	41.5781s	41.6002s	41.7502s	02m 46.4668s	216.259
26	Second Day	12	Tora Takagi	41.9566s	42.0766s	41.9391s	41.9661s	02m 47.9384s	214.364
27	Bump Day	13	Greg Ray	41.5787s	41.5843s	41.5312s	41.4794s	02m 46.1736s	216.641
28	Bump Day	91	Buddy Lazier	41.8520s	41.8075s	41.8020s	41.8947s	02m 47 3562s	215.110
29	Bump Day	12T	Jeff Simmons	41.9466s	41.9269s	41.8926s	41.8449s	02m 47.6110s	214.783
30	Bump Day	33	Richie Hearn	42.1853s	42.1253s	42.0666s	42.0712s	02m 48.4484s	213.715
31	Bump Day	98	P.J. Jones	42.1900s	42.2008s	42.1667s	42.1753s	02m 48.7328s	213.355
32	Bump Day	25	Marty Roth	42.3489s	42.3592s	42.4601s	42.6638s	02m 49.8320s	211.974
33	Bump Day	18	Robby McGehee	42.7690s	42.4820s	42.5364s	42.3202s	02m 50.1076s	211.631

Pole Day = **May 15**
Second Day = **May 16**
Bump Day = **May 23**

ANDRETTI **GREEN RACING BOUNCED** back from the relative disappointment of finishing second and third at Indianapolis by securing its second one-two finish of the season as Tony Kanaan's 7-Eleven Dallara/Honda headed pole-winner Dario Franchitti's ArcaEx car in the Bombardier 500 at Texas Motor Speedway. Kanaan's second victory of the season catapulted him back ahead of yet another AGR teammate, Dan Wheldon, in the season-long points chase.

"What an unbelievable night for the whole Team 7-Eleven," said Kanaan. "I came so close to winning this race last year and I just didn't want to finish second again. I really wanted to finish the job this time and we did it. Everyone on the team did a great job all weekend long and it showed tonight. Every win means a lot but this one is very, very sweet right now."

Kanaan dominated a typically dramatic race on the high-banked 1.5-mile oval, leading 145 of the 200 laps. But he had to fight for his win. First of all he had to overcome a tardy first pit stop when the vent hose stuck momentarily. Then he fell to third place after the final round of yellow-flag pit stops with less than 20 laps remaining. The Brazilian, though, made short work of both Helio Castroneves (Marlboro Team Penske Dallara/Toyota) and Wheldon's Klein Tools/Jim Beam Dallara/Honda before stretching away toward the finish line, with Franchitti in tow.

"Unless he made a mistake and gave up the inside [line] I wasn't getting by," noted a pragmatic Franchitti, who was nonetheless delighted with his first IndyCar Series pole and a career-best finish to date.

Castroneves had taken the lead after eschewing the opportunity to make a pit stop during the fifth and final caution period, but the strategy failed to pay off when he ran out of fuel just two laps shy of the finish and wound up 12th.

Facing page: A victorious Tony Kanaan. Above from top: The Brazilian race-winner; Dan Wheldon takes to the pits.

"Sometimes a gamble like that pays off," noted the Brazilian, who struggled with his car's handling all night long, "but it wasn't meant to be tonight."

Also out of luck was Wheldon, who attempted a similar ploy but fell victim to gearbox failure just ten laps from the finish. The Englishman's disappointment represented the first time he had failed to finish among the top eight since Michigan in July 2003.

Alex Barron, meanwhile, enjoyed a stellar run for Red Bull Cheever Racing, climbing from the back of the grid (he had failed to complete his qualifying run due to gearbox failure) to third as the highest-placed Chevrolet representative. "We knew we could move up, we just didn't know how far," said the American. "We were at the right place at the right time, able to overtake a lot of cars around the outside."

Sam Hornish Jr. put a string of three poor results behind him by guiding his Marlboro Team Penske Dallara/Toyota to fourth ahead of Adrian Fernandez, who showed how well he was coming to grips with the IndyCar Series despite a late start to his campaign.

Indy 500 winner Buddy Rice qualified second and circulated among the leaders until tangling with Darren Manning with less than 20 laps to go. Top rookie Kosuke Matsuura also ran well again, qualifying a strong fourth and leading his first laps in competition before being sidelined by electrical woes.

IRL IndyCar® Series Race 5: Bombardier 500 at Texas Motor Speedway
Saturday, June 12, 2004

Place	Driver	Car	Nat.	Car Name	C/E/T	Laps Comp.	Running/ Reason Out	Q. Speed (mph)	Q. Time	Starting Position	IRL Pts.	Total IRL Pts.	IRL Standing	IRL Awards ($)	Designated Awards ($)	Total Awards ($)
1	Tony Kanaan	11	BR	Team 7-Eleven	D/H/F	200	Running	208.511	25.1210s	3	53	210	1	100,400	18,500	118,900
2	Dario Franchitti	27	GB	ArcaEx	D/H/F	200	Running	209.609	24.9894s	1	40	108	9	82,900	10,750	93,650
3	Alex Barron	51	USA	Red Bull Cheever Racing	D/C/F	200	Running	No speed	No time	22	35	117	8	69,600	2,250	71,850
4	Sam Hornish Jr.	6	USA	Marlboro Team Penske	D/T/F	200	Running	207.319	25.2654s	11	32	119	7	56,500	0	56,500
5	Adrian Fernandez	5	MEX	Quaker State Telmex Tecate	G/H/F	200	Running	207.574	25.2344s	9	30	80	16	51,600	0	51,600
6	Vitor Meira	17	BR	Rahal Letterman Team Centrix	G/H/F	200	Running	207.116	25.2902s	13	28	69	17	45,600	0	45,600
7	Greg Ray	13	USA	Access Motorsports	G/H/F	200	Running	206.204	25.4020s	15	26	84	15	44,400	0	44,400
8	Darren Manning	10	GB	Target Chip Ganassi Racing	G/T/F	200	Running	206.583	25.3554s	14	24	124	5	43,300	0	43,300
9	Felipe Giaffone	24	BR	Team Purex/Dreyer & Reinbold	D/C/F	200	Running	204.888	25.5652s	19	22	37	23	43,300	2,000	45,300
10	Tora Takagi	12	J	Pioneer Mo Nunn Racing	D/T/F	200	Running	204.889	25.5651s	18	20	108	9	42,000	0	42,000
11	Al Unser Jr.	20	USA	Patrick Racing	D/C/F	198	Running	204.807	25.5753s	20	19	32	24	40,800	0	40,800
12	Helio Castroneves	3	BR	Marlboro Team Penske	D/T/F	197	Running	207.994	25.1834s	6	18	146	3	39,600	0	39,600
13	Dan Wheldon	26	GB	Klein Tools/Jim Beam	D/H/F	190	Gearbox	207.197	25.2803s	12	17	175	2	38,500	0	38,500
14	Scott Dixon	1	NZ	Target Chip Ganassi Racing	G/T/F	182	Accident	205.899	25.4397s	16	16	122	6	37,100	0	37,100
15	Buddy Rice	15	USA	Rahal Letterman Argent/Pioneer	G/H/F	181	Accident	208.755	25.0916s	2	15	144	4	36,000	0	36,000
16	Kosuke Matsuura (R)	55	J	Panasonic/ARTA	G/H/F	141	Mechanical	208.360	25.1392s	4	14	95	12	34,900	0	34,900
17	Mark Taylor (R)	2	GB	Menards/Johns Manville Racing	D/C/F	125	Accident	207.420	25.2531s	10	13	67	19	33,600	0	33,600
18	Scott Sharp	8	USA	Delphi	D/T/F	125	Engine	203.740	25.7092s	21	12	90	13	33,600	0	33,600
19	Bryan Herta	7	USA	XM Satellite Radio	D/H/F	113	Mechanical	208.001	25.1826s	5	12	103	11	32,400	0	32,400
20	Tomas Scheckter	4	SA	Pennzoil Panther	D/C/F	48	Mechanical	207.725	25.2160s	8	12	85	14	31,300	0	31,300
21	Ed Carpenter (R)	52	USA	Red Bull Cheever Racing	D/C/F	46	Accident	207.855	25.2003s	7	12	64	20	31,300	0	31,300
22	A.J. Foyt IV	14	USA	Conseco/A.J. Foyt Racing	D/T/F	38	Accident	205.100	25.5387s	17	12	68	18	31,300	0	31,300
													Total	1,000,000	33,500	1,033,500

Time of race: 1h 53m 24.1239s. Average speed: 153.965 mph. Margin of victory: 0.2578s.

Fastest lap: #17 Vitor Meira (Race lap 3, 211.483 mph, 24.7679s). Fastest leading lap: #11 Tony Kanaan (Race lap 200, 208.848 mph, 25.1278s).

MBNA Pole Award: #27 Dario Franchitti (209.609 mph, 24.9894s). The Marlboro Lap Leader Award: #11 Tony Kanaan. Firestone Performance Award: #11 Tony Kanaan.

Caution flags: Laps 26-30, #10 Manning and #52 Carpenter, contact in T1; laps 38-44, #14 Foyt, contact in T4; laps 46-56, #52 Carpenter, contact in T4; laps 126-133, #2 Taylor, contact in backstretch; laps 180-185, #15 Rice and #10 Manning, contact in T3 and #1 Dixon and #5 Fernandez, contact in pit out. Total: 5 caution flags, 37 laps.

Lap leaders: Dario Franchitti, 1-22; Tony Kanaan, 23-27; Franchitti, 28-33; Kanaan, 34-97; Kosuke Matsuura, 98-105; Sam Hornish Jr., 106; Greg Ray, 107-109; Helio Castroneves, 110-111; Kanaan, 112-128; Buddy Rice, 129-134; Kanaan, 135-177; Rice, 178; Kanaan, 179-181; Dan Wheldon, 182-187; Kanaan, 188-200. Total: 14 lead changes among 8 drivers.

Lap leader summary: Tony Kanaan, 6 times, 145 laps led; Dario Franchitti, 2 times, 28 laps led; Kosuke Matsuura, 1 time, 8 laps led; Buddy Rice, 2 times, 7 laps led; Dan Wheldon, 1 time, 6 laps led; Greg Ray, 1 time, 3 laps led; Helio Castroneves, 1 time, 2 laps led; Sam Hornish Jr., 1 time, 1 lap led.

Legend: R – IndyCar Series Rookie. Chassis legend: D – Dallara (15); G – Panoz G Force (7). Engine legend: C – Chevrolet (6); H – Honda (9); T – Toyota (7). Tire legend: F – Firestone (22).

RICHMOND

THE **SUNTRUST INDY CHALLENGE AT** Richmond International Raceway proved to be a race of two distinct halves. The opening 113 laps were dominated by Toyota, which had claimed its first pole of the season through the efforts of Helio Castroneves. Later, however, the Honda contingent came to the fore. Dario Franchitti led a race-high 79 laps, but it was Andretti Green Racing teammate Dan Wheldon who took advantage of an inspired strategic call to claim his second victory of the year.

The Englishman, who had celebrated his 26th birthday just four days earlier, endured a difficult time in practice and qualifying, posting only the 20th best time. Wheldon wasn't a factor during the early stages of the 250-lap Saturday night race either, mired well back in the pack as Castroneves led the way.

Buddy Rice qualified second for Rahal Letterman Racing and headed the chase initially before being passed by the second Marlboro Team Penske Dallara/Toyota of Sam Hornish Jr. The two-time IndyCar Series champion then overtook his teammate on lap 38, and continued

to hold the upper hand until lap 110 when a brief rain shower brought out the caution flags.

Most of the leaders elected to make pit stops, but several differing strategies were already being employed. Franchitti was among those to have taken on service during an earlier caution, and duly took the lead. The Scotsman was chased

at the restart by Castroneves, Tomas Scheckter (Pennzoil Panther Racing Dallara/Chevrolet) and Hornish. Darren Manning, too, looked strong until running foul of some slower traffic and finding the wall with his Target Panoz G-Force.

Scheckter and Hornish also came to grief on the ultra-tight 0.75-mile speedway, ending their hopes of victory by tangling at the exit of Turn Two on the 188th lap. Caution again.

Franchitti and the other leaders took the opportunity to make pit stops, and this time Castroneves won the battle on pit lane after choosing not to take on fresh Firestone tires.

Left: Dan Wheldon celebrates his victory. Bottom left: Buddy Rice and Helio Castroneves pose with their cars. Clockwise from right: Castroneves holds aloft his MBNA Pole Award; Wheldon crosses the finish line; before executing a victory burn-out.

Ahead of them both, however, were Wheldon, Vitor Meira (Rahal Letterman Team Centrix Panoz G Force/Honda) and Rice, all of whom had stopped earlier and were intent on stretching their fuel loads to the finish.

Two more accidents in the closing stages assisted their ploy, one of which involved Franchitti and fellow Briton Mark Taylor, who qualified an excellent fourth in the second Panther Racing Dallara/Chevrolet but struggled throughout the race with poor handling. An irate Franchitti, like Hornish earlier, lost several laps while repairs were made.

One final incident between Greg Ray and Ed Carpenter ensured that the race would be settled under caution without a restart. But Wheldon was simply happy to be have secured the win.

"You wouldn't have picked us to win based on our starting spot, but that is a credit to everyone involved in the team," said Wheldon's team manager Tony Cotman, who devised the strategy that enabled his charge to emerge victorious.

Castroneves actually beat Meira to the finish line, but the pass was later nullified by the race stewards following a miscue that resulted in the yellow lights being left on as the white and green flags were displayed. Castroneves had to be content with third.

IRL IndyCar® Series Race 6: SunTrust Indy Challenge at Richmond International Raceway
Saturday, June 26, 2004

Place	Driver	Car	Nat.	Car Name	C/E/T	Laps Comp.	Running/ Reason Out	Q. Speed (mph)	Q. Time	Starting Position	IRL Pts.	Total IRL Pts.	IRL Standing	IRL Awards ($)	Designated Awards ($)	Total Awards ($)
1	Dan Wheldon	26	GB	Klein Tools/Jim Beam	D/H/F	250	Running	164.935	16.3701s	20	50	225	2	100,800	0	100,800
2	Vitor Meira	17	BR	Rahal Letterman Team Centrix	G/H/F	250	Running	169.901	15.8916s	8	40	109	14	82,900	0	82,900
3	Helio Castroneves	3	BR	Marlboro Team Penske	D/T/F	250	Running	171.202	15.7708s	1	35	181	3	69,700	10,000	79,700
4	Bryan Herta	7	USA	XM Satellite Radio	D/H/F	250	Running	170.182	15.8654s	7	32	135	8	56,400	0	56,400
5	Tony Kanaan	11	BR	Team 7-Eleven	D/H/F	250	Running	168.987	15.9776s	10	30	240	1	51,600	0	51,600
6	Buddy Rice	15	USA	Rahal Letterman Argent/Pioneer	G/H/F	250	Running	170.782	15.8096s	2	28	172	4	45,700	0	45,700
7	Adrian Fernandez	5	MEX	Quaker State Telmex Tecate	G/H/F	250	Running	167.597	16.1101s	16	26	106	15	44,400	0	44,400
8	Scott Dixon	1	NZ	Target Chip Ganassi Racing	G/T/F	250	Running	170.405	15.8446s	6	24	146	5	43,200	0	43,200
9	Scott Sharp	8	USA	Delphi	D/T/F	248	Running	167.161	16.1521s	17	22	112	12	43,200	2,000	45,200
10	Felipe Giaffone	24	BR	Team Purex/Dreyer and Reinbold	D/C/F	248	Running	166.841	16.1831s	18	20	57	21	42,100	2,000	44,100
11	A.J. Foyt IV	14	USA	Conseco/A.J. Foyt Racing	D/T/F	248	Running	162.799	16.5849s	21	19	87	18	40,700	0	40,700
12	Dario Franchitti	27	GB	ArcaEx	D/H/F	247	Running	168.334	16.0395s	12	21	129	9	39,700	7,500	47,200
13	Sam Hornish Jr.	6	USA	Marlboro Team Penske	D/T/F	246	Running	170.623	15.8244s	4	17	136	6	38,500	10,000	48,500
14	Kosuke Matsuura (R)	55	J	Panasonic ARTA	G/H/F	246	Running	168.260	16.0466s	13	16	111	13	37,100	0	37,100
15	Greg Ray	13	USA	Access Motorsports	G/H/F	245	Running	166.461	16.2200s	19	15	99	16	36,000	0	36,000
16	Ed Carpenter (R)	52	USA	Red Bull Cheever Racing	D/C/F	244	Running	168.132	16.0588s	14	14	78	20	34,800	0	34,800
17	Tomas Scheckter	4	SA	Pennzoil Panther	D/C/F	222	Accident	170.592	15.8272s	5	13	98	17	33,600	0	33,600
18	Mark Taylor (R)	2	GB	Menards/Johns Manville Racing	D/C/F	217	Accident	170.683	15.8188s	3	12	79	19	33,600	0	33,600
19	Tora Takagi	12	J	Pioneer Mo Nunn Racing	D/T/F	157	Handling	169.241	15.9536s	9	12	120	11	32,400	0	32,400
20	Darren Manning	10	GB	Target Chip Ganassi Racing	G/T/F	132	Accident	168.924	15.9835s	11	12	136	7	31,200	0	31,200
21	Al Unser Jr.	20	USA	Patrick Racing	D/C/F	119	Handling	158.601	17.0238s	22	12	44	22	31,200	0	31,200
22	Alex Barron	51	USA	Red Bull Cheever Racing	D/C/F	9	Accident	167.945	16.0767s	15	12	129	9	31,200	0	31,200
													Total:	**1,000,000**	**31,500**	**1,031,500**

Time of race: 1h 38m 10.6077s. Average speed: 114.589 mph. Margin of victory: Under caution.

Fastest lap: #6 Sam Hornish Jr. (Race lap 238, 169.419 mph, 15.9368s). Fastest leading lap: #26 Dan Wheldon (Race lap 240, 165.597 mph, 16.3046s).

MBNA Pole Award: #3 Helio Castroneves (171.202 mph, 15.7708s). The Marlboro Lap Leader Award: #27 Dario Franchitti. Firestone Performance Award: #6 Sam Hornish Jr.

Caution flags: Laps 11-21, #51 Barron, contact T2; laps 67-78, debris; laps 110-130, moisture; laps 133-138, #4 Scheckter, contact T4; laps 189-200, #6 Hornish and #4 Scheckter, contact T2; laps 223-232, #2 Mark Taylor and #27 Franchitti, contact T2; laps 246-250, #52 Carpenter and #13 Ray, contact T2. Total: 7 caution flags, 77 laps.

Lap leaders: Helio Castroneves, 1-37; Sam Hornish Jr., 38-113; Dario Franchitti, 114-192; Dan Wheldon, 193-250. Total: 3 lead changes among 4 drivers.

Lap leader summary: Dario Franchitti, 1 time, 79 laps led; Sam Hornish Jr., 1 time, 76 laps led; Dan Wheldon, 1 time, 58 laps led; Helio Castroneves, 1 time, 37 laps led.

Legend: R – IndyCar Series Rookie. Chassis legend: D – Dallara (15); G – Panoz G Force (7). Engine legend: C – Chevrolet (6); H – Honda (9); T – Toyota (7). Tire legend: F – Firestone (22).

KANSAS

THE FOURTH OF JULY TURNED OUT to be a red-letter day for Rahal Letterman Racing. And for Honda. Three Honda-powered cars led the field at the start of the Argent Mortgage Indy 300 at Kansas Speedway, and 200 laps later there were six Honda Indy V8s at the front of field, headed by Rahal Letterman teammates Buddy Rice and Vitor Meira.

"There was no question that much of the success at Rahal Letterman this year is due to Buddy being on board," said 1986 Indianapolis 500 Champion Bobby Rahal. "With Vitor coming in, I think it adds a one-two punch. Really, we got two great young guys who work very, very closely together. The results are a reflection of that."

The race reached an exciting climax as Rice and Meira spent virtually the entire final ten laps in wheel-to-wheel formation, trading the point several times before, appropriately, the American crossed the finish line a scant 0.0051 secs ahead for the second-closest finish in IndyCar Series history.

"It's great to race each other cleanly," said Rice. "That's how it's supposed to happen, so I'm glad I could do it with my teammate."

"We're the happiest guys because it was one and two for Team Rahal," added Brazil's Vitor Meira following his second runner-up finish in as many races. "I wanted the win pretty bad

but not to the point to do anything stupid. So I'll take second."

Rice and Meira led a combined 120 laps, but Andretti Green Racing's Tony Kanaan also made his presence felt. The series point-leader led for 75 laps before finishing close behind in third place, unable to find a way past Rahal Letterman's two Panoz G Force cars.

"They did what they were supposed to do," said Kanaan, after claiming his sixth straight top-five result. "I would have done the same if I was

there with my teammates. It's the way it is. It's a long championship and we just need to keep thinking points, points and points."

Kanaan, in turn, was shadowed by two of his own stablemates: Dario Franchitti and Bryan Herta. The result was especially satisfying for Franchitti who had started from the back of the pack following a post-qualifying engine change. The fourth AGR Dallara/Honda of Dan Wheldon also might have been in contention but for a miscue in the pit lane which cost him a lap. Wheldon still salvaged a ninth-place finish. Sixth was taken by Adrian Fernandez, while Helio Castroneves took the consolation of being the best non-Honda, finishing in seventh ahead of Sam Hornish Jr.'s identical Marlboro Team Penske Dallara/Toyota.

"In the first stint, the Marlboro Team Penske car had understeer and oversteer, so we made a front-wing adjustment during our pit stop which was an improvement," related Castroneves. "We just tried to stay in the draft and we were able to run in the top ten, but we just didn't have enough to catch the leaders."

The race was slowed by only two cautions, firstly when Scott Sharp and Tora Takagi made contact just after the green flag was shown, and then on lap 175 when rookies Jeff Simmons and Kosuke Matsuura made contact in Turn One. None of the drivers was injured.

Main picture: Buddy Rice and Vitor Meira lead wheel-to-wheel. Far left: Rice takes the win. Above left: Rice with his trophy. Left: Rice in the pits.

IRL IndyCar® Series Race 7: Argent Mortgage Indy 300 at Kansas Speedway
Sunday, July 4, 2004

Place	Driver	Car	Nat.	Car Name	C/E/T	Laps Comp.	Running/ Reason Out	Q. Speed (mph)	Q. Time	Starting Position	IRL Pts.	Total IRL Pts.	IRL Standing	IRL Awards ($)	Designated Awards ($)	Total Awards ($)
1	Buddy Rice	15	USA	Rahal Letterman Pioneer/Argent	G/H/F	200	Running	210.141	26.0396s	1	53	225	3	105,000	17,500	122,500
2	Vitor Meira	17	BR	Rahal Letterman Team Centrix	G/H/F	200	Running	209.342	26.1391s	3	40	149	10	86,500	10,000	96,500
3	Tony Kanaan	11	BR	Team 7-Eleven	D/H/F	200	Running	209.681	26.0968s	2	35	275	1	72,500	0	72,500
4	Dario Franchitti	27	GB	ArcaEx	D/H/F	200	Running	208.646	26.2262s	21*	32	161	7	58,600	0	58,600
5	Bryan Herta	7	USA	XM Satellite Radio	D/H/F	200	Running	208.210	26.2812s	9	30	165	5	53,400	0	53,400
6	Adrian Fernandez	5	MEX	Quaker State Telmex Tecate	G/H/F	200	Running	208.020	26.3051s	10	28	134	12	47,100	2,000	49,100
7	Helio Castroneves	3	BR	Marlboro Team Penske	D/T/F	200	Running	209.120	26.1668s	6	26	207	4	45,800	0	45,800
8	Sam Hornish Jr.	6	USA	Marlboro Team Penske	D/T/F	199	Running	209.262	26.1491s	4	24	160	8	44,600	0	44,600
9	Dan Wheldon	26	GB	Klein Tools/Jim Beam	D/H/F	199	Running	207.151	26.4155s	12	22	247	2	44,600	0	44,600
10	Alex Barron	51	USA	Red Bull Cheever Racing	D/C/F	199	Running	207.668	26.3497s	11	20	149	10	43,300	2,000	45,300
11	Darren Manning	10	GB	Target Chip Ganassi Racing	G/T/F	198	Running	206.364	26.5162s	18	19	155	9	41,900	0	41,900
12	Scott Dixon	1	NZ	Target Chip Ganassi Racing	G/T/F	197	Running	206.990	26.4361s	15	18	164	6	40,700	0	40,700
13	A.J. Foyt IV	14	USA	Conseco/A.J. Foyt Racing	D/T/F	197	Running	207.016	26.4327s	14	17	104	17	39,600	0	39,600
14	Ed Carpenter (R)	52	USA	Red Bull Cheever Racing	D/C/F	197	Running	206.894	26.4483s	16	16	94	19	38,100	0	38,100
15	Tomas Scheckter	4	SA	Pennzoil Panther	D/C/F	196	Running	209.138	26.1646s	5	15	113	16	36,900	0	36,900
16	Felipe Giaffone	24	BR	Team Purex Dreyer & Reinbold	D/C/F	191	Running	207.098	26.4223s	13	14	71	21	35,700	1,000	36,700
17	Townsend Bell	2	USA	Menards/Johns Manville Racing	D/C/F	189	Running	208.839	26.2020s	7	13	13	27	34,400	0	34,400
18	Kosuke Matsuura (R)	55	J	Panasonic ARTA	G/H/F	172	Accident	208.652	26.2255s	8	12	123	15	34,400	0	34,400
19	Jeff Simmons (R)	20	USA	Patrick Racing	D/C/F	172	Accident	205.761	26.5939s	19	12	26	26	33,100	0	33,100
20	Scott Sharp	8	USA	Delphi	D/T/F	0	Accident	206.495	26.4994s	17	12	124	14	31,900	500	32,400
21	Tora Takagi	12	J	Pioneer Mo Nunn Racing	D/T/F	0	Handling	204.741	26.7264s	20	12	132	13	31,900	500	32,400

* Changed engines following qualifying.

Total: 1,000,000   33,500   1,033,500

Time of race: 1h 42m 56.6727s. Average speed: 177.183 mph. Margin of victory: 0.0051s.

Fastest lap: #4 Tomas Scheckter (Race lap 188, 210.723 mph, 25.9677s). Fastest leading lap: #17 Vitor Meira (Race lap 81, 210.611 mph, 25.9815s).

MBNA Pole Award: #15 Buddy Rice (210.141 mph, 26.0396s). The Marlboro Lap Leader Award: #15 Buddy Rice. Firestone Performance Award: #17 Vitor Meira.

Caution flags: Laps 1-5, #8 Sharp and #12 Takagi, accident T4; laps 175-185, #20 Simmons and #55 Matsuura, accident T1. Total: 2 caution flags, 16 laps.

Lap leaders: Buddy Rice, 1-6; Tony Kanaan, 7-56; Rice, 57-58; Kanaan, 59-64; Vitor Meira, 65-66; Kanaan, 67-74; Meira, 75-106; Rice, 107-108; Sam Hornish Jr., 109-111; Kanaan, 112-122; Rice, 123-159; Castroneves, 160-161; Rice, 162-191; Meira, 192; Rice, 193-194; Meira 195; Rice, 196-198; Meira, 199, Rice, 200. Total: 18 lead changes among 5 drivers.

Lap leader summary: Buddy Rice, 8 times, 83 laps led; Tony Kanaan, 4 times, 75 laps led; Vitor Meira, 5 times, 37 laps led; Sam Hornish Jr., 1 time, 3 laps led; Helio Castroneves, 1 time, 2 laps led.

Legend: R – IndyCar Series Rookie. Chassis legend: D – Dallara (15); G – Panoz G Force (6). Engine legend: C – Chevrolet (6); H – Honda (8); T – Toyota (7). Tire legend: F – Firestone (21).

NASHVILLE

Facing page: Race-winner Tony Kanaan.
This picture: Crunch time in the pit lane.

TONY KANAAN USED A TIME-HONORED recipe comprising good race strategy, street smarts, a touch of aggression and even a slice of luck to emerge as the winner of a bruising Firestone Indy 200 at Nashville Superspeedway. The victory was his third of the season for Andretti Green Racing and helped pad his IRL IndyCar Series points advantage to 61 over AGR teammate Dan Wheldon, who finished a disappointing 13th.

Honda maintained its series stranglehold with a seventh win in eight races, although Toyota claimed second through fourth, while Chevrolet earned fifth thanks to an impressive run by Townsend Bell in his second IndyCar Series start.

Buddy Rice displayed his qualifying prowess once again by snatching his fourth pole position with Bobby Rahal and David Letterman's Pioneer/ Argent Mortgage Panoz G Force/Honda. Teammate Vitor Meira secured the other front row starting position in his similar Team Centrix machine.

It was Meira who got the jump at the start. Indeed the gifted Brazilian led the first 113 laps and, having finished second in the previous two races, seemed set for a well-deserved maiden victory. Alas, it was not to be. During a routine pit stop under caution, Meira was waved out before the refueling hose had been disconnected. He jumped on the brakes but stalled the engine and had fallen to 15th by the time he could resume. Undaunted, Meira blitzed through to fifth over the next 30 laps, regularly circulating faster than Rice, the new race leader. Sadly, he lost time with another pit lane

miscue, then suffered a gearbox failure that left him with only fourth gear for the closing stages.

"We had a misunderstanding in the pits and we made some mistakes," noted Meira with remarkable *sang-froid*. "Everyone here knew the Centrix Honda was the car to beat. Buddy and I ran away from the pack, but things don't always go your way."

Rice, too, had mixed fortunes. He lost the lead to Wheldon when the Englishman elected not to change tires during a routine pit stop, under yellow, on lap 165, and was doing his best to regain the advantage when the pair made contact in Turn Two. Miraculously, both men managed to regain control of their errant cars and were able to continue. But the damage was done. Rice required a pit stop

for attention to a disfigured wing and Wheldon lost a lap while changing a punctured tire.

The incident allowed Kanaan to take the lead for the first time, and he drove cagily over the final 20 laps to ensure there was no way a charging Sam Hornish Jr. could sneak past and deny him the win. The second Marlboro Team Penske Dallara/ Toyota of Helio Castroneves finished close behind in third, followed by Darren Manning (Target Panoz G Force/Toyota) and Bell, who shone aboard Panther Racing's Menards/Johns Manville Dallara/Chevy.

Mark Taylor, who had lost his ride to Bell following the Richmond race, also drove well on his return to the series, claiming seventh in his first drive with Greg Ray's Access Motorsports team.

IRL IndyCar® Series Race 8: Firestone Indy 200 at Nashville Superspeedway
Saturday, July 17, 2004

Place	Driver	Car	Nat.	Car Name	C/E/T	Laps Comp.	Running/ Reason Out	Q. Speed (mph)	Q. Time	Starting Position	IRL Pts.	Total IRL Pts.	IRL Standing	IRL Awards ($)	Designated Awards ($)	Total Awards ($)
1	Tony Kanaan	11	BR	Team 7-Eleven	D/H/F	200	Running	199.804	23.4230s	5	50	325	1	100,400	0	100,400
2	Sam Hornish Jr.	6	USA	Marlboro Team Penske	D/T/F	200	Running	199.003	23.5172s	9	40	200	5	82,900	0	82,900
3	Helio Castroneves	3	BR	Marlboro Team Penske	D/T/F	200	Running	198.801	23.5411s	11	35	242	4	69,600	0	69,600
4	Darren Manning	10	GB	Target Chip Ganassi Racing	G/T/F	200	Running	199.108	23.5048s	6	32	187	7	56,500	0	56,500
5	Townsend Bell	2	USA	Menards/Johns Manville Racing	D/C/F	200	Running	198.747	23.5475s	12	30	43	24	51,600	0	51,600
6	Buddy Rice	15	USA	Rahal Letterman Pioneer Argent	G/H/F	200	Running	201.231	23.2568s	1	28	253	3	45,600	10,000	55,600
7	Mark Taylor (R)	13	GB	Access Motorsports	G/H/F	200	Running	197.237	23.7278s	18	26	105	19	44,400	2,000	46,400
8	Scott Dixon	1	NZ	Target Chip Ganassi Racing	G/T/F	200	Running	199.027	23.5144s	8	24	188	6	43,300	0	43,300
9	Kosuke Matsuura (R)	55	J	Panasonic ARTA	G/H/F	200	Running	198.381	23.5910s	14	22	145	14	43,300	0	43,300
10	Adrian Fernandez	5	MEX	Quaker State Telmex Tecate	G/H/F	200	Running	198.701	23.5530s	13	20	154	12	42,000	0	42,000
11	Tora Takagi	12	J	Pioneer Mo Nunn Racing	D/T/F	200	Running	196.653	23.7983s	20	19	151	13	40,800	0	40,800
12	Vitor Meira	17	BR	Rahal Letterman Team Centrix	G/H/F	200	Running	200.967	23.2874s	2	21	170	10	39,600	17,500	57,100
13	Dan Wheldon	26	GB	Klein Tools/Jim Beam	D/H/F	199	Running	199.992	23.4009s	4	17	264	2	38,500	0	38,500
14	Scott Sharp	8	USA	Delphi	D/T/F	199	Running	198.162	23.6170s	15	16	140	15	37,100	0	37,100
15	Felipe Giaffone	24	BR	Team Purex Dreyer & Reinbold	D/C/F	198	Running	197.237	23.7278s	19	15	86	21	36,000	0	36,000
16	A.J. Foyt IV	14	USA	Conseco/A.J. Foyt Racing	D/T/F	190	Running	193.125	24.2330s	22	14	118	17	34,900	0	34,900
17	Alex Barron	51	USA	Red Bull Cheever Racing	D/C/F	178	Suspension	197.993	23.6372s	16	13	162	11	33,600	0	33,600
18	Bryan Herta	7	USA	XM Satellite Radio	D/H/F	161	Accident	200.955	23.2888s	3	12	177	8	33,600	0	33,600
19	Tomas Scheckter	4	SA	Pennzoil Panther	D/C/F	108	Accident	198.829	23.5378s	10	12	125	16	32,400	0	32,400
20	Dario Franchitti	27	GB	ArcaEx	D/H/F	65	Gearbox	199.089	23.5071s	7	12	173	9	31,300	0	31,300
21	Jaques Lazier	20	USA	Patrick Racing	D/C/F	64	Mechanical	197.400	23.7082s	17	12	12	28	31,300	0	31,300
22	Ed Carpenter (R)	52	USA	Red Bull Cheever Racing	D/C/F	60	Accident	196.399	23.8290s	21	12	106	18	31,300	0	31,300
													Total:	1,000,000	29,500	1,029,500

Time of race: 1h 55m 34.6367s. Average speed: 134.975 mph. Margin of victory: 0.3375s.

Fastest lap: #17 Vitor Meira (Race lap 146, 198.084 mph, 23.6263s). Fastest leading lap: #17 Vitor Meira (Race lap 59, 197.806 mph, 23.6596s).

MBNA Pole Award: #15 Buddy Rice (201.231 mph, 23.2568s). The Marlboro Lap Leader Award: #17 Vitor Meira. Firestone Performance Award: #17 Vitor Meira.

Caution flags: Laps 10-13, debris; laps 35-42, debris; laps 62-72, #52 Carpenter, accident T4; laps 110-118, #4 Scheckter, accident T2; laps 163-176, #7 Herta, accident T2 and #14 Foyt, tow-in; laps 179-181, #26 Wheldon, #15 Rice, contact T2; laps 185-187, #26 Wheldon, lost tire T4. Total: 7 caution flags, 52 laps.

Lap leaders: Vitor Meira, 1-113; Buddy Rice, 114-165; Dan Wheldon, 166-181; Tony Kanaan, 182-200. Total: 3 lead changes among 4 drivers.

Lap leader summary: Vitor Meira, 1 time, 113 laps led; Buddy Rice, 1 time, 52 laps led; Tony Kanaan, 1 time, 19 laps led; Dan Wheldon, 1 time, 16 laps led.

Legend: R – IndyCar Series Rookie. Chassis legend: D – Dallara (15); G – Panoz G Force (7). Engine legend: C – Chevrolet (6); H – Honda (9); T – Toyota (7). Tire legend: F – Firestone (22).

MILWAUKEE

THE INDYCAR SERIES' FIRST-EVER VISIT to the historic Milwaukee Mile resulted in a popular maiden success for Dario Franchitti. The Scotsman qualified only seventh for the Menards A.J. Foyt Indy 225 but worked his #27 ArcaEx Dallara/Honda steadily forward, and in the closing stages fought off challenges from both two-time IndyCar Series Champion Sam Hornish Jr. and 2004 Indy 500 Champion Buddy Rice to score an especially satisfying victory.

"This win means a lot, both to me and the ArcaEx team, especially to come at a special track like The Milwaukee Mile," said Franchitti, 31, who sat out much of the 2003 season after a motorcycle accident had necessitated back

From top: Dario Franchitti salutes the Milwaukee crowd; and receives his prize.

surgery. "To come back after taking a year off and win this race makes it pretty special."

Vitor Meira secured the second pole of his career with Rahal Letterman Racing's Team Centrix Panoz G Force/Honda, but his advantage was short-lived as series leader Tony Kanaan (Team 7-Eleven Dallara/Honda) took the lead going into Turn Three on the very first lap. Hornish, too, was on the move early. The Ohio native started fourth in his Marlboro Team Penske Dallara/Toyota, but by lap 17 was up into the lead and soon putting some distance between himself and his pursuers.

The first caution period of the afternoon came after 39 laps when Scott Sharp performed a quick non-contact spin in Turn Four. Everyone took the opportunity to make their first pit stops of the day – except Bryan Herta, who became the third different leader. Herta's XM Satellite Radio Dallara/Honda continued to pace the field at the restart, but Andretti Green Racing's strategy backfired when Herta was obliged to make a pit stop under green after 80 laps and fell a lap behind the leaders before he could resume.

Hornish's teammate, Helio Castroneves, took up the running after Herta's stop, but only until lap 106, when Franchitti moved past. Franchitti held the point until lap 147, when the final round of pit stops – triggered by a single-car accident involving Darren Manning – saw him beaten out of the pits by Hornish. Franchitti, though, immediately swept past at the restart and began to inch his way clear. Rice also passed Hornish, on lap 202, and was beginning to put some pressure on Franchitti when Jaques Lazier crashed Pat Patrick's Dallara/Chevrolet to bring out the day's fifth caution. But Franchitti made no mistakes at the restart, with seven laps remaining, and held off Rice by 0.6590 secs at the checkered flag to claim Andretti Green Racing's sixth win of the season.

"I would have preferred not to see the caution," said Rice, who moved up to second in the IRL point standings behind fourth-place finisher Kanaan. "But I'm not sure that changes the outcome at all. I mean, Dario was strong. It was going to take a lot to get by him."

Hornish secured his second successive appearance on the podium by claiming third, while Meira finished hot on Kanaan's heels in fifth. Townsend Bell maintained his strong form by earning his second top-six result in just three attempts since joining Panther Racing. Bell also was once again the top Chevrolet finisher.

Tony Kanaan in his 7-Eleven Dallara/Honda machine.

IRL IndyCar® Series Race 9: Menards A.J. Foyt Indy 225 at The Milwaukee Mile
Sunday, July 25, 2004

Place	Driver	Car	Nat.	Car Name	C/E/T	Laps Comp.	Running/ Reason Out	Q. Speed (mph)	Q. Time	Starting Position	IRL Pts.	Total IRL Pts.	IRL Standing	IRL Awards ($)	Designated Awards ($)	Total Awards ($)
1	Dario Franchitti	27	GB	ArcaEx	D/H/F	225	Running	167.312	21.8394s	7	53	226	6	100,400	7,500	107,900
2	Buddy Rice	15	USA	Rahal Letterman Pioneer Argent	G/H/F	225	Running	168.272	21.7149s	3	40	293	2	82,900	0	82,900
3	Sam Hornish Jr.	6	USA	Marlboro Team Penske	D/T/F	225	Running	168.258	21.7167s	4	35	235	5	69,600	0	69,600
4	Tony Kanaan	11	BR	Team 7-Eleven	D/H/F	225	Running	168.597	21.6730s	2	32	357	1	56,500	0	56,500
5	Vitor Meira	17	BR	Rahal Letterman Team Centrix	G/H/F	225	Running	169.338	21.5781s	1	30	200	7	51,600	10,000	61,600
6	Townsend Bell	2	USA	Menards/Johns Manville Racing	D/C/F	225	Running	165.826	22.0351s	12	28	71	22	45,600	0	45,600
7	Alex Barron	51	USA	Red Bull Cheever Racing	D/C/F	225	Running	164.162	22.2585s	15	26	188	11	44,400	2,000	46,400
8	Adrian Fernandez	5	MEX	Quaker State Telmex Tecate	G/H/F	224	Running	168.001	21.7499s	6	24	178	12	43,300	2,000	45,300
9	Bryan Herta	7	USA	XM Satellite Radio	D/H/F	224	Running	165.878	22.0282s	11	22	199	9	43,300	0	43,300
10	Kosuke Matsuura (R)	55	J	Panasonic ARTA	G/H/F	223	Running	159.973	22.8413s	20	20	165	13	42,000	0	42,000
11	Ed Carpenter (R)	52	USA	Red Bull Cheever Racing	D/C/F	223	Running	164.278	22.2428s	14	19	125	18	40,800	0	40,800
12	Helio Castroneves	3	BR	Marlboro Team Penske	D/T/F	222	Running	168.093	21.7380s	5	18	260	4	39,600	10,000	49,600
13	Felipe Giaffone	24	BR	Team Purex Dreyer & Reinbold	D/C/F	221	Running	165.210	22.1173s	13	17	103	20	38,500	1,000	39,500
14	Mark Taylor (R)	13	GB	Access Motorsports	G/H/F	221	Running	163.669	22.3255s	16	16	121	19	37,100	0	37,100
15	Scott Sharp	8	USA	Delphi	D/T/F	218	Running	161.537	22.6202s	19	15	155	15	36,000	500	36,500
16	A.J. Foyt IV	14	USA	Conseco/A.J. Foyt Racing	D/T/F	214	Running	161.869	22.5738s	18	14	132	17	34,900	0	34,900
17	Jaques Lazier	20	USA	Patrick Racing	D/C/F	205	Accident	166.375	21.9625s	9	13	25	28	33,600	0	33,600
18	Dan Wheldon	26	GB	Klein Tools/Jim Beam	D/H/F	147	Mechanical	164.068	22.2712s	21*	12	276	3	33,600	0	33,600
19	Darren Manning	10	GB	Target Chip Ganassi Racing	G/T/F	143	Accident	166.080	22.0014s	10	12	199	9	32,400	0	32,400
20	Tora Takagi	12	J	Pioneer Mo Nunn Racing	D/T/F	110	Electrical	162.847	22.4383s	17	12	163	14	31,300	0	31,300
21	Tomas Scheckter	4	SA	Pennzoil Panther	D/C/F	32	Gearbox	166.829	21.9027s	8	12	137	16	31,300	500	31,800
22	Scott Dixon	1	NZ	Target Chip Ganassi Racing	G/T/F	0	Did not start	164.420	22.2236s	DNS**	12	200	7	31,300	0	31,300
													Total:	1,000,000	33,500	1,033,500

* Moved due to engine change. ** Did not start due to accident during qualifying.

Time of race: **1h 46m 49.4110s.** Average speed: **128.272 mph.** Margin of victory: **0.6590s.**

Fastest lap/Fastest leading lap: **#27 Dario Franchitti** (Race lap 127, 160.229 mph, 22.8049s).

MBNA Pole Award: **#17 Vitor Meira** (169.338 mph, 21.5781s). The Marlboro Lap Leader Award: **#27 Dario Franchitti.** Firestone Performance Award: **#3 Helio Castroneves.**

Caution flags: Laps 39-45, #8 Sharp, spin T4; laps 47-50, #14 Foyt, accident T4; laps 112-121, debris; laps 144-154, #10 Manning, accident T2; laps 212-218, #20 Lazier, accident T2. **Total: 5 caution flags, 39 laps.**

Lap leaders: Tony Kanaan, 1-16; Sam Hornish Jr., 17-42; Bryan Herta, 43-80; Helio Castroneves, 81-105; Dario Franchitti, 106-113; Castroneves, 114; Franchitti, 115-146; Hornish, 147-154; Franchitti, 155-225. **Total: 8 lead changes among 5 drivers.**

Lap leader summary: Dario Franchitti, 3 times, 111 laps led; Bryan Herta, 1 time, 38 laps led; Sam Hornish Jr., 2 times, 34 laps led; Helio Castroneves, 2 times, 26 laps led; Tony Kanaan, 1 time, 16 laps led.

Legend: R – IndyCar Series Rookie. Chassis legend: D – Dallara (15); G – Panoz G Force (7). Engine legend: C – Chevrolet (6); H – Honda (9); T – Toyota (7). Tire legend: F – Firestone (22).

MICHIGAN

THE **MICHIGAN INDY 400 AT MICHIGAN**
International Speedway was all about Tony
Kanaan – well, at least for the first 189 of
200 laps. The IRL IndyCar Series point leader's
7-Eleven Dallara/Honda was headed only briefly
during a mid-race caution period and seemed
poised to score its fourth win of the season. But
Buddy Rice (Rahal Letterman Pioneer/Argent Panoz
G Force/Honda) had been stalking the #11 Andretti
Green Racing machine, and slipped past on lap 190
when Kanaan was implored by his team to conserve
fuel as the race headed towards its climax.

Try as he did, Kanaan was unable to redress
the balance in the final ten laps. Several times he
nosed alongside his rival as they duelled for the
victory, but each time Rice was able to rebuff
the high-speed challenge. The American finally
crossed the line a scant 0.0796 secs in front.

"I don't think I could have hit the gas [pedal]
any harder," quipped Rice after snaring his third

Above and below: Buddy Rice takes top honors after edging
Tony Kanaan on lap 190.

win of the year and reducing Kanaan's
championship lead to 57 points with six races
remaining. "It was on the floor all the way."

Not surprisingly, Kanaan was upset at losing
a race he seemed to have in his pocket: "I had
a very strong car," he declared. "I led over 180
laps and didn't win the race, so that hurts. I was
told to conserve fuel, so I did. As a result I couldn't
battle for the win. It hurts right now but I know
that after a couple hours I'll be over it and ready
to look towards another opportunity."

Kanaan's Andretti Green Racing teammate,
Dan Wheldon, overcame a sequence of three
disappointing races to finish a strong third, just
edging out Sam Hornish Jr. in the fleetest of the
Toyota-powered cars. Vitor Meira and Bryan
Herta continued Honda's dominance by finishing
fifth and sixth.

Scott Dixon also enjoyed a solid drive to
seventh place for Target Chip Ganassi Racing.
The New Zealander, who had been forced to
miss the previous race at Milwaukee following
two massive crashes during practice and
qualifying, rebounded well to qualify third
at MIS, and remained among the leaders
all afternoon.

For the third successive race, Townsend Bell was the top Chevrolet finisher, in eighth, with Panther Racing's Menards/Johns Manville Racing Dallara. Panther teammate Tomas Scheckter also looked menacing in the early stages, vaulting from 13th on the grid to second inside the first 25 laps. But the South African's appalling sequence of misfortune continued as he was hit from behind by Tora Takagi during his first scheduled pit stop. Scheckter resumed, albeit three laps in arrears, and finished an unrepresentative 19th.

Adrian Fernandez's hopes of a top finish were squandered by not one but two pit lane incidents, which resulted in a drive-through penalty and a 12th-place finish. Super Aguri Fernandez Racing teammate Kosuke Matsuura qualified a magnificent second in his similar Panoz G Force/Honda, but endured a difficult race and could manage only 17th.

Ed Carpenter (Red Bull Cheever Racing Dallara/Chevrolet) emerged as the top rookie finisher in 14th.

Above: Vitor Meira tangles with Dan Wheldon in the pits – but both drivers managed to complete the race.

IRL IndyCar® Series Race 10: Michigan Indy 400 at Michigan International Speedway
Sunday, August 1, 2004

Place	Driver	Car	Nat.	Car Name	C/E/T	Laps Comp.	Running/ Reason Out	Q. Speed (mph)	Q. Time	Starting Position	IRL Pts.	Total IRL Pts.	IRL Standing	IRL Awards ($)	Designated Awards ($)	Total Awards ($)
1	Buddy Rice	15	USA	Rahal Letterman Pioneer Argent	G/H/F	200	Running	214.018	33.6421s	6	50	343	2	100,400	0	100,400
2	Tony Kanaan	11	BR	Team 7-Eleven	D/H/F	200	Running	215.871	33.3533s	1	43	400	1	82,900	27,500	110,400
3	Dan Wheldon	26	GB	Klein Tools/Jim Beam	D/H/F	200	Running	213.821	33.6730s	8	35	311	3	69,600	0	69,600
4	Sam Hornish Jr.	6	USA	Marlboro Team Penske	D/T/F	200	Running	214.179	33.6168s	4	32	267	5	56,500	0	56,500
5	Vitor Meira	17	BR	Rahal Letterman Team Centrix	G/H/F	200	Running	214.089	33.6309s	5	30	230	7	51,600	0	51,600
6	Bryan Herta	7	USA	XM Satellite Radio	D/H/F	200	Running	213.699	33.6922s	9	28	227	8	45,600	0	45,600
7	Scott Dixon	1	NZ	Target Chip Ganassi Racing	G/T/F	200	Running	214.328	33.5934s	3	26	226	9	44,400	0	44,400
8	Townsend Bell	2	USA	Menards/Johns Manville Racing	D/C/F	200	Running	213.852	33.6681s	7	24	95	22	43,300	0	43,300
9	Scott Sharp	8	USA	Delphi	D/T/F	200	Running	211.211	34.0891s	18	22	177	14	43,300	2,000	45,300
10	Helio Castroneves	3	BR	Marlboro Team Penske	D/T/F	200	Running	No speed	No time	20*	20	280	4	42,000	0	42,000
11	Alex Barron	51	USA	Red Bull Cheever Racing	D/C/F	199	Running	212.400	33.8983s	14	19	207	11	40,800	0	40,800
12	Adrian Fernandez	5	MEX	Quaker State Telmex Tecate	G/H/F	199	Running	213.452	33.7312s	10	18	196	12	39,600	0	39,600
13	Darren Manning	10	GB	Target Chip Ganassi Racing	G/T/F	199	Running	213.263	33.7611s	12	17	216	10	38,500	0	38,500
14	Ed Carpenter (R)	52	USA	Red Bull Cheever Racing	D/C/F	199	Running	212.329	33.9096s	15	16	141	18	37,100	0	37,100
15	A.J. Foyt IV	14	USA	Conseco/A.J. Foyt Racing	D/T/F	199	Running	211.843	33.9874s	16	15	147	17	36,000	0	36,000
16	Felipe Giaffone	24	BR	Team Purex Dreyer & Reinbold	D/C/F	199	Running	No speed	No time	21*	14	117	20	34,900	0	34,900
17	Kosuke Matsuura (R)	55	J	Panasonic ARTA	G/H/F	199	Running	214.718	33.5324s	2	13	178	13	33,600	0	33,600
18	Jaques Lazier	20	USA	Patrick Racing	D/C/F	198	Running	210.290	34.2384s	19	12	37	26	33,600	0	33,600
19	Tomas Scheckter	4	SA	Pennzoil Panther	D/C/F	197	Running	213.146	33.7796s	13	12	149	16	32,400	0	32,400
20	Tora Takagi	12	J	Pioneer Mo Nunn Racing	D/T/F	197	Running	210.159	34.2597s	22*	12	175	15	31,300	0	31,300
21	Mark Taylor (R)	13	GB	Access Motorsports	G/H/F	195	Running	211.318	34.0719s	17	12	133	19	31,300	0	31,300
22	Dario Franchitti	27	GB	ArcaEx	D/H/F	123	Engine	213.318	33.7524s	11	12	238	6	31,300	0	31,300

* Moved due to engine changes after qualifying. Total: 1,000,000 | 29,500 | 1,029,500

Time of race: 2h 11m 46.7517s. Average speed: 182.123 mph. Margin of victory: 0.0796s.

Fastest lap: #10 Darren Manning (Race lap 117, 216.578 mph, 33.2444s). Fastest leading lap: #11 Tony Kanaan (Race lap 81, 215.439 mph, 33.4202s).

MBNA Pole Award: #11 Tony Kanaan (215.871 mph, 33.3533s). Marlboro Lap Leader Award: #11 Tony Kanaan. Firestone Performance Award: #11 Tony Kanaan.

Caution flags: Laps 39-44, debris; laps 110-114, debris; laps 124-130, #3 Castroneves and #17 Meira, contact frontstraight; laps 156-161, #4 Scheckter, tow-in. Total: 4 caution flags, 24 laps.

Lap leaders: Tony Kanaan, 1-125; Buddy Rice, 126-127; Darren Manning, 128-131; Kanaan, 132-189; Rice, 190-200. Total: 4 lead changes among 3 drivers.

Lap leader summary: Tony Kanaan, 2 times, 183 laps led; Buddy Rice, 2 times, 13 laps led; Darren Manning, 1 time, 4 laps led.

Legend: R – IndyCar Series Rookie. Chassis legend: D – Dallara (15); G – Panoz G Force (7). Engine legend: C – Chevrolet (6); H – Honda (9); T – Toyota (7). Tire legend: F – Firestone (22).

Adrian Fernandez celebrates victory with a burn-out.
Below: Buddy Rice with his MBNA Pole Award.

KENTUCKY

A **DRIAN FERNANDEZ SCORED** a narrow victory in a thrilling Belterra Casino Indy 300 at Kentucky Speedway, but the biggest winner on the day was Honda which claimed not only the top seven finishing positions but also an astonishing tenth consecutive victory. The result was enough to clinch Honda's first-ever IRL Manufacturer's Championship title. Fernandez's delight, meanwhile, was compounded by rookie teammate Kosuke Matsuura finishing an excellent fourth.

"It was a great weekend," beamed Fernandez after claiming his first victory since joining the IRL IndyCar Series in March. "I am very happy for the team. They deserved this win and worked very hard to get us a better car. I take my hat off to them for the fantastic job they did, and also to Kosuke for finishing fourth. I am very

happy for Honda and want to congratulate them on winning the Manufacturer's Championship today. It was a fantastic day for everyone."

For the fourth time in 11 races, points leader Tony Kanaan led the most laps, a total of 126, but the Brazilian's hopes of victory faded in the final segment when his car mysteriously lost speed. Even so, Kanaan emerged with a fifth-place finish – his tenth top-five in a row – to maintain a healthy 50-point advantage in the championship stakes.

"It was a long day," said Kanaan, "so when you come back to buy a result like this with all of the struggles, it's pretty good."

Good strategy provided the key to Fernandez's success. He lost some ground during his second pit stop, but made exemplary use of a fresh set of Firestone tires following a caution period with

just over 50 laps remaining. The Mexican veteran charged from sixth to first inside a handful of laps, then held off a determined challenge from Buddy Rice for the win. Fernandez's margin of victory was a slender 0.0581 secs – a car's length.

Dan Wheldon's Klein Tools/Jim Beam Dallara finished a very close third behind the pair of Panoz G Force cars, while Matsuura belied his rookie status with a mature drive to fourth in Super Aguri Fernandez Racing's Panasonic/ARTA Panoz G Force. The Japanese driver's previous best result had been an eighth at his home race in Motegi.

Dario Franchitti and Vitor Meira completed the Honda rout, while Ed Carpenier earned kudos as the best non-Honda, claiming eighth in Red Bull Cheever Racing's Dallara/Chevrolet.

Several other Chevrolet runners had shown well, however, including Panther Racing teammates Tomas Scheckter and Townsend Bell. Scheckter posted one of his patented charges, climbing from 13th to the lead before bad luck struck again. This time, for the second race in a row, the South African's challenge was ended by a pit lane mishap, when a slipping clutch caused his car to lurch forward uncontrollably before the refueling process had been completed. Fortunately, no one was injured in the ensuing conflagration. Bell also moved up among the top five before overstepping the limit and finding the wall after 157 laps.

A dismal day for Toyota saw Brit Darren Manning as its best-placed finisher, tenth, aboard Target Chip Ganassi Racing's Panoz G Force.

Clockwise from above: Tony Kanaan and Buddy Rice with their crews; Tomas Scheckter; Adrian Fernandez with the trophy.

IRL IndyCar® Series Race 11: Belterra Casino Indy 300 at Kentucky Speedway
Sunday, August 15, 2004

Place	Driver	Car	Nat.	Car Name	C/E/T	Laps Comp.	Running/ Reason Out	Q. Speed (mph)	Q. Time	Starting Position	IRL Pts.	Total IRL Pts.	IRL Standing	IRL Awards ($)	Designated Awards ($)	Total Awards ($)
1	Adrian Fernandez	5	Mex	Quaker State Telmex Tecate	G/H/F	200	Running	215.326	24.7439s	4	50	246	9	100,400	2,000	102,400
2	Buddy Rice	15	USA	Rahal Letterman Pioneer Argent	G/H/F	200	Running	216.016	24.6648s	1	40	383	2	82,900	10,000	92,900
3	Dan Wheldon	26	GB	Klein Tools/Jim Beam	D/H/F	200	Running	214.275	24.8653s	11	35	346	3	69,600	0	69,600
4	Kosuke Matsuura (R)	55	J	Panasonic ARTA	G/H/F	200	Running	214.327	24.8592s	10	32	210	13	56,500	0	56,500
5	Tony Kanaan	11	BR	Team 7-Eleven	D/H/F	200	Running	215.731	24.6974s	2	33	433	1	51,600	17,500	69,100
6	Dario Franchitti	27	GB	ArcaEx	D/H/F	200	Running	215.181	24.7605s	5	28	266	6	45,600	0	45,600
7	Vitor Meira	17	BR	Rahal Letterman Team Centrix	G/H/F	200	Running	214.724	24.8132s	7	26	256	7	44,400	0	44,400
8	Ed Carpenter (R)	52	USA	Red Bull Cheever Racing	D/C/F	200	Running	212.976	25.0169s	14	24	165	16	43,300	2,000	45,300
9	Bryan Herta	7	USA	XM Satellite Radio	D/H/F	200	Running	No speed	No time	21	22	249	8	43,300	0	43,300
10	Darren Manning	10	GB	Target Chip Ganassi Racing	G/T/F	200	Running	214.697	24.8164s	8	20	236	11	42,000	0	42,000
11	Alex Barron	51	USA	Red Bull Cheever Racing	D/C/F	200	Running	212.051	25.1260s	17	19	226	12	40,800	0	40,800
12	Helio Castroneves	3	BR	Marlboro Team Penske	D/T/F	200	Running	215.029	24.7780s	6	18	298	4	39,600	0	39,600
13	Scott Dixon	1	NZ	Target Chip Ganassi Racing	G/T/F	200	Running	214.647	24.8221s	9	17	243	10	38,500	0	38,500
14	Sam Hornish Jr.	6	USA	Marlboro Team Penske	D/T/F	199	Running	215.592	24.7134s	3	16	283	5	37,100	0	37,100
15	Jaques Lazier	20	USA	Patrick Racing	D/C/F	199	Running	211.968	25.1359s	19	15	52	23	36,000	0	36,000
16	Felipe Giaffone	24	BR	Team Purex Dreyer & Reinbold	D/C/F	199	Running	212.032	25.1283s	18	14	131	20	34,900	1,250	36,150
17	Scott Sharp	8	USA	Delphi	D/T/F	199	Running	212.433	25.0808s	16	13	190	14	33,600	750	34,350
18	A.J. Foyt IV	14	USA	Conseco/A.J. Foyt Racing	D/T/F	199	Running	212.937	25.0215s	15	12	159	18	33,600	0	33,600
19	Mark Taylor (R)	13	GB	Access Motorsports	G/H/F	199	Running	213.878	24.9114s	12	12	145	19	32,400	0	32,400
20	Tora Takagi	12	J	Pioneer Mo Nunn Racing	D/T/F	198	Running	211.068	25.2430s	20	12	187	15	31,300	0	31,300
21	Townsend Bell	2	USA	Menards/Johns Manville Racing	D/C/F	157	Accident	No speed	No time	22	12	107	21	31,300	0	31,300
22	Tomas Scheckter	4	SA	Pennzoil Panther	D/C/F	137	Fuel Fire	213.091	25.0034s	13	12	161	17	31,300	0	31,300
													Total:	1,000,000	33,500	1,033,500

Time of race: 1h 38m 20.7207s. Average speed: 180.588 mph. Margin of victory: 0.0581s.

Fastest lap: #17 Vitor Meira (Race lap 196, 216.411 mph, 24.6198s). Fastest leading lap: #5 Adrian Fernandez (Race lap 90, 214.980 mph, 24.7837s).

MBNA Pole Award: #15 Buddy Rice (216.016 mph, 24.6648s). Marlboro Lap Leader Award: #11 Tony Kanaan. Firestone Performance Award: #11 Tony Kanaan.

Caution flags: Laps 34-39, debris; laps 139-147, #4 Scheckter, pit fire; laps 158-164, #2 Bell, accident T2. Total: 3 caution flags, 22 laps.

Lap leaders: Tony Kanaan, 1-89; Adrian Fernandez, 90; Buddy Rice, 91; Fernandez, 92; Kanaan, 93-127; Tomas Scheckter, 128-136; Dan Wheldon, 137-142; Kanaan, 143-144; Rice, 145-151; Fernandez, 152-200. Total: 9 lead changes among 5 drivers.

Lap leader summary: Tony Kanaan, 3 times, 126 laps led; Adrian Fernandez, 3 times, 51 laps led; Tomas Scheckter, 1 time, 9 laps led; Buddy Rice, 2 times, 8 laps led; Dan Wheldon, 1 time, 6 laps led.

Legend: R – IndyCar Series Rookie. Chassis legend: D – Dallara (15); G – Panoz G Force (7). Engine legend: C – Chevrolet (6); H – Honda (9); T – Toyota (7). Tire legend: F – Firestone (22).

A packed house at Pikes Peak International Raceway.

PIKES PEAK

DARIO **FRANCHITTI OVERCAME** a miscue in the pits to score a fine victory in the Honda Indy 225. The race sponsor once again secured all three places on the podium – for the third successive race – with Franchitti's ArcaEx Dallara/Honda chased home by the similarly powered Quaker State Telmex Tecate Panoz G Force of Adrian Fernandez and Dan Wheldon's Klein Tools/Jim Beam Dallara.

Franchitti started on the outside of the second row after qualifying had been rained out and the grid decided according to practice times. Andretti Green Racing's Tony Kanaan and Dan Wheldon led from the get-go, but the yellow caution lights flashed on almost immediately when Buddy Rice spun into the wall on the back straightaway.

"I just lost it coming out of [Turn] Two," said the perplexed Indy 500 winner, who was uninjured. "I don't know. That's just the way it goes."

Franchitti jumped into second place soon after the restart, and then took the lead from Kanaan on lap 30. But AGR wasn't having things all its own way. The two Marlboro Team Penske Dallara/Toyotas were also making their presence felt. Sam Hornish Jr. worked his way steadily forward after starting ninth, and on lap 60 he claimed the point from Franchitti. Ten laps later Helio Castroneves took second in the second Penske machine.

The Hondas proved a little more frugal than the Toyotas, allowing Franchitti to regain the advantage when Hornish peeled off into the pit lane for a scheduled service after 79 laps. The

Scotsman stayed out for four more laps before making his first stop. Then came his only hiccup of the day, when he was waved out fractionally early, the refueling vent hose still attached to his car. Fortunately, a potential catastrophe was averted when Franchitti immediately jumped on the brakes, although not before vent man Mike Miller had been sent tumbling, injuring his knee ligaments.

The mishap derailed Franchitti's progress only slightly, and by lap 132 he had repassed Hornish for the lead. Barring one lap when he made his final pit stop – this time without drama – Franchitti was on top for the remainder of the 225-lap race.

"The engineers at Andretti Green Racing have worked very hard to give us a good one-mile [track] car and obviously we have an advantage with the Honda engine," noted the Scotsman after taking his second victory of the year. "I had a good rhythm out there and these low-grip situations [given the Colorado altitude] definitely suit my driving style."

Hornish's hopes of a top finish were dashed when he hit the wall after 157 laps. The ever-unlucky Tomas Scheckter ran as high as second before his Panther Racing Pennzoil Dallara/Chevy succumbed to a broken drive-shaft. So Fernandez emerged to take second ahead of Wheldon, Darren Manning, who equaled his career-best finish to date for Target Chip Ganassi Racing, and Kanaan, who, following Rice's early demise, was content to finish a safe fifth and extend his championship lead to 68 points with just four races remaining. Kanaan also led his 813th lap of the year, eclipsing Tony Stewart's previous single-season record, set in 1997.

Clockwise from left: Dan Wheldon and Dario Franchitti on the podium; Dario lifts the trophy; Brian Herta and Scott Sharp fight it out.

IRL IndyCar® Series Race 12: Honda Indy 225 at Pikes Peak International Raceway
Sunday, August 22, 2004

Place	Driver	Car	Nat.	Car Name	C/E/T	Laps Comp.	Running/ Reason Out	Q. Speed (mph)	Q. Time	Starting Position*	IRL Pts.	Total IRL Pts.	IRL Standing	IRL Awards ($)	Designated Awards ($)	Total Awards ($)
1	Dario Franchitti	27	GB	ArcaEx	D/H/F	225	Running	172.916	20.8193s	4	53	319	5	100,800	7,500	108,300
2	Adrian Fernandez	5	MEX	Quaker State Telmex Tecate	G/H/F	225	Running	171.591	20.9674s	7	40	286	7	82,900	2,000	84,900
3	Dan Wheldon	26	USA	Klein Tools/Jim Beam	D/H/F	225	Running	173.586	20.7390s	2	35	381	3	69,700	0	69,700
4	Darren Manning	10	GB	Target Chip Ganassi Racing	G/T/F	225	Running	171.675	20.9698s	8	32	268	10	56,400	0	56,400
5	Tony Kanaan	11	BR	Team 7-Eleven	D/H/F	225	Running	174.311	20.6527s	1	30	463	1	51,600	0	51,600
6	Helio Castroneves	3	BR	Marlboro Team Penske	D/T/F	225	Running	172.395	20.8823s	5	28	326	4	45,700	0	45,700
7	Vitor Meira	17	BR	Rahal Letterman Team Centrix	G/H/F	225	Running	173.149	20.7913s	3	26	282	8	44,400	0	44,400
8	Jaques Lazier	20	USA	Patrick Racing	D/C/F	225	Running	168.917	21.3122s	14	24	76	23	43,200	2,000	45,200
9	Bryan Herta	7	USA	XM Satellite Radio	D/H/F	224	Running	172.308	20.8928s	6	22	271	9	43,200	0	43,200
10	Alex Barron	51	USA	Red Bull Cheever Racing	D/C/F	224	Running	168.311	21.3890s	16	20	246	12	42,100	0	42,100
11	Ed Carpenter (R)	52	USA	Red Bull Cheever Racing	D/C/F	224	Running	167.230	21.5272s	20	19	184	16	40,700	0	40,700
12	Townsend Bell	2	USA	Menards/Johns Manville Racing	D/C/F	223	Running	168.388	21.3792s	15	18	125	21	39,700	0	39,700
13	Kosuke Matsuura (R)	55	J	Panasonic ARTA	G/H/F	221	Running	No speed	No time	22	17	227	13	38,500	0	38,500
14	Mark Taylor (R)	13	GB	Access Motorsports	G/H/F	221	Running	167.786	21.4559s	18	16	161	19	37,100	0	37,100
15	Scott Sharp	8	USA	Delphi	D/T/F	221	Running	167.666	21.4712s	19	15	205	14	36,000	0	36,000
16	Felipe Giaffone	24	BR	Team Purex Dreyer & Reinbold	D/C/F	219	Running	169.705	21.2133s	12	14	145	20	34,800	0	34,800
17	Tomas Scheckter	4	SA	Pennzoil Panther	D/C/F	161	Half Shaft	169.424	21.2485s	13	13	174	17	33,600	0	33,600
18	Sam Hornish Jr.	6	USA	Marlboro Team Penske	D/T/F	157	Accident	171.665	20.9711s	9	12	295	6	33,600	10,000	43,600
19	Tora Takagi	12	J	Pioneer Mo Nunn Racing	D/T/F	101	Handling	168.050	21.4222s	17	12	199	15	32,400	0	32,400
20	Scott Dixon	1	NZ	Target Chip Ganassi Racing	G/T/F	93	Handling	171.445	20.9980s	10	12	255	11	31,200	0	31,200
21	A.J. Foyt IV	14	USA	Conseco/A.J. Foyt Racing	D/T/F	53	Handling	165.688	21.7276s	21	12	171	18	31,200	0	31,200
22	Buddy Rice	15	USA	Rahal Letterman Pioneer Argent	G/H/F	0	Accident	171.437	20.9990s	11	12	395	2	31,200	0	31,200
													Total:	**1,000,000**	**21,500**	**1,021,500**

* Starting lineup determined by combined practice speeds after qualifying was cancelled due to rain.

Time of race: 1h 34m 56.9156s. Average speed: 142.182 mph. Margin of victory: 2.2429s.

Fastest lap: #26 Dan Wheldon (Race lap 173, 169.109 mph, 21.2880s). Fastest leading lap: #27 Dario Franchitti (Race lap 171, 167.651 mph, 21.4732s).

The Marlboro Lap Leader Award: #27 Dario Franchitti. Firestone Performance Award: #6 Sam Hornish Jr.

Caution flags: Laps 1-7, #15 Rice, accident T2; laps 121-129, debris; laps 158-167, #6 Hornish, accident T4. Total: 3 caution flags, 26 laps.

Lap leaders: Tony Kanaan, 1-29; Dario Franchitti, 30-59; Sam Hornish Jr., 60-78; Franchitti, 79-83; Hornish, 84-131; Franchitti, 132-160; Kanaan, 161; Franchitti, 162-225. Total: 7 lead changes among 3 drivers.

Lap leader summary: Dario Franchitti, 4 times, 128 laps led; Sam Hornish Jr., 2 times, 67 laps led; Tony Kanaan, 2 times, 30 laps led.

Legend: R – IndyCar Series Rookie. Chassis legend: D – Dallara (15); G – Panoz G Force (7). Engine legend: C – Chevrolet (6); H – Honda (9); T – Toyota (7). Tire legend: F – Firestone (22).

NAZARETH

The final caution came with just six laps to go, when Czech Republic driver Tomas Enge – a former Formula 3000 champion making his IRL debut with Patrick Racing – spun and crashed in Turn Four, taking the unbelievably unfortunate Tomas Scheckter with him into the wall.

Against the odds, the safety crews cleared up the debris in time for a one-lap scramble to the checkered flag. Kanaan (Team 7-Eleven Dallara)

had the upper hand at the final restart – which was remarkable in itself, since he had started stone-cold last after suffering a rare engine failure in qualifying – but the Brazilian was unable to hold off the fired-up Fernandez (Quaker State/ Tecate/Telmex Panoz G Force) in a thrilling finish. Still, second place for Kanaan was enough to put the coveted championship title beyond the reach of his rivals.

Once again the beleaguered Tomas Scheckter finds the wall.

IRL IndyCar® Series Race 15: Toyota Indy 400 at California Speedway
Sunday, October 3, 2004

Place	Driver	Car	Nat.	Car Name	C/E/T	Laps Comp.	Running/ Reason Out	Q. Speed (mph)	Q. Time	Starting Position	IRL Pts.	Total IRL Pts.	IRL Standing	IRL Awards ($)	Designated Awards ($)	Total Awards ($)
1	Adrian Fernandez	5	MEX	Quaker State Telmex Tecate	G/H/F	200	Running	215.270	33.4463s	4	50	415	4	100,400	2,000	102,400
2	Tony Kanaan	11	BR	Team 7-Eleven	D/H/F	200	Running	No speed	No time	21	40	578	1	82,900	0	82,900
3	Dan Wheldon	26	GB	Klein Tools/Jim Beam	D/H/F	200	Running	213.861	33.6667s	13	35	498	2	69,600	0	69,600
4	Sam Hornish Jr.	6	USA	Marlboro Team Penske	D/T/F	200	Running	216.062	33.3237s	3	32	374	7	56,500	0	56,500
5	Buddy Rice	15	USA	Rahal Letterman Pioneer Argent	G/H/F	200	Running	214.824	33.5158s	6	30	473	3	51,600	0	51,600
6	Dario Franchitti	27	GB	ArcaEx	D/H/F	200	Running	214.344	33.5908s	9	28	394	6	45,600	0	45,600
7	Helio Castroneves	3	BR	Marlboro Team Penske	D/T/F	200	Running	217.479	33.1067s	1	29	408	5	44,400	27,500	71,900
8	Scott Dixon	1	NZ	Target Chip Ganassi Racing	G/T/F	199	Running	216.301	33.2869s	2	24	327	10	43,300	0	43,300
9	Townsend Bell	2	USA	Menards/Johns Manville Racing	D/C/F	199	Running	213.603	33.7074s	16	22	171	21	43,300	0	43,300
10	Mark Taylor (R)	13	GB	Access Motorsports	G/H/F	199	Running	214.030	33.6402s	11	20	206	19	42,000	2,000	44,000
11	Scott Sharp	8	USA	Delphi	D/T/F	199	Running	213.824	33.6725s	14	19	258	14	40,800	0	40,800
12	Ed Carpenter (R)	52	USA	Red Bull Cheever Racing	D/C/F	198	Running	214.086	33.6314s	10	18	233	16	39,600	0	39,600
13	Kosuke Matsuura (R)	55	J	Panasonic ARTA	G/H/F	198	Running	213.077	33.7906s	20	17	268	13	38,500	0	38,500
14	Tora Takagi	12	J	Pioneer Mo Nunn Racing	D/T/F	196	Running	211.629	34.0218s	19	16	245	15	37,100	0	37,100
15	Tomas Scheckter	4	SA	Pennzoil Panther	D/C/F	193	Accident	213.993	33.6459s	12	15	218	17	36,000	0	36,000
16	Tomas Enge (R)	20	CZ	Patrick Racing	D/C/F	190	Accident	212.010	33.9606s	17	14	14	29	34,900	0	34,900
17	Bryan Herta	7	USA	XM Satellite Radio	D/H/F	188	Running	214.345	33.5907s	8	13	348	8	33,600	0	33,600
18	Alex Barron	51	USA	Red Bull Cheever Racing	D/C/F	185	Accident	213.815	33.6740s	15	12	294	12	33,600	0	33,600
19	A.J. Foyt IV	14	USA	Conseco/A.J. Foyt Racing	D/T/F	178	Accident	214.686	33.5374s	7	12	212	18	32,400	0	32,400
20	Felipe Giaffone	24	BR	Team Purex Dreyer & Reinbold	D/C/F	173	Clutch	211.697	34.0108s	18	12	195	20	31,300	0	31,300
21	Vitor Meira	17	BR	Rahal Letterman Team Centrix	G/H/F	170	Gearbox	215.141	33.4664s	5	12	344	9	31,300	0	31,300
22	Darren Manning	10	GB	Target Chip Ganassi Racing	G/T/F	0	Did not start	215.822	33.3608s	DNS*	12	323	11	31,300	0	31,300
													Total:	1,000,000	31,500	1,031,500

* Did not start due to accident during qualifying.

Time of race: **2h 14m 12.5029s.** Average speed: **178.826 mph.** Margin of victory: **0.0183s.**

Fastest lap: **#17 Vitor Meira** (Race lap 17, 216.959 mph, 33.1860s). Fastest leading lap: **#3 Helio Castroneves** (Race lap 84, 215.252 mph, 33.4491s).

MBNA Pole Award: **#3 Helio Castroneves** (217.479 mph, 33.1067s). The Marlboro Lap Leader Award: **#3 Helio Castroneves.** Firestone Performance Award: **#3 Helio Castroneves.**

Caution flags: Laps 9-13, #17 Meira, contact in T2; laps 173-177, debris; laps 179-181, #14 Foyt, accident T2; laps 187-191, #51 Barron, accident in T2; laps 194-198, #4 Scheckter and #20 Enge, accident T4. Total: **5 caution flags, 23 laps.**

Lap leaders: Adrian Fernandez, 1-10; Mark Taylor, 11-14; Dan Wheldon, 15; Helio Castroneves, 16; Wheldon, 17; Castroneves, 18-50; Sam Hornish Jr., 51; Fernandez, 52-53; Castroneves, 54-89; Fernandez, 90-91; Castroneves, 92-127; Fernandez, 128; Hornish, 129-130; Tony Kanaan, 131-133; Castroneves, 134-164; Kanaan, 165; Fernandez, 166; Wheldon, 167-168; Hornish, 169; Castroneves, 170-177; Kanaan, 178-192; Fernandez, 193; Kanaan, 194-199; Fernandez, 200. Total: **23 lead changes among 6 drivers.**

Lap leader summary: Helio Castroneves, 6 times, 145 laps led; Tony Kanaan, 4 times, 25 laps led; Adrian Fernandez, 7 times, 18 laps led; Mark Taylor, 1 time, 4 laps led; Dan Wheldon, 3 times, 4 laps led; Sam Hornish Jr., 3 times, 4 laps led.

Legend: **R** – IndyCar Series Rookie. Chassis legend: **D** – Dallara (15); **G** – Panoz G Force (7). Engine legend: **C** – Chevrolet (6); **H** – Honda (9); **T** – Toyota (7). Tire legend: **F** – Firestone (22).

TEXAS II

HELIO **CASTRONEVES HAD TO PAY** a hefty price for his long overdue first victory of the season. But on balance, it was well worthwhile.

The season finale at Texas Motor Speedway boiled down to a two-lap shoot-out following a terrifying accident that led to Alex Barron being taken to the hospital, suffering from a mild concussion. For the third time in the season's final four races, Castroneves had led the most laps, and after slipping to seventh in the closing stages two weeks earlier in California, he was determined not to allow a repeat scenario in the Chevy 500.

So, rather than waiting until he was past the usual cones which mark the beginning of the restart acceleration zone, the Brazilian gunned his Marlboro Dallara/Toyota a little early and

took off like a scalded cat. His rivals cried "foul!" – and race officials later agreed – but Castroneves held off the combined challenge from Andretti Green Racing teammates Tony Kanaan and Dan Wheldon to take the checkered flag.

"We did it – finally!" exclaimed the two-time Indy 500 champion after scoring his first win since Nazareth in 2003. "It's great momentum [for the off-season]. These guys are awesome – not only Marlboro Team Penske, but all our associates, especially Toyota. You guys worked your butts off to make today happen. I'm so proud of everyone."

The triumph was equally gratifying for Toyota, which secured its first win since the very first race of the season and finally ended Honda's win streak at 14.

Toyota, indeed, was strong all weekend, with Castroneves securing his fourth consecutive pole and teammate Sam Hornish Jr. starting alongside him on the front row. Between them, the pair led 157 of the 200 laps, although Hornish's hopes of repeating his season-opening win were dashed by an electrical failure after 163 laps.

Other strong performances were posted by Adrian Fernandez, who claimed his fifth top-five finish in the last six races, and Tomas Scheckter, who was again the strongest of the Chevrolets. The South African set the second fastest time in qualifying, only for his run to be disallowed due to a technical infringement. Undaunted, Scheckter was working his way steadily toward the front when his engine failed abruptly.

Top Honda runners Wheldon and Kanaan both took turns out in front during the closing stages, but Castroneves regained the advantage on lap 180 and was still out in front when the yellow lights flashed on five laps later. For the second time during the weekend, Dario Franchitti had suffered a broken rear wheel on his ArcaEx Dallara/Honda, which spun around and collected Barron's Red Bull Dallara/Chevy on its way to a heavy impact with the wall.

The wreckage cleared, Castroneves bolted to the victory, while Kanaan stole second place from Wheldon in the dash to the finish line. The race stewards later determined that Castroneves had jumped the restart, issuing a stiff penalty of $50,000 and the loss of 15 championship points, but the results stood and the victory was his.

Facing page, from top: Helio Castroneves takes the checkered flag; Castroneves celebrates his victory. Above, clockwise from top: Castroneves was a worthy victor; Adrian Fernandez in the pits; Alex Barron crashes out.

IRL IndyCar® Series Race 16: Chevy 500 at Texas Motor Speedway
Sunday, October 17, 2004

Place	Driver	Car	Nat.	Car Name	C/E/T	Laps Comp.	Running/ Reason Out	Q. Speed (mph)	Q. Time	Starting Position	IRL Pts.	Total IRL Pts.	IRL Standing	IRL Awards ($)	Designated Awards ($)	Total Awards ($)
1	Helio Castroneves	3	BR	Marlboro Team Penske	D/T/F	200	Running	215.996	24.2504s	1	53	446†	105,000	17,500	122,500	
2	Tony Kanaan	11	BR	Team 7-Eleven	D/H/F	200	Running	213.105	24.5794s	8	40	618	1	86,500	0	86,500
3	Dan Wheldon	26	GB	Klein Tools/Jim Beam	D/H/F	200	Running	213.402	24.5452s	7	35	533	2	72,500	0	72,500
4	Vitor Meira	17	BR	Rahal Letterman Team Centrix	G/H/F	200	Running	214.316	24.4405s	3	32	376	8	58,600	0	58,600
5	Adrian Fernandez	5	MEX	Quaker State Telmex Tecate	G/H/F	200	Running	212.959	24.5963s	10	30	445	5	53,400	12,000	65,400
6	Scott Dixon	1	NZ	Target Chip Ganassi Racing	G/T/F	200	Running	213.954	24.4819s	5	28	355	10	47,100	0	47,100
7	Mark Taylor (R)	13	GB	Access Motorsports	G/H/F	200	Running	212.324	24.6699s	14	26	232	17	45,800	0	45,800
8	Scott Sharp	8	USA	Delphi	D/T/F	200	Running	212.558	24.6427s	13	24	282	13	44,600	2,000	46,600
9	Townsend Bell	2	USA	Menards/Johns Manville Racing	D/C/F	200	Running	212.939	24.5986s	21	22	193	21	44,600	0	44,600
10	A.J. Foyt IV	14	USA	Conseco/A.J. Foyt Racing	D/T/F	200	Running	212.855	24.6083s	11	20	232	18	43,300	0	43,300
11	Felipe Giaffone	24	BR	Team Purex Dreyer & Reinbold	D/C/F	199	Running	209.304	25.0258s	18	19	214	20	41,900	0	41,900
12	Tora Takagi	12	J	Pioneer Mo Nunn Racing	D/T/F	198	Running	211.284	211.284s	16	18	263	15	40,700	0	40,700
13	Tomas Enge (R)	20	CZ	Patrick Racing	D/C/F	198	Running	211.295	24.7900s	15	17	31	27	39,600	0	39,600
14	Alex Barron	51	USA	Red Bull Cheever Racing	D/C/F	185	Accident	213.057	24.5850s	9	16	310	12	38,100	0	38,100
15	Dario Franchitti	27	GB	Arca Ex	D/H/F	184	Accident	213.219	24.5663s	19**	15	409	6	36,900	0	36,900
16	Bryan Herta	7	USA	XM Satellite Radio	D/H/F	173	Handling	213.675	24.5139s	6	14	362	9	35,700	0	35,700
17	Sam Hornish Jr.	6	USA	Marlboro Team Penske	D/T/F	163	Electrical	215.097	24.3518s	2	13	387	7	34,400	0	34,400
18	Tomas Scheckter	4	SA	Pennzoil Panther	D/C/F	105	Mechanical	215.831	24.2690s	20*	12	230	19	34,400	0	34,400
19	Kosuke Matsuura (R)	55	J	Panasonic ARTA	G/H/F	59	Gearbox	212.713	24.6247s	12	12	280	14	33,100	0	33,100
20	Buddy Rice	15	USA	Rahal Letterman Pioneer Argent	G/H/F	42	Electrical	214.194	24.4545s	4	12	485	3	31,900	0	31,900
21	Ed Carpenter (R)	52	USA	Red Bull Cheever Racing	D/C/F	3	Accident	210.852	24.8421s	17	12	245	16	31,900	0	31,900

† Point total reflects penalty for jumping restart on Lap 198. * Qualifying time disallowed. ** Started back-up car after accident during final practice.　　　Total: 1,000,000　　31,500　1,031,500

Time of race: 1h 49m 32.2547s. Average speed: 159.397 mph. Margin of victory: 0.3732s.

Fastest lap: #7 Bryan Herta (Race lap 83, 214.923 mph, 24.3715s). Fastest leading lap: #3 Helio Castroneves (Race lap 200, 211.108 mph, 24.8120s).

MBNA Pole Award: #3 Helio Castroneves (215.996 mph, 24.2504s) The Marlboro Lap Leader Award: #3 Helio Castroneves Firestone Performance Award: #5 Adrian Fernandez

Caution flags: Laps 4-11, #52 Carpenter, accident backstretch; laps 106-114, #4 Scheckter, spray; laps 165-169, #6 Hornish, stalled pit entrance. laps 185-197, #27 Franchitti and #51 Barron, accident T4. Total: 4 caution flags, 35 laps.

Lap leaders: Helio Castroneves, 1-56; Sam Hornish Jr., 57-59; Scott Sharp, 60-62; Dario Franchitti, 63-64; Dan Wheldon, 65; Castroneves, 66-91; Adrian Fernandez, 92; Castroneves, 93; Fernandez, 94-110; Hornish, 111-160; Vitor Meira, 161; Tony Kanaan, 162-166; Wheldon, 167-179; Castroneves, 180-200. Total: 13 lead changes among 8 drivers.

Lap leader summary: Helio Castroneves, 4 times, 104 laps led; Sam Hornish Jr., 2 times, 53 laps led; Adrian Fernandez, 2 times, 18 laps led; Dan Wheldon, 2 times, 14 laps lead; Tony Kanaan, 1 time, 5 laps lead; Scott Sharp, 1 time, 3 laps lead; Dario Franchitti, 1 time, 2 laps lead; Vitor Meira, 1 time, 1 lap lead.

Legend: R – IndyCar Series Rookie. Chassis legend: D – Dallara (15); G – Panoz G Force (6). Engine legend: C – Chevrolet (6); H – Honda (9); T – Toyota (6). Tire legend: F – Firestone (22).

THIAGO MEDEIROS:
MR. FOCUSED

WORDS BY **MARY BIGNOTTI MENDEZ**

IN **COMMON WITH TOP ATHLETES** in any sporting endeavor, champion racecar drivers must dedicate themselves to strict training regimens to stay competitive. They are disciplined in their physical fitness workouts, diet and social activities. Thiago Medeiros is no exception. And in 2004, his intense focus and dedication paid off with his first major professional championship title.

In his sophomore campaign, Medeiros dominated the 2004 Menards Infiniti Pro Series season, achieving six wins and eight poles in 12 events. Along the way he displayed his mastery of the short and intermediate-length ovals, as well as the superspeedways. He led at some stage in all but one of the races and paced the field for 588 laps out of a possible 850 (over 69 percent). His final points tally saw him finish 134 markers clear of second-placed Paul Dana.

"I couldn't ask for a better season," said a jubilant Medeiros, who hopes to follow in the footsteps of past

Eighth overall was taken by Al Unser Jr.'s son, "Just Al", who joined Keith Duesenberg Racing in time for the fourth race at Kansas and amassed six top-five finishes in eight starts. Unser, 22, earned no fewer than five third-place finishes and also snared the pole at Michigan. Although he never led a lap, he was always in the mix with the leaders. Surgery for a broken left thumb resulting from a dirt bike mishap caused Unser to miss the California race.

The top ten championship placings were completed by Giebler, who was unable to raise the finance to complete a full season despite winning the opener for Keith Duesenberg Racing, and veteran Billy Roe, who, at 47, was more than twice the age of most of his competitors. The former IndyCar Series driver claimed a best of fourth at Nashville in his seven starts for Kenn Hardley Racing.

Jeff Simmons raised the Hardley team's profile by taking the pole at Pikes Peak and finishing second at Chicago. The gifted American also finished a strong second in a one-off appearance with A.J. Foyt's team at the series' blue ribboned race at the Indianapolis Motor Speedway in May.

Final Points Standing

Pos.	Driver	Nat.	Team	Points
1	Thiago Medeiros	BR	Sam Schmidt Motorsports	513
2	Paul Dana	USA	Hemelgarn 91 Johnson Motorsports	379
3	Arie Luyendyk Jr.	HOL	Sam Schmidt Motorsports/AFS Racing	330
4	P.J. Chesson	USA	Mo Nunn Racing	317
5	Leonardo Maia	BR	Brian Stewart Racing	292
6	Jesse Mason	CAN	Brian Stewart Racing	283
7	Rolando Quintanilla	MEX	Roquin Motorsports	264
8	Al Unser	USA	Keith Duesenberg Racing	252
9	Phil Giebler	USA	Keith Duesenberg Racing	215
10	Billy Roe	USA	Kenn Hardley Racing	164
11	Brad Pollard	USA	Kenn Hardley Racing/Sam Schmidt Motorsports	152
12	Jeff Simmons	USA	A.J. Foyt Racing/Kenn Hardley Racing	150
13	Gary Peterson	USA	AFS Racing	112
14	James Chesson	USA	Mo Nunn Racing	95
15	Travis Gregg	USA	Sam Schmidt Motorsports	89
16	Matt Beardsley	USA	Beardsley Motorsports/Roquin Motorsports	88
17	Marty Roth	CAN	Roth Racing/Brian Stewart Racing	79
18	Jon Herb	USA	Racing Professionals	67
19	Taylor Fletcher	USA	Bullet-Team Motorsports/Roquin Motorsports	52
20	P.J. Abbott	USA	Sam Schmidt Motorsports/Keith Duesenberg Racing	48
21	Cory Witherill	USA	Hemelgarn 91 Johnson Motorsports	41
22	Scott Mayer	USA	Sam Schmidt Motorsports	38
23	Jay Drake	USA	AFS Racing	32
24	Tony Turco	USA	Brian Stewart Racing	32
25	Ross Fonferko	USA	Keith Duesenberg Racing	26
26	Racer Kashima	J	Sam Schmidt Motorsports	17
27	Ryan Hampton	USA	Brian Stewart Racing	16

All drove Dallara chassis with Infiniti Q45 engines and Firestone tires.